THE
BUTTERFLY
&
THE
BULLDOZER

A Letter to My Grandchildren

"Just Some of My Friends", Rick's sculptures

Edited by Ed Boyer & Eva Richards
Proofreading by Norma Jean Sanders and Carol Chastang
Graphic Design by Ellen C. Brown

Printed in the USA

ISBN-13: 978-1500214425

FOREWORD

The first time I saw Rick Richards, he was dressed up as Paul Revere, astride a beautiful galloping horse on the bright green baseball diamond in Dodger Stadium. It was the summer of 1976, I was 19 years old, and a new Soka Gakkai International member.

Back in the day, SGI members staged these elaborate shows—culture festivals—in venues that ranged from community parades to Madison Square Garden. This Dodger Stadium show was a celebration of America's Bicentennial. As Rick rode around the stadium infield and tipped his hat to the cheering crowd—and he really knew how to work an audience—I was struck by how happy he looked. It was as if he were in heaven—or better yet, the state of Buddhahood, savoring every second of those few minutes, riding a horse while determined to encourage each person there to chase after their wildest dreams.

That was almost 40 years ago. Yet that memory of the guy on the horse—I didn't even know his name—stuck with me for a long time. And I felt he was trying to tell everyone there, "Do what you love. Live Boldly. Never give up on your dream!"

It was around that time when I took Eva Muñoz—my friend since second grade—to her first Buddhist meeting. Twelve years later she met Rick.

I was wary of Rick when I met him. I hadn't connected the dots between Rick, "the guy who was taking up the space in Eva's life that was once mine," and Rick the encouraging guy on the horse. Yet I respected him. In a town like L.A., where your connections and possessions are the barometers for your worth, Rick, despite often living on the outs (or in his car, his residence when

7

he met Eva), carried himself with a dignity and sense of purpose that made me see how misplaced my values were.

Rick had so many talents, but I had no idea he was a writer! That was my experience with Rick…just when I thought I'd figured him out, he'd throw a curve. His true stories in "The Butterfly and the Bulldozer" about the eccentric souls he met on his travels are funny and memorable. I admire the courage it took for him to share—with an amazing attention to detail and an enviable power of recollection—his tormented relationships with his parents.

I had no idea the book would affect me the way it did. Rick, with his words, did a great job of shaking me, as if to wake me up to say, "You deserve to become absolutely happy, no matter what!" I was shocked to find my eyes tearing up at several places in the book. And I was also moved to step up my own Buddhist practice. Again, that's Rick's determination at work.

This book really is about love. And love is something we're all looking for—be it in a cause to embrace, a mentor to trust and follow, a path to take that will lead others toward a life of fulfillment, joy and no regrets, or a beloved friend to laugh and cry with.

As he did 38 years ago during the Dodger Stadium show, Rick's sincere spirit continues to encourage me.

Carol Chastang
Bowie, MD

Rick at Dodger stadium portraying Paul Revere
at a SGI-USA culture festival.

WHY NOW?

On my son's 33rd birthday, August 30, 2008, after dinner at a nearby restaurant with his mother, sister and some friends, I got home to find three messages from him. He sounded a little frantic.

"Dad, are you at home?"

I immediately returned his call.

"Yes."

"Stay there. I'll be right over."

Five minutes later he came in the house carrying a 20-inch iMac.

"I want to give this to you in appreciation for the gift of my life."

I was blown away. It's very hard for me to accept gifts or compliments. Usually, I have some smart-ass remark. I was speechless.

We had talked a number of times about my getting a computer and starting to write. And he really wanted me to get out of the age of "the dinosaur." In this time of the internet, iPhones, Twitter and . . . whatever else they come up with by the time you read this, I feel very much out of place. If something doesn't have an eraser on it, I don't know what to do. So now I have this beautiful computer. He could have given me a pony, but no. I've been challenged by someone I admire and love very much, and I had better get with it. Here I go, and I don't want to stop. And I won't.

Back to the question as to why at this stage of my life do I have this desire? Will it create any value other than satisfy my own ego? Can I use it to accomplish my greatest dream, which is to contribute with the entirety of my life to a world of true peace?

Two years before, I had become very sick and there was little expectation on the doctors' part that I would survive. During that time I had many thoughts going through my mind, and one of them was that I might never meet my grandchildren.

Perhaps some day my daughter Kelli or my son Drew will have a child or two. Should that become the case, then the only things those children might know about their grandfather would be memories by the parents.

Now that I have this challenge, what do I want to write? I decided I wanted to tell stories that will be encouraging to those potential grandchildren's lives. If I would ever consider myself an expert in anything, it could only be in my own experience of myself. I can't experience the experience of others. I may be able to relate to them, but only from the outside or in my heart. I'll never experience their experience of themselves.

There is a wonderful teaching in Buddhism called the "Lotus Sutra." The most widely read and best known is the Chinese version by the Central Asian monk Kumarajiva. This version has been acknowledged as the most authoritative. The English translation I will refer to is by Burton Watson.[1] In the 16th chapter of the "Lotus Sutra" there is a phrase that has always fascinated me.

> *"Sometimes I speak of myself, sometimes others;*
> *sometimes I present myself, sometimes others;*
> *sometimes I show my own actions;*
> *sometimes those of others.*
> *All that I preach is true and not false."[1]*

In my quest to communicate with the children of my children, I felt that writing about my own experience would be the best thing to do. At the same time, I realize that if I were to name all the people, all the places and all the things I have done and seen, it would be better told if I changed a few names to avoid inadvertently hurting anyone. I'm getting excited about this adventure. I can only hope this new passion of mine will be readable and will cause one to want to read on.

I have always thought "The Butterfly and the Bulldozer" would be a good title for a book. I will probably have to explain it as a semi-autobiographical personal historical novel. Then of course comes the question, "Who cares?" Which means that I'm answering my own question that I posed earlier. Why? Why now? Because I want to . . . and that's that. I hope that this time will be spent creating value. I'm going to have a wonderful time. I hope to have a grandchild or two, that's it. That's why I want to write.

---

[1] *The Lotus Sutra,* trans. Burton Watson (New York: Columbia University Press, 1993), 226

I probably should say that I know nothing about computers, but I just might know where some of the keys are. So now that you know that I really don't know what I am doing, but I do know I want to say hello to my grandchildren, yet unborn. This writing could be considered a letter to them... just in case.

Rick & his mother

1

MOTHER
The First Eight Years

To reach the conclusion first is probably not the best way to start a story, but I must say this: my mother is one of the greatest treasures I have in my life. Without her I would never have arrived at the level of happiness I am experiencing now. With that said, the next sentence would make it seem that I stand on my head a lot.

It's really sad, but I find it very difficult to remember any love or warmth from my mother during my first eight years of life. Most of my time was spent trying to keep out of her way. Out of sight was my best bet in those days. It seemed that I wasn't capable of doing anything right in her eyes, and it didn't take long to figure out that I just wasn't worth anything. She'd say, "You're more trouble than you're worth." I bought it. At the same time I knew there was something wrong in that. I wanted her to love me, but no matter how hard I tried, it never produced the result I was looking for. All I wanted was a hug or maybe a smile to let me know I was more than "pathetic."

We lived in a row house in a small town outside of Philadelphia. I had a little room with a raked or slanted roof on the second floor at the top of the stairs. The bed was small; it had a mattress with a hard plastic-like cover with designs of trains and animals on a blue background. Never any sheets, no pillow, but there was an old blanket I could get under. On the wall, a clock made of wood. I hated that clock. The ticking was so loud I couldn't get to sleep. I wanted to kill it. I should have broken it. Then I would have paid the price. I felt like I was caught in some kind of a trap.

The ticking of the clock made me feel like the clock was using me as a target. The numbers had a house painted between them. The bottom of each house was facing the middle of the clock. Throughout my childhood I would have bad dreams about that clock. I'd get caught in the world of the clock and couldn't get out. Sometimes the whole thing would be turning counter clockwise with me running to catch up to it, and then sometimes it would suddenly reverse and be chasing me. The good part of the dream was that neither one of us ever caught up with the other.

That room, my room, was converted into a kitchen when my grandmother moved in with us. I called her Nana. She was the only person in my life who showed me any kind of affection. I remember her calling me "precious." What a contradiction for someone who already knew he was "pathetic." I wasn't even six years old when we lived in that house, but already I didn't have a "my room" any more. It didn't seem fair. I could never feel bad about Nana getting my room for a kitchen. It seemed that my mother was finding another way for me to get farther out of her sight.

What do you do with the kid? You put him in a box in

the basement. You have someone build a plywood box with a floor and a door and you move him and the bed down there. I was always being sent to the cellar. I felt that I was being sent to the dungeon. I used to sit on the second step from the top of the stairs leading to the kitchen. I looked through the crack under the door, watching the feet of whomever, as they walked around. When it was time for my appearance to eat, she would unlock the door and I could come out. It's like letting your dog in for the night, except that I had to go out again, back to the dungeon.

My mother never knew it, but I had a pet. It was a wonderful rubber toy horse that used to gallop up and down the mountains and take me for a ride over the top of my blanket that I draped over my legs. All I had to do was shift my legs around and I would be coming out from behind a rock in another part of the "Wild West." I wished I had a partner to ride the range with me. My horse was my best friend.

At the end of a hallway that led to the alley in back of the house, I could look through the bars on the window in the door to the rest of the world. Looking through that window was a time for dreaming. All I had to do was stand on a box, hold on to the bars and wonder what was out there. Would I ever be able to go and find out? I could hear noises coming from outside and sometimes I would see people walk by. Who were they and where were they going? One day I heard a lot of yelling. I went to the door to see a dog being stoned to death by some of the kids from the neighborhood. I couldn't do anything. I just stood there watching. I was probably 4 years old or maybe 5. I think it caused a trauma in my heart. How could someone do something like that? Many years later I had the same reaction watching movies where a horse or a dog or any animal would get hurt.

That dog and I shared a common path. His death entered my heart, and for years I wondered where his life had gone. I think that was the beginning of my wondering where my life was. Where would it go if I were to die? That image is as clear today as the day I saw it. I tried to tell my mother about the dog but she just said, "Mind your own business. Stop trying to cause trouble."

One Halloween while living there, though I wasn't allowed to go out trick-or-treating, I remember that my mother was wearing a sheet over her head trying to look like a ghost when some kids came to the door. She either said something to them or they just didn't like her from something she said or did in the past. They grabbed the sheet and pulled her out the door onto the landing at the top of the steps. They ran like hell and she screamed like bloody murder. Shortly after that we moved. It was also around this time that I remember sitting on the stairs going up to the second floor when a man came to the door and into the house to talk to my mother. Before long she was yelling at him and he left. I'm not sure, but I think it was my father. Why he would have come there I don't know. I'd like to think it was to see me. No such luck. It was probably that he just wanted to get laid.

I have a couple of pictures of my mother when she was young, and I have to admit she looked hot and ready. She was athletic and loved to dance. I also have a picture of her and my father taken on the day they got married. I can certainly see what would catch his eye and cause his shorts to move.

From what I could gather over the years, he was the stud of his neighborhood, and between the two of them there probably were a lot of sparks. It didn't last too long though. My father came to the hospital the day I was born, put my name on the birth certificate and left. He never came back. But we stayed in that house until around my sixth birthday though I don't remember ever having a birthday party when I was a kid. I just remember my age because my mother would always mention it when I did something that got her mad.

"You're four years old. You should know better."

"Snap out of it stupid. You don't have the brains that God gave a goose. You're six. You should be able to spell brat by now."

After six years in that little row house with my personal dungeon, we moved. I can't explain the reason for it, but we moved to a three-story house with a very large back yard, a separate garage, and a huge tree that had a swing already hanging from it. I don't know what happened to Nana at that time, but she didn't come with us.

My mother must have come across some money. As I look back on the situation it must have been a good-sized bump for her to be able to afford that much of a change in lifestyle. Not long after that, she brought a dog home. His name was Porky. I was excited. Now I would have a friend to play with and to talk to. That didn't last long. Porky would start to pee anytime someone would give him attention. Two days later he disappeared. I can only guess what happened to him. Later, I was given a kitten by the neighbors who lived on the street right behind us. I named him Skippy after the peanut butter. It was my intention that we would stick together forever. He would sit up on his back legs and box with me. And he liked to talk with me. I was his best friend and he was mine.

I came home from school one day and went looking for Skippy but couldn't find him. Thinking that he had gone into the neighbors' garden, I went to the swing to wait for him. Because the ropes of the swing were so long, I could swing to great heights. At the top of one of the best swings, I looked over to the side of the house and could see something on the ground that was out of place. Even now as I remember this, I can feel a little something coming up in my heart. I walked toward what I had seen from the swing. It was Skippy. There were bees crawling in his eyes. It was ugly. I buried him behind the garage. I cried a lot and then it was over. I never told my mother about this and she never asked about the cat.

Later on in my life I snuck into a movie house to see a Roy Rogers film. Trigger was the most beautiful horse in the world to me, and as I sat watching "My Pal Trigger," I was hit with one of the most devastating experiences I ever had. Roy had to shoot Trigger's mother. I think this was close to the last time in my life I cried. The dog being stoned, Porky disappearing, Skippy and now Trigger's mother took me beyond tears for a long time. Mixed in with all this was the story of "Old Yeller." The dog had rabies and they had to shoot him. I had heard about "Bambi" and to this day I still haven't seen that one. Won't either. Life was beginning to seem like a story with a lot of unanswered questions. Where did Nana go? Why did Skippy have to die? Why was I a pain in my mother's ass?

With the new house, and the new neighborhood, came

new ways of living. Within walking distance were the stores and shops. Everything was of the Mom and Pop variety. I remember a train station, a bowling alley, a school, a butcher shop and a couple of bars or pubs. I also remember I had to go to the local dentist. I bit his thumb when he tried to sneak a needle in my mouth. Don't do that.

The bars and pubs got my attention as they became the primary location of my mother's evenings. There was one bar called Shark's and another called The Friendly Tavern. The Friendly Tavern was just that. A husband and wife team owned it. My mother became a regular there and so did I. I had responsibilities. One was to sit on a stool next to my mother until she needed it for someone who was to be the "friend" for the night. The other was to accept the handful of slugs that were given to me by the owners so I would go off and play the games when the friend would arrive. I still have a great passion for pinball. There was another important task to perform—"be seen but not heard."

After a while I found a way to get attention and a friend. From the time we moved into the neighborhood, just about the time I turned 6, until my eighth birthday, I became the kid behind the bar. I ended up being able to mix just about every drink they made: Old Fashioneds, martinis, daiquiris, Manhattans. The husband and wife became my mentors of the bar life. Their names were Chick and Laura. All I had to do was watch them and do as they did. These trips to the Friendly Tavern went on for two years. I became very good at my job. I became especially good at following the example of the teachers. I noticed that every time they mixed a drink, there would be a little extra left over. Of course you don't throw it out. Either you waited and gave it to the customer or you finished it off yourself. The owners loved to have a sip or two of these leftovers. Me too. I was a good student. The booze became my friend. I really liked the taste of the different drinks. I especially liked the effect. I liked the way it made me feel. There are all kinds of friends, but booze doesn't get near the top of the list. Eventually, it showed me where the bottom was. But then again, maybe that is what you should expect from a good friend.

I don't know how many times I walked behind my mother and her "friend for the night" as we made our way back to our house. She was attracted to men in uniform and they to her. I remember Frank. He was a conductor on the train. I remember a police officer, a couple of men in the armed services, and the butcher who worked in the market across the street. The butcher must have changed into a fresh set of clothes before he came to the tavern. I knew he was the butcher but he looked like a cook to me. His name was Ray. He was a regular. We'd get back to the house. I'd be told to go straight to my room on the top floor.

One night a couple of police officers were at the house. I was hiding in the dark when one of them apparently said something about her breasts and she invited him to find out for himself. I just remembered that as I was writing this paragraph. My home life, as I look back on it, was more like a circus with my mother being the ringmaster and the men were the performers. Who was I?

I had pretty thick skin by the time I was 8. So much pain and confusion and disappointment came my way. I just had to almost step out of my mind and watch it come down. I withdrew from my reality in order to survive in my world. Not being wanted or needed or loved wasn't anything out of the ordinary. Fuck 'em.

Most of the good memories that come to mind in the early days with my mother usually started upside-down. One day she told me that I had to go to the hospital to have my tonsils removed. I didn't know what a tonsil was, but I did know that a hospital had a lot to do with pain. She waited to break this news to me after we were already headed there. One of her "friends" was driving. They were having a good time while I sat in the back seat thinking that this has got to be bad. I don't know how long we were driving. I just remember it felt like it was forever. Then out of nowhere we pulled into a parking lot and we were at the circus. It was the Circus Vargas and she was giving me a gift. Hopalong Cassidy and his horse Topper were the headliners. She said something like, "This is because you've been a good boy." I didn't know the word "bullshit" in those days. Probably a good thing. "Hoppy" rode around the ring twice and threw out "Hoppy Bars" to the crowd. Didn't get one of them, but I still have my tonsils.

My mother liked to bowl. I would have to go to the alley with her and sit still while she had her fun. The sound of the pins going down was so loud it made me want to run. It was too much. She would get really mad when she saw how it affected me. I was ruining her ability to have a good time. We went to the Jersey shore one summer. When the waves crashed on the beach, it took me right back to the bowling alley. From that day on I don't think I ever went in the water. A pool is ok. Just don't expect me to go surfing in the ocean

14

and have to listen to the waves break.

Either on or around my eighth birthday, my mother took me out to the home of the couple that owned the Friendly Tavern. For some strange reason I believed that it was to be a party for me. They had a beautiful home that I think must have been a farm of some sort. There was a barn and a very big yard that probably had been a pasture or a very large garden. They also had a dog. He was a Saint Bernard. I played with him for a while before being told to come in the house and go to the basement. This was a good basement. It was a full bar with lots of games, Pinball and one-armed bandits, a jukebox and a dartboard. I loved that dartboard. Imagine what my target was.

Imagination was a very important ingredient of my survival in those early days of my life. That instinct to survive carried me to a lot of places and I have met a palette of interesting people along the way. Earlier I mentioned that my mother was a great treasure in my life. Being able to learn so many lessons in life was caused by the relationship we had. To this day I am forever grateful. My life would have been entirely different if I had grown up with a family filled with love and respect for each other. I can honestly say, looking back over my history, I wouldn't change it. That's hindsight talking, not the 8 year old. Not too much foresight was available either. I didn't see the next step coming.

After being told to come back in the house and go to the basement, my mother finally came to the top of the stairs and called for me to come up. We went out the back door. I saw there was a car with two people sitting in it but didn't pay a lot of attention until my mother opened the trunk of her car and pulled out a suitcase. Then I got the news: "You are going to live with these people, and you had better behave yourself or there will be a price to pay. Get in the car."

This may sound a bit dramatic . . . but it seemed that my life paused for a minute. I could see them. They didn't get out of their car, a station wagon. He had a ball of cotton tucked in the socket where his right eye had been. It was being held in place with what looked like scotch tape. She was very thin and had bleached blond hair. Later, I noticed she had let the nails on her pinky fingers grow very long and would use them to clean her ears. I got in the car as told. As we drove off, I could see my mother turn her back to me and walk toward the house. This was wrong. This wasn't the way to live.

I didn't take my eyes off her. She never turned her head toward me. She went back into the house. My life felt like it was being pulled from the earth like an unwanted weed. The further away from the house we got the stronger the pull became as the roots tried to fight to stay in the ground. Almost from the moment the house was out of sight, I became aware I was someone else. I certainly was no longer my mother's son. I hated the word "mother." I hoped she would feel this pain I had in my heart.

There's a place in the back of my mind I could go anytime I wished. No one else has ever been there. No one is invited. It's safe there. People free. I can call on the friends of my heart and mind. They never desert me. They never hurt me. They don't lie; they don't cheat. They don't hate me. They don't exist. My friends are my imagination and they don't question me. You can't have too many friends. They taught me to be my own best friend.

This was when I knew there would never be anyone in my life that I would depend on for anything. Ever. I was in the basement of my life. Another dungeon. I also suspected, somewhere in the back of my heart, that there was a tower of treasures above me, and that I had to discover the way to the top. There had to be a way out of this hell.

I had already experienced enough disappointment to wonder if this was to be the "forever" future. On one level I knew that this wasn't the way of life I wanted to live but because I had been through so much rejection by now and had managed to want to survive, I somehow found hope in my heart. It wasn't always there but when I needed it, it would appear. Without this hope, I don't know what the end results of my life would have been. Today this hope is one of my secret weapons that enables me to fight any and all negative functions that appear in my life. Hope is another great friend.

2

AGE 8
And Beyond

It was quite a transition from hoping I was going to be having my first birthday party ever to realizing I was being turned over to a couple of people who needed a maid but bought a kid to do the chores around the house and live in their basement. They needed someone to shovel the coal to keep the furnace going so they wouldn't get cold at night. There must have been some kind of exchange of money made with my mother. I remember the wife saying on more than one occasion, "You're not worth it."

Those words could just as easily have come from the mouth of my mother. The husband had lost an eye working in the shipyards during World War II. A piece of steel flew in his eye from some welding that was being done near him. He lost his balance or equilibrium. They came up with a brilliant idea, "Buy me a kid." When I didn't meet their expectations or give them something to smile about, I would have to sit on a stool and watch them eat. I felt right at home. The scene had changed, but the nature of the characters trying to lead my life hadn't.

The wife was the dominant one in the family. The nails on her little fingers must have been an inch long. She loved to point with them. She would point me to the stool or the basement. Of course part two of any punishment was that I didn't get to eat. It amazes me to this day how fast one can adjust to different circumstances.

The stool was in the dining room. From that vantage point I made a couple of discoveries. One was that an open carton of Chesterfields looked like a gift to me. "Pinky" and "One Eye" both smoked. My mother smoked. I was already 8 years old and had been in love with booze of all kinds for about two years. It must have been time for me to start smoking. Another great discovery was that they liked having a glass of wine with their dinner and throughout the rest of the night. Over the course of the evening he would mellow out and she would get meaner. While on the stool, if I was able to shift it to just the right position, I could see the television reflected in the mirror. Right after "Kukla, Fran and Ollie" there was "Frontier Playhouse." Even pigs can have a heaven.

The house was about 50 yards from the B&O Railroad. Every chance I got, I stole a pack of those Chesterfields and headed for the tracks. There were always a couple of freight cars parked off to the side that begged for me to climb in. From that first time sitting and smoking in those cars, I dreamed about hopping on when the train was moving and leaving the past behind. It was getting colder at night so I decided to wait till the winter turned to spring. Sitting and dreaming and smoking—especially when it was raining—was wonderful. I loved that rain, especially with thunder.

That first cigarette got me so dizzy I couldn't see straight. The problem was I liked it. Took another 53 years before I stopped. Sometimes I would sit under the car and wait for a train to come along. The sound was deafening, but the rhythm and sound of the wheels clicking on the tracks, the shaking of the ground mesmerized me. This was totally different than the bowling alley. The rhythm, the harmony and the fact that the train was going somewhere seemed to call out to me in song. Later when I rode the rails, I would almost always be lulled into a meditative state with the sound and the motion of the train. Today it's the sound of horses' hooves striking the ground when walking or galloping that will stop me in my tracks. Those sounds register in my heart and cause my mind to travel. In my mind I can go anywhere. It can be more refreshing than a vacation.

The dining room turned out to be a workroom for the husband. Before his accident he was an avid fly fisherman, making his own rods, tying his own flies. Another reason to buy a kid was to support his fishing habit. After he lost his eye, he couldn't make his own fishing tackle. He trained me. After showing some talent in tying flies and helping make the rods, he decided that we should build a rowboat in the basement. He was the planner and I was the laborer. Probably not the greatest pool of talent around, but it was the best their money could buy. He sketched the boat out on the wall at the bottom of the stairs. I marked out the measurements. Their car was that station wagon. We went to the lumberyard, bought the materials, and he and I stashed it in the basement. Pinky Fingers hated the smell of sawdust and construction as it made its way into the kitchen, but other than complain a little, she didn't try to put a stop to it. I think she and One Eye had hooks into each other, and they liked it that way. Could it be love and lust?

That basement was my room. It was good to have my own room again—especially when it came with a coal furnace and a boat yard. And the basement was where they kept their healthy supply of wine—Mogen David and Manischewitz. Four one-gallon bottles to a case, and they probably had six or eight cases down there at a time. The coldest place in the basement was under the stairs coming from the kitchen, right next to the door leading outside, up the concrete steps through the storm doors. It was easy. I was the one who would be called upon to bring a bottle up when needed, so no one was any wiser when I would let them know there just were so many left. Smart as a whip was I. I didn't know there were other wines in the world. I loved that wine. It helped keep me comfortable during those winter nights, and it made up for a few missed meals.

The wife, Pinky, and I didn't get along at all. One of her tasks for me was to take the margarine that was packaged in clear bags with a red dot in the middle that I would have to break and knead into the rest of whatever else was in that bag. I don't remember giving her cause, but one day she came up behind me and pulled at my ear. I turned very quickly and slammed the bag into her stomach and knocked her back. She froze with the long nail pointed at me. She said she saw something in my ear and wanted to get it. Those long fingernails of hers were weapons. She used them as her badge of identity. I watched her clean out her husband's ears one night. I think it turned them on. They would soon be on their way upstairs.

I remember them going to church only once. I had to go with them. They put me in a Bible class while they went into the service. All I'll say is that I must have asked too many questions or I asked the wrong questions. I do know that the husband and wife were told to never bring me back there. How stupid is it to ask a kid to believe something that he can't see or experience? Just have faith they said.

"Faith in what? Why?"

"Because the Bible says so."

It just didn't make sense to me. It would be like asking me to love my mother. How could I? There was nothing there for me to love. Shortly after that the wife approached me with the family Bible and started to read something out of it. I took it out of her hands, tore out a couple pages and threw the book at her. She swung her arm at me and caught me with one of her pinky fingers above the eye and cut me. I scared the hell out of her with a stare. From that day on I could just look at her with that stare, and she was as mellow as a kitten.

Back to the boat building . . . he had the tools and knowledge and me. I didn't have too much gratitude in those days, but today I appreciate the fact that I learned how to use my hands and a few tools while we went about building the boat. And then there was the "Promise."

"When we get this boat done I'm going to teach you how to fish."

He was going to teach me how to fish. Nobody ever took the time to teach me anything. I didn't even learn how to tie my shoes correctly until I was in the Army. No one

ever took the time. That's OK. I didn't want to owe anything to anyone anyway.

Throughout that entire winter we worked on that boat.
I took pride in what I was doing. I wanted to build the best
boat I could. And I was going to learn how to fish. There
were a couple of problem areas. Once we got it done we had
to varnish it inside and out at least three times. I think I can
still smell that varnish now. I felt like I was varnishing my
lungs inside and out. I slept with that odor. If that house still
stands I'm sure the varnish is still in the air.

Another more complicated problem was that we couldn't
get the damn boat out of the cellar. It just wouldn't fit
through the door and up the steps. We tried and tried. There
were only a couple of choices.

"Let's see if we could go up the stairs and through the
kitchen."

No," she said, with no room for a change of mind.

"We could take part of the boat apart."

"No," he said. "Let's cut a wedge of concrete out of the
foundation and take it out that way."

And we did. The newest problem was that he couldn't
handle the sledgehammer with any accuracy. I was supposed
to hold the chisel while he swung the hammer. Seeing him
take a practice swing convinced me.

"No," I said.

I did it, the hammer, the chisel and me. He had a rig for
putting the boat on top of the station wagon. He bought oars
and everything was ready to go. Sunday morning he and I
were going to get up at four in the morning, have biscuits
with gravy and drive to a lake somewhere in New Jersey and

fish. I was really excited. I didn't have many things to look forward to in those days, but this was different. I was going to learn to fish. That whole winter I had learned all I could, but it was all in my mind. Now it was time to experience it. I was ready.

The lake was beautiful. Pine trees were all around. Just to hear the sounds of nature at that time of the morning . . . it was as if life was taking its first breath. I'll never forget it. The habit of listening and smelling the air in the morning became a great discovery for me. We unloaded the boat. I held my breath realizing that we really didn't know if it would float.

It did.

"All right kid, the first thing you need to know is how to row a boat and not make waves or noise. We want to slowly troll around the lake until we find the right location. The fish like to eat early in the day. Any noise or disturbance will scare them away."

I put all the concentration I could muster into becoming the best boat rower ever. My mother had once said to me, "You're a half-ass. You do everything half-assed. If you're going to do something, do it right or don't do it at all."

We went fishing three times. Each time I rowed the boat. Never once did he even hint that I could pick up a rod. By the last trip I was ready to rock that boat and throw him in the water. I was sure I could drown him. But I didn't. By this time it was spring. The days were getting warm, and I was just getting ready to head for the tracks and get on a freight car. I'd been watching the trains pretty closely through the winter. I knew I'd had enough of these people. Time to go.

Time to leave for places unknown. The trains were waiting. I decided to find some real horses. Time to make a dream come true.

I went to school that last day of the third grade. I passed. I also had packed a paper bag with all I owned the night before. A pair of jeans, a couple shirts, underwear and a toothbrush and probably a couple other things that I can't remember. I also had a warm jacket they had bought me and a hat that covered my ears. When I got back to the house, I scored a couple packs of Chesterfields.

I had been there for almost a year and every day I thought about leaving. Not too long ago I was asked what was going on in my mind when it became time to leave. I really don't know. It wasn't as if I wanted to strike out at someone. I think I already knew this was my life or fate or destiny, and that it was a lot more important to take care of myself instead of trying to take it out on someone else. I had stopped thinking someone was going to take care of me. I did know that I was on a hunt. I wanted to find a path that would lead me to something I could enjoy.

I am a hunter. I've been hunting love and warmth and acceptance all my life. Now I look back and I clearly see that I was going in the wrong direction to find it. I thought it was out there or in someone's arms or approval. Now I know it's inside me. The heart of a hunter is hope. Now it's my hope to encourage anyone, or to put it more honestly, everyone, to go on an internal journey. Without the rejections in my life, I probably would not have taken this journey.

Should I say it?

"Thank you, Mother?"

3

HI-YO
Trigger

I came into this life with a love of horses. It seems all of us have some sort of love or maybe fear of something from the day we are born. I know that I carried a lot of baggage when I arrived. Some of which seemed impossible to imagine that this could have been of my own doing, but my love for horses was more than just welcomed.

I don't remember how old I was. I had to be around 6 or 7 years old. I was riding in the back seat of a car with my mother and one of her so-called boyfriends somewhere outside of Philadelphia. There were about six horses grazing along the fence by the side of the road when I stuck my head out the window and let out with the best impression of a horse's whinny I could muster. It seemed like a miracle, but all of a sudden one of the horses started to run and was trying to catch up to the car. It's impossible to describe the feeling that I had in my heart. I felt as if I was experiencing a oneness with a horse's mind and heart. At that time in my life nothing could have given me more comfort. Looking back, I think this was the first sense of self-identity I had that seemed to register on the happy side of life.

Without getting into all the details, I'll just say that my so-called childhood seemed to be a consistent struggle for survival. Whether it was for food or shelter or some kind of love, I was always on the lookout for some sort of relief from the life that I was living. Horses were like family to me. It never fails that when I see a horse, the sun seems to appear from within my heart. Watching a horse run is seeing poetry dance. When you're with him, heart and soul, it's as if you're sailing through the sky on a cloud.

The moment I hopped the B&O, away from One Eye and Pinky Finger, I was on a journey without a destination that lasted for about seven years. I made my way up and down the East Coast trying to find that "something" that makes a person live on. The people I met were some of the most amazing characters life could produce. Each moment was everything to them. The intensity in their lives at any given moment was so powerful it made me want to emulate it. Listening and watching these travelers of timelessness as they occupied the space they claimed for their lives forever plays in my mind. They caused me to wonder, "What is the meaning of my life? Why these circumstances? Why now? Why here at this moment?" There had to be some reason or purpose that I was alive. I'm so glad I was born with a curious nature. All this time I would let my love for horses take me to the next farm or stable or racetrack—anywhere there was a horse. It is my great fortune to have this love for these magnificent animals. They were also the key to my survival.

I had family in Philadelphia, but I never contacted them. The last thing I wanted was to be forced to go back to a place where I knew there never would be any love and everything would be a bitter hell. It's strange, but I did think of Philly as my home town. Every once in a while I'd find myself there, wondering why. Maybe there's an invisible string of destiny that's a mental and even physical path. It's as if the string is a route on a map toward the past or the future.

During one of my stays in Philly, I came across a horse harnessed to a junk wagon. He was waiting by the curb while his owner was looking for goods. I liked him immediately. He wore a hat and was glad to meet someone who wanted to be friends. It wasn't long before his owner came back to the wagon. Two things were quickly apparent as he walked up to the horse, patted his neck and said something to the effect, "Won't be long. We'll be done for the day, and we'll eat and maybe get a treat." Then he asked, "Who's your friend?" I liked that. This man talked to his horse as you would to a buddy. He then introduced us. "This is Tony. What's your name?"

I told him my name was something. I don't think I ever used my real name in those days. Today, I'm not sure why. It had to be either that I was afraid someone would try to trace me back to my mother, or it was just a part of the game I played with my mind, thinking I could hide from the world. It got me in trouble more than once when I couldn't remember what I had called myself. Sometimes I would forget what name I had used and wouldn't answer when they would call out to me.

I wish I could remember the name of Tony's owner. He was very tall, very skinny and very black. And he had a smile that was at least as wide as the wagon itself. I immediately felt comfortable as we talked about Tony and horses for a while. He had to move on and finish his route for the day. I was probably 10 or 11 around this time. He must have sensed that I was on my own when he asked if I wanted to ride in the wagon. He had about five more stops he had to make.

"If you don't have anything to do, you can come with me and meet my family. I'll be done pretty soon. I'm hungry. You hungry?"

I think I was always hungry. "Yes, Sir. Thank you." Yes sir, no sir or yes ma'am, no ma'am was drilled into me from the beginning. I should be grateful to my mother for at least one good habit. It has served me well throughout my life. He didn't ask questions about where I came from or where I was going. He seemed to trust that I wasn't a risk.

Ninety-nine percent of the time I would put up a wall from within my life that said "No Trespassing." One reason was that I didn't want anyone to know how I conducted my life. For instance, getting my hands on cigarettes was always a problem. Very seldom did I have any money so I would either steal them or con someone into giving me some. One of my most successful schemes was to go to a cigarette vending machine, knowing no one was watching, and start pulling on the handle until I got someone's attention. I didn't look like a kid who smoked so when I told them my mother sent me for a pack of Camels, nine times out of 10 they believed that I had put the money in the machine, and they would open it up and give me a pack.

Sometimes I would have to find a substitute for cigarettes. I don't know how I came up with this crazy way to get a smoke but I did. Before they came up with plastic straws, they were made of wax and paper. If I couldn't come up with a real cigarette, I would go to a drug store, sit at the soda fountain like I was going to order something and grab a handful of those straws that were always sitting in a glass jar on the counter. I'd stick them under my clothes and if the soda jerk came up to me I'd just say, "I think I lost my money. I'll be back." I almost always had matches so I'd tear the straw in half and light it up. I learned the hard way to always remember to blow out the fire before that first great inhale. I probably inhaled enough wax in my system that I could put a hell of a shine on a shoe.

When I met Tony and his owner, I felt a sense of ease I hadn't experienced very often. That wall of anger wasn't there. His trust and acceptance of me gave me a feeling of peace and well-being. Other than the warmth I felt and exchanged with horses, this was a new experience for me.

We got to his house and unloaded the wagon with the things he wanted to try and sell or maybe keep for himself. I did my best to help as we unhitched Tony, put him in his stall and moved the wagon into the garage. The house wasn't very big, and it was located right in the middle of the block with stores and buildings all around it.

"Let's eat," he said.

The moment he opened the door it was like getting hit with the kitchen. I love the smell of horses, but the aroma of this food made me salivate and caused my stomach to growl. We went inside and he introduced me to his wife and daughter. I can't remember the daughter's name, but I remember she kept looking at me as if I was some kind of invader. The wife though, she was wonderful. She asked my name and I'm pretty sure I must have said the same thing as I told the husband because there was no surprised expression from him. Again, there were no really personal questions.

She said, "You can call me Colored Edith."

I asked, "Why colored?"

She said, "Because I am."

She made me laugh and I felt real comfortable. I wish you could have heard this woman laugh. She sounded like happy rolling thunder. When she laughed, you laughed. You couldn't help it.

"You look hungry. Sit down. Maybe you want to wash your hands first."

I knew that wasn't a question. There was chicken, mashed potatoes and peas. And then . . . there was the gravy. I think it was mushroom gravy. As I write this I can taste that dinner. It was as good as it gets. Colored Edith kept telling me to eat more and more. I ate until I was so uncomfortable I was afraid I was going to get sick. At first, I felt awkward. I wasn't comfortable eating with other people, so I stalled until someone made a move, and I would follow their lead. Pretty soon they began to talk about family stuff, and I felt out of place. I thanked them for the dinner and said that I had to go.

"Where are you going?"

Colored Edith looked at me with an eye that said, "Don't lie to me."

"Why don't you stay here tonight? Have breakfast in the morning, and then be on your way?"

There are times when I have met someone for the first time, and I would feel an immediate sense of danger. My entire life felt like it was on alert. That happened frequently.

Not this time. First, with the husband and then with Colored Edith, I felt like this would be one of those rare occasions when I was attracted to someone like a magnet. Even the thought of staying for breakfast, which would normally have felt like a trap to me, was like a warm blanket.

I was told I could sleep with Tony if I wanted. This man and woman seemed to understand my heart. Colored Edith got a couple of blankets and put them down next to me. I sat inside with the family for a while, but I wasn't able to feel like I should be there. I asked if I could go out with Tony.

"Of course, son, make yourself at home. Use the bathroom if you need to."

I slept like a rock that night, Tony and me. The garage or barn was missing one half of the door. Tony's stall was off to the side of the garage barn. It had been a room used for tools or something. The walls of the stall were insulated with bales of straw. There was a large area where the straw was piled high in case Tony wanted to lay down. To this day, I've never heard this about any other horse, but if he wanted to take a dump or pee, he would just go out to the yard area and do his business like a housebroken dog and then he'd come back. Who taught him this? It was something I would have thought Colored Edith could come up with, but I didn't ask. Should have. All these years I've wondered. Many years later my son and I went out in the backyard of our house and had a "longest pee contest." There was something very bonding about peeing on a tree with my son. I wonder if Tony inspired this.

My determination to leave the next morning changed at breakfast. We had scrambled eggs with biscuits and that gravy. It was the best breakfast I ever had. "My husband wants me to ask if you would stay around for a couple of days and help him with his route. Just help with some of the heavy stuff. Do you think you could? We'll give you all you can eat and a dollar a day. It would be good for Tony to have a friend also."

I pretended to think about it for a couple of seconds.

"Yes, Ma'am. Thank you."

I did everything I could to show my appreciation. I never ate so well before and didn't for a long time after. It was a wonderful experience to be a part of this family. Even though the daughter and I never exchanged words, every once in a while we'd catch each other glancing at the other. I think we almost laughed once, but that was as far as we would go. Too bad.

I remember Colored Edith telling me almost daily, "There's no one in the tub if you wanted to use it."

I soon realized that meant that she thought it was time for me to take a bath. It was the way she said it. She made me feel like I was someone she really cared about. I will never forget her. Thinking about her is always accompanied with a warm feeling in my heart. I believe she really liked me and perhaps it was one of the first times in my life that I experienced a look toward the future that might include a relationship with love. She is one of the most outstanding people in my life. Her husband also made me feel like an equal. He taught me the value of "pieces of the earth." That's what he called the stuff, the junk, as we would put it in the wagon. He asked me if I wanted to learn to harness Tony up to the wagon.

What a privilege. "Yes, Sir."

I volunteered to clean up Tony's backyard.

Tony was a good friend. He had been in the family for well over twenty years. They didn't know how old he really was. He was someone I could talk to about anything and he never seemed to think anything was unimportant. There was a little stool that I would bring into his stall so we could talk. He would lower his head and nuzzle my hair. Sometimes I would whisper to him and he would put his nose next to my face and take in a breath. I would lightly blow into his nostril. It was like a kiss. He was also a good friend to their family. I noticed that whenever the daughter or wife was around Tony, they would pet and rub him with great love. They treated him like one of the family. In his heart, I know that he knew that he was. I can't prove it, but he always seemed to be listening to whatever someone was saying.

When we would go out to work in the morning, he knew which direction he had to go and which streets to turn onto on Monday, on Tuesday and Wednesday. He knew the route for each of the days of the week. Everyone should have a horse like Tony. I stayed there for a couple weeks and then I knew I had to go. There was something in that family that I wanted in my heart, but it wasn't the right time or place. Saying good-bye was very difficult but it had to be done. I almost didn't, but Colored Edith knew. She looked at me one morning and just said, "Don't ever pass this house without coming in."

"Yes, Ma'am."

That was it. I went out on the route, but before getting to the house I asked if we could stop for a minute. We pulled over and I gave the man a long hug.

"Thank you, Sir".

I jumped off the wagon and went up to Tony. By this time I was starting to well up inside. I hugged him as he rested his head on my shoulder. He also knew. I kissed his nose and took off running down the street. I still hate good-byes. I never passed that house again. I couldn't.

Time to move on. Where I was going, I don't know. What I did know was I had to keep my eye out for horses. I felt happy and secure around horses and horse people. It was either a little before or a little after spending time with Tony and his family that I snuck into a movie house when I saw that Roy Rogers and Trigger were playing there. The movie was "My Pal Trigger." I'd do anything to watch that horse. Just give me a chance. I sat there holding my breath waiting for Trigger. The story line tells how Roy got his horse. Trigger's mother had just given birth to him when a cougar attacked. Roy came to her rescue but it was too late. She had been hurt so bad there was nothing that could be done. Roy took his rifle and shot her. I was traumatized. It was impossible to me that anyone could ever do that. It left a mark on my heart that still makes me feel sick. I've grown older but the pain is still that of the boy. It was quite a while before I forgave Roy.

For three summers in a row I worked at a stable of rental horses on the shore of Lake Erie. I was about 12 or 13 when a trucker who had picked me up somewhere near Pittsburgh stopped to eat and gas up at a truck stop outside of Erie, Pennsylvania. I think he even bought me a hot dog. I went outside to wait for him while he finished his lunch, and I saw a trailer of horses parked on the lot. I went over to say hello, and when the driver and his friend came out, I asked where they were going. They told me they were hauling the horses over to a stable by Lake Erie that supplied horses for riding. One thing led to another and I asked if I could go with them and see if I could get a job working at the stable. I found the driver who had gotten me to the truck stop in the first place and had bought me the hot dog, and I said, "Thank you."

I got a ride with the horses and I was on my way. I love the smell of horseshit!

If I were to say I loved barns as much as I love horses, I'd be lying. But I do love barns. It's like feet and shoes; we just go together. We were meant for each other. When we pulled up to the stables, I felt like it just had to be my next home. I don't think I had any doubts that I was going to stay there for a while. It's one thing to love the smell of horses but put together with the fragrance of a barn, you have aromatherapy for cowboys. I was so happy to be there that when I found the man running the place and asked for a job, he couldn't say no. He knew he was going to get a lot of work out of me and that I would love it. Later, I found out he owned the barn, and he and his family lived nearby.

They must have had about forty or more horses that they supplied to the camps—YMCA, YWCA, private camps plus groups that would come up for the day or weekend and camp out. Sometimes I got to take the campers, who were about my own age, out on the trails. I didn't like people my own age. If their families could afford to send them to camp, I knew they weren't my type. I just kept my mouth shut unless it came to the horses. I liked the fact that I got along better with the horses than they did. It put me on a different level.

They all went to school and could probably run circles around me with their brains. So I just never let them into my world.

There was one horse that was so tall I would literally have to climb up the saddle like I was climbing a rope. His name was Coalie. He was my horse for all three summers. Another good friend. Can't have too many good friends. It wasn't an immediate bond. Sometimes you have to slowly get to their heart. Eventually, the trust will appear. Never give up. I was told Coalie was 17 hands high and had been a hunter. His stable mate and best friend was a white pony. I don't know his name, but he was a pretty good size and was probably just right for me. But I didn't ride ponies. Not me. Horses only.

We were out on a ride one day shortly after a rain when we came across a little ditch that had collected quite a bit of water. Another of the stable workers had the lead and took everyone across slowly to avoid any problem. I was the follow up. After everyone crossed, I stayed back for a minute or so and decided to cross at a slow canter. Coalie seemed to like the idea but didn't let me know that he decided to jump this little ditch. It's not his fault that when we reached the other side his front legs slid out from under him and caused him to take in a deep breath and go into a stretching position. It also wasn't his fault that the girth snapped so that the saddle and I did a summersault, landed in the ditch and left me soaked from head to toe. I'm not sure if horses can laugh, but Coalie stopped, turned around, and just stared at me. I think he may have been a little bored with life and this broke the monotony for him. With a little help from the leader, I rode him back to the barn bareback with the saddle on my lap. I think this little event was the turning point for Coalie and me. From then on he seemed to be glad to see me when I would come up to him.

During those summers, I lived in a tent with a couple of the men who also worked at the stables. Storms would suddenly appear out of nowhere over the lake. When it rained it would pour buckets. The sound of the thunder and lightning, the rain beating on the tent, it was like a symphony of living nature for me. The music of nature, how happy I was to listen. I looked forward to the rains. When the rides for the day would be cancelled, I'd stay in the barn with the horses. It was a special kind of day. The other workers and I would sit around and just listen to the changes in the sound of the rain beating like a drum or thumping on the ground. The smells of the barn and weather mixed together and hung in the air. Sometimes steam would rise like clouds and disappear. The horses were grateful for the company. Walking around and talking gently to each of them, touching them with love, those are the magic memories of my childhood.

It's very difficult to remember everywhere I went, everything I did and everyone I met. One year between either the first and second or second and third summer at the Erie stables, I spent a winter making my way toward the south, headed for the warm weather. After hitching a number of rides, I was let off near a rail station and decided I was going to hop a ride. Instead, I ran into what had to be a hobo camp. It was located in a wooded area that was pretty much off the beaten path of the nearby homes and stores.

I think this place was a long term residence for quite a few people, and others came and would stop on their way from one place to another. It was almost like a little town without houses and buildings. There were women there and even a couple of children. These were families who either chose or were forced to live this way, but I really don't think I heard anyone complain. I stood on the outside of what I thought was the boundary, taking it all in when someone waved to me to come over.

Someone was cooking potatoes in a fire they had started in an old trunk of a tree. This was a community fire pit. Someone pulled a potato out of the fire and threw it to me. I know what a "hot potato" feels like. I caught that thing and threw it back. They threw it again, and this time I caught it and began to toss it in the air enough times to cool it off. I mustn't have been the first one to do that because a bunch of the people around the fire started to laugh. I ate that baked potato with great joy and appreciation.

What amazed me about that whole experience was the way everyone shared whatever they had with the rest. I didn't know it then, but this was a society of people who worked together for the welfare of all. That first night I had all I could eat, and one of the women invited me to use a blanket and sleep in their area with her children. The next day a couple of the men talked to me about working with them. They had a system for making a little money and/or getting free food. Having a kid with them made it go a lot easier when they made their rounds in the town looking for odd jobs or a handout of food. Some of the women would do the same thing with their daughters. I learned a lot of social lessons there that didn't really come to play until much later in my life. I also fell in love with raw potatoes. I liked them baked as well, but it was the raw potato I liked best.

One summer, thumbing my way toward the lake, I was let off in Cincinnati, Ohio, across the street from the Cincinnati Gardens. It was a skating rink during the day and a sports arena at night, as well as an arena for traveling shows like the Ice Follies and such. The first thing that caught my eye was a billboard announcing that the Gene Autry Show was to open in about a week. He had a horse named Champion. Here I go again. I ended up going around to the back of the Gardens and talking to a man who worked there. He introduced me to the manager, and I ended up with a job sweeping up around the concession area.

They needed someone to help in the skate shop. "That's me," I said.

I learned how to sharpen the skates, both figure and hockey. The next thing I knew the Gardens management bought me a pair of Levis and a shirt and had me put them on because I was to have my picture taken with Gene Autry. Why, I don't know, but I still have a copy of that picture. I was around 14 or maybe 13. As well as Champion, there was another horse, or I should say pony, named Champ Jr. Their markings were almost identical. They were friendly and we got along. His handlers wouldn't let me work with them. But whenever possible, I was right there watching and learning. To this day, I'm proud that I have always considered myself to be a student. I love to look and listen, watch and learn. Giving consideration to what I see and hear causes me to think before I speak. I'm no expert but I'm going to keep that as one of my good habits.

In my quest for horses, a place to stay and something to eat, I found that movie theaters were a pretty good target when I wanted something on a temporary basis. I had a knack for sneaking into the movies. Whenever I saw that a Roy Rogers film was playing, there was no way that you could keep me from going to the movies that day. Trigger was the star; Roy was just lucky to be the rider. There was nothing more beautiful than to see that animal on the screen, a Golden Palomino. and what an athlete. To this day, even though I have seen and ridden some of the finest horses ever to arrive on this earth, there just isn't anything that can replace that horse in my heart. He's number one as far as I am concerned.

So there I was sharpening ice skates, wearing the new clothes and I had a picture of Gene Autry and me. I was hiding out each night inside the Gardens, taking showers in the dressing rooms when everyone had left. And then I found out that Roy Rogers, King of the Cowboys, and Trigger, the Smartest Horse in the Movies, were coming to town in two weeks. What's a boy to do? Wait for Trigger? Silly question. What else could be more important? Time sure seemed to stand still while I waited for Trigger.

During this time between Gene Autry and Trigger, something pretty amazing happened to my life. I think I fell in love. Not really *love love*, but a love of some sort.

One afternoon I was doing some of the chores that were a part of the work when I was walking past the skating rink on my way to somewhere in the Gardens, and I glanced over at the skaters. I saw something that has forever been in the recesses of my mind and that I have no trouble recalling at anytime, anywhere. I saw one of the most beautiful women in the world. I should really say I saw the most beautiful legs in the world as she danced on the ice. I stopped in my tracks as she seemed to flow over the ice in slow motion. Never before had a woman or girl gotten my attention like this. She took my breath away.

I found myself dreaming about things I never considered before. She was quite a bit older than me, but that didn't matter. That figure, moving with the grace of wind, was the most gorgeous picture I had ever seen in that short life of mine. I think she even made me forget about Trigger for a while.

I didn't realize I had drawn her attention until I noticed she was skating directly toward me. She had apparently seen me around on other days because she asked if I worked there. Over the next week, before the skating had to be stalled while the Roy Rogers show was being set up, we became friends. She was my introduction to the world of women. I knew that world existed but it was a dark world until then, and I had little interest in going there.

Friends may be the wrong word to describe this short relationship. It was an introduction to a part of my being that I had never considered before. If this incident in my life hadn't occurred, I may have never been able to grow to have the respect and appreciation and curiosity and love for women that I now have. I think that one of the greatest challenges in my life, long term, has been to understand the minds of women and they way they think. They just aren't like us. They are women. And thanks to those legs on the ice, I have been forever curious. The lady and I never said good-bye.

Finally two trucks arrived with all that was needed for the show. One truck had all the tack, a run for the dog, portable stalls for horses and a jeep named Nellybelle. The other truck held the animals—the dog Bullet, Dale Evans' horse Buttermilk and Trigger Jr. And then . . . there was Trigger. Be cool.

I could tell who was in charge immediately. It was the wrangler and trainer whose name I didn't know until years later. I went right up to him and said, "Excuse me, sir. I want to shovel Trigger's shit."

He looked at me like I was going to be trouble. After a pause he got a little grin on his face and said, "Help me set up the stalls."

That was all I needed. I did my best not to stare at Trigger too much, and I did everything I could to make myself indispensible. Of course I wasn't allowed near the horses as they brought them off the trailer, but after I set up the run for Bullet, the trainer let me put a leash on the dog and put him in the run. While the two men working with the wrangler got the horses in their stalls and gave them some feed, I decided to bring the tack out of the truck and set it up on the stands. I found the cleaning equipment, wiped everything down and started doing everything I could to make sure the trainer would notice how hard I worked. After they unloaded the jeep I even started to dust it off. Become indispensible, that was my goal. I also wanted him to see how much I appreciated the opportunity. Do anything to get closer to Trigger.

The first show was to start around 2 p.m. the next day, which must have been a Saturday. In the mean time everything was set up. The wrangler went to check out the arena. I followed him. I didn't want to miss a thing. The Cincinnati Gardens was the home for a hockey farm team for the Montreal Canadiens. The walls for the ice rink were still in place.

They covered the floor the same way they would for a rodeo. The trainer went inside the rink checking everything for the show. I kept out of the way but wanted to be sure he knew I was there. He came over to me and asked, "Can you ride kid?" I kept my cool, took a beat, thought for a second and answered, "You'll have to tell me, Sir." It must have been the right answer because after a couple of beats he said to me, "Put a long rein on Buttermilk and bring him out here."

I felt like my heart got struck by lightning. I brought Buttermilk out, and he started to stretch him out. After a while he said, "Get another line and bring out Junior." I did and after about 20 minutes he said, "Put Buttermilk back and bring out Trigger." There I go. I should tell you I felt like crying with the tears of joy only something like this could bring out of me. As I walked up to Trigger and stood there for a minute, I knew he knew just how much I loved him. Then we went to the arena and the wrangler gave me the lead for Junior. He took Trigger, walked him out in a circle, brought him up to a trot, then to a light canter, and I just went into dreamland. "Take Junior back and bring me Trigger's saddle. Not the silver one. Bring me the working one." I started to go a little nuts at that point.

Saddled up and ready was the most beautiful animal in the world.

"All right, climb up and I'll adjust the stirrups."

I melted into that saddle like cheese on a hamburger. I was made to be there and I knew it. And it didn't matter to me if no one else would ever know. "Just walk him out for a while." After I took him around the arena once and was bringing him back he said, "Let's see a slow canter." I

44

remember bringing him up and just going for the greatest ride man had ever dreamed. I took it on my own to cut to a couple smaller circles and into a figure eight. How long we rode I don't know. It was as if the world was in slow motion. When my heart and the horse's heart are one, it's a dance, a wonderful dance that is never forgotten. "All right bring him back and walk once more, and we'll put him away before he sweats." I took him back, unsaddled him and brushed him down myself. Trigger helped me unlock a treasure that was hidden deep inside my life. It would be a long time before I found appreciation and gratitude for a human's life like I felt towards him.

For the next week I rode all three horses twice a day to stretch them out, and I also got to groom them. The other two men who worked with the trainer were more than glad to let me do just about anything I wanted. They knew they had a gift in me. That whole experience has been a bragging point my entire life. I'm sure I've told that story more times than I can count. Just ask my children. I'll just mention Trigger and immediately you know they have seen that movie too many times. But there is just a little more. You might call it an update.

In 1969 the mother of my children and I bought our first house. It just so happened that the previous owner was Pat Brady, who had worked in many of the films and the television series "The Roy Rogers Show." He had died earlier but his mother lived next door. During the Cincinnati adventure I had met Mr. and Mrs. Rogers, but that was little more than a handshake. Maybe a month after moving into the house, I was looking out the kitchen window when I saw the Rogers walking up to the house next door to visit Mr. Brady's mother.

Skip to 1972 and I'm walking my dog, Jesse James, in Griffith Park when I saw a horse that stopped me in my tracks. The horse was an Andalusian by the name of Califa. His rider and owner was Budd Boetticher. Budd could see that I couldn't take my eyes off his horse. He asked me if I could ride.

"You'll have to tell me, Sir."

Works every time. He invited me back to his barn, and I stayed and rode his horses for about four or five years. During that time Budd felt that he had to call on a trainer to help with some dressage cues for Califa. The trainer he called was the wrangler who was with Trigger in Cincinnati. His name was Glenn Randall and to this day, although he has passed, his reputation is as one of the best ever. I think that man could teach a horse to spit. At first he didn't remember me, but as the day wore on he did recall the time and maybe me. Just a little more please.

A few years ago, maybe 2004, Cheryl Rogers, the daughter of Roy and Dale wrote a book about her dad and his history. There was a chapter on Trigger. She said that her dad always spoke of only one Trigger, but that there were more. There were three at the top of the order. There was Trigger and Trigger Jr., unrelated by blood. And there was another called Little Trigger. Little Trigger was very smart and had the most tricks. He was the one who would go on the personal tours with the shows. All these years I've not only been telling a lie, but I believed it myself. It's what you call a real bummer. Except for the fact that the experience I had in my heart was as honest and as real as the sun that shines in the sky.

In August of 2006 I found out that I had Non-Hodgkin's Lymphoma. It was a pretty aggressive cancer. After 21 chemos, a stem cell transplant and the many side effects of medications, particularly steroids, I was in a very fragile condition. Although I have gained a lot of my health back, there is still some discomfort. The steroids affected my bones and muscles especially in my left leg. One thought that would come up every so often was would I ever be able to step up and take a seat on a horse again. No illness will ever take the cowboy out of this heart.

About August, 2007, I was doing my morning prayers and a surge rushed through me. I knew it was time to stop thinking about it and do something. Able to drive again, I got behind the wheel and headed straight for the Los Angeles Equestrian Center. I went to the rental barn and asked for a favor.

"Would you let me try to get up on one of your horses?"

I explained my situation to the woman who was running the place.

"Of course. Just sign a release and you have to use the steps to mount."

She called out to a young man, who was about 9 or 10 years old, the same age I was when I was hoping for any chance to hang out with horses.

"Roberto, bring out Diablo."

Watching that young man flashed me back to my childhood. You could see on his face the love for horses. It takes a skunk to really know another skunk. I knew this boy immediately. Trying to mount from the step was difficult. I couldn't get my right leg to swing over. I asked if I could try from the ground. Diablo was wearing a Mexican saddle and I had to use just about every ounce of my strength to pull myself up. But I got there. I was back in the saddle again. Maybe I'm a little over the edge, but for a minute there I think it may have been a little more exciting than getting up on Trigger . . . my Trigger . . . Trigger. In my mind there is only one Trigger. I agree with Roy.

4

CHARACTERS
Welcomed

It didn't dawn on me to keep track of my age. Too many other things occupied my mind. I truly didn't want to steal food or things, but I always had to be on the lookout for something to eat or a jacket to keep warm. I became good at getting what I needed when I needed it. You can't imagine how easy it is to find a jacket and or a hat hanging up in a diner or restaurant. It was my attitude that allowed me to get away with so much. If I saw something I needed, I claimed it in my mind. I walked up like I owned it, took it, didn't run and bring attention and that was that. It was mine. The problem was that I didn't know that I would be spending the rest of my life paying it back. The cause and effect law is never far behind.

With the same ease I had walking up to someone and offering to shovel horseshit, I could go to the back door of a restaurant or diner and offer to wash dishes for a meal. I almost always ended up with more food than I could eat. Meatloaf and potatoes are still one of my favorite meals. It didn't happen too often but if they would say "no," I'd ask for a raw potato. Even without any money in my pocket I'd ask,

"How much for a potato?" They'd usually give me two. Love those raw potatoes. My daughter, Kelli, loves them as well. Where did she get that from?

On the south side of a bridge in North Carolina sat a diner where I got a great meal of fried chicken and mashed potatoes and mixed vegetables. They liked my work enough that they offered me a job working in the kitchen washing dishes and cleaning up. I was there for a couple of days when someone told me about a place called Cowtown. It was in New Jersey where cowboys from the East Coast would go to practice their rodeo skills. I had to go. I thanked the people at the restaurant and made my way there. Chasing what? I don't know. I must have been looking for family. Horses were again leading my life. By this time I had pretty much made up my mind that I was going to head for Hollywood before too long. Most all the movies I had ever seen had cowboys and horses. Where else was I to go? Acting couldn't be that hard, especially from the back of a horse. Made sense to me. Maybe I would run into Trigger again.

As I was leaving the restaurant, the man who gave me the chance at the job, a big old guy by the name of Pots, made me a really great sandwich. He had even offered to let me stay at his place, but I couldn't go that far with him. I trusted him but I just didn't want a friend who would want to know who I was. I still was very uncomfortable with that kind of relationship with anyone. If it had been a woman I may have answered differently.

This woman thing was getting more of my attention all the time. I was beginning to make a study of them. How many different ways can a woman make her hips move when she walks? Why are they so interesting to watch? It doesn't matter if they are walking away from you or coming right at you, they jiggle and sway in such a way they just take your attention away from whatever else you're doing or saying. It was crazy and I was beginning to really love it, but not as much as horses. At least I don't think so. No, they're just different. Long live different!

I left the diner with my sandwich in a bag and immediately stuck out my thumb and walked toward the bridge. There was a very narrow walkway to make my way across the bridge on foot. Just before I started to cross, a car stopped. I had done quite a bit of hitchhiking by this time and was always aware that I had to be on guard whenever I met anyone for the first time.

A couple of years before, I snuck into a movie house to get out of the rain and sat next to an older man. Most everyone in the theatre was a kid my age, around 10 or 11. I didn't think too much about it until the man reached over and touched my leg. I had nothing in my past to educate me for this kind of encounter, but my instinct took over and I elbowed him in the arm and got out of there. I stayed in the theatre but my heart was racing like a motor. It scared the hell out of me and set up an alarm system in my head that served me well.

The bridge wasn't very long, but before we got to the other side he reached over and started to put his hand on my leg. Before he got there I saw it coming, and with my right fist I hit him in the neck with every ounce of strength I had. His response caused his car to run into the curb on our side of the bridge, but he kept going until we got to the other side and pulled over. I immediately got out and slammed the door shut. He drove off and I lost my sandwich. I continued on my way north a little wiser and a little more distrustful of strangers.

It must have been in 1955 or 56 that I found my way to Cowtown, and once again I was comfortable. Horse people are a special breed. All I ever had to do was let them know I wanted work. No questions, lots of love for horses, lots of horseshit, very little bullshit. Could always sleep with the tack or feed. Hay isn't just for horses. Makes a great bed.

Early on I recognized that women were much more effective at getting the best out of a horse. Men usually try to conquer horses by controlling them with fear or punishment. They think they've got to dominate and show them who's boss. Women on the other hand, as a general rule, go for the heart. They ask the horse to do something rather then demand it to obey. When asked with a little TLC, horses respond as if you linked up with their heart.

I once watched an old man break a coke bottle over the head of a horse he couldn't control. There was nothing I could do. The bottle was filled with water. The horse thought it was his own blood running down his face. The man had broken his spirit. From that day on there was no joy in his heart. When a horse knows you respect and appreciate him, he'll do his very best to become a partner in anything you want to do. Animals have as much right to enjoy life as we do. Over the years I've learned more from women than men about the nature and character of horses. I want to tell you about one woman in particular, a real character.

It must have been in the spring or summer of my 15th

year when I got to Cowtown. A cowboy by the name of Will had given me a job helping with his stock. He was about 60 and had been on the rodeo circuit for many years. He was too old and too banged up to compete any more but was training horses and would work other people's animals as well as train and sell his own.

One day he said to me, "Keep your eyes open for a green pickup with a stove on the back. Betty's going to be here in a bit."

Pretty soon a truck pulled up with a woman driving who had to be in her 50's. She got out and almost knocked me over with her appearance. She was beautiful. Great body. Stood tall in tight jeans, a cowboy's shirt, boots and a hat that looked like it got caught in a buffalo stampede. Her face had more lines in it than a map. If you liked dried fruit, she would be right up your alley.

Betty loved horses and cowboys. Apparently she had been all over this country when she was a young trick rider. She performed at rodeos, fairs, and Wild West shows, whatever. By the time she reached her 20's, she'd found she loved cowboys as much or more than horses. She decided she enjoyed riding the men as much or maybe more than the horses. She stayed on the rodeo circuit, but as a "paid date." Betty loved her work and loved meeting new people. She loved to travel and party. For her, it was the best of all worlds. By the time she was well into her 40's, the wear and tear had begun to show and it became difficult to make a living. She went back to her roots—horses.

Will had called Betty to give her the names and numbers of a couple of his friends who could use her services. Betty had created a career for herself that included horses and cowboys. Horses can be very valuable, especially for breeding. Supplying good bloodlines for stud services brings in a lot of money. It's important to take good care of the health and appearance of these animals. Betty knew that she had a built-in market if she could supply a service. Service had always been her priority. The cowboys were never disappointed with her companionship. Why not take care of the horses with the same attention and affection she showed the cowboys?

She bought the pickup, put a small oil stove on the back, a couple soft sponges, the best soap and shampoo, towels, etc. "Betty's Bath" was born. It's very important to be sure that your horse is very clean and free of debris before breeding. Today you would probably compare it to detailing your car. When tending to the mares, getting them ready, Betty treated them with the same passion and attention she wished for herself. But the stallions were her specialty. Sand, dirt or pebbles can get caught up in the sheath of a stallion. Great care has to be taken to see they are removed without scratching the animal.

With care and pride, Betty became very popular with both horse and owner. She went overboard in her efforts to make sure each was satisfied with her performance. The horse would respond to that warm soft soapy sponge and the skill of Betty's hands with the excitement you would expect of a young man seeing the beauty of a nude woman for the first time. Starting with soaking the sponge in her bucket, she would gently reach up and beginning with his balls, begin his bath. Most of the time the relationship between horse and bather would reach a conclusion that was satisfactory for both. There was one occasion when Betty was called on to bathe one of these wonderful stallions who wasn't going to be servicing a mare that day. And with the owner's permission she went beyond the normal bath and took this animal to a conclusion you could only wish had happened to yourself. He could have knocked over a wagon with his relief. Have you ever seen a horse go cross-eyed?

Sitting there on her little stool was Betty, getting wet all over as the owner and handlers watched with glee. When she was done, with the horse in dreamland quivering in delight, she would ask, "Who's next?"

Smiles all around. I never got up close and personal with Betty, but it would have been wonderful to get wet with her. I heard Betty died when she slipped in the shower and hit her head while she was giving a bath to a pony named Tony. Don't believe everything you hear. At least that's what someone told me once. Sometimes cowboys tell tall tales.

Another unforgettable character was a man named Roy. I'm not sure of his last name but it started out with "Sea"-something. Seashell or Seagraves or Siegel, what it was exactly, I don't remember, but it struck me as odd that I met him at an old marina near the Chesapeake Bay. I was looking to work for a couple of bucks or a meal or something. I found someone who looked like he was in charge and asked him if I could do something to make a couple dollars. He just said, "Go talk to that man over there. His name is Roy Sea-something."

The man he was pointing at was putting up a ladder that had a platform that must have been designed for use on boats in dry dock. Watching the man as I walked over, I noticed he had quite a limp. The bad leg, the left one, moved all right, but it must have been about four or five inches shorter than the other. It seemed a little odd to me that on the left foot he wore a brown street shoe while on the right he wore a bright blue deck shoe. He walked flat with the right one, but with the left he walked as high on his toes as he could, but it was still quite a limp.

After I said hello and asked for a little work, he asked me how old I was. I probably lied and told him I was around 11 or 12. I think I was 10 or 11. He asked me to get him a pack of cigarettes from the little grocery store just outside the marina area. Great, at the least I figured I could get a cigarette from him if nothing else. The other important benefit of going for the cigarettes was I would be given a pack of matches with them. Matches were a great tool and toy for me, a necessity of my life. I headed for the store with the two dollars he handed me. I thought about running off with the two dollars for a second, but figured I could do a lot better if I stuck around and got a job for a little while.

While living with One Eye and Pinky Fingers, I discovered this love for matches. Not only did I need them for lighting the cigarettes I stole, but they also became a toy that I could make things with. I loved the power of kitchen matches. I took a stash of them with me when I left. But it was book matches that became a treasure of creativity. Taking the match and splitting the stem, separating the paper down to the head a couple of times, I could make little figures of stick people and pose them in different positions. Or I could spread two pieces out like wings, twist the middle section, spin it in my fingers and get the match to fly like a helicopter.

Even today I like to have a pack of matches on me. I'm still making those little people, and now I like to split the paper and run it under my fingernails. It just feels s-o-o-o good. It's a lot like the sensational feeling you get when using a Q-Tip to clean out your ears after a shower.

When I got to the store I bought the smokes, Viceroys, I think. Thinking about it now, I don't remember anyone ever refusing to sell cigarettes to me. Of course I didn't buy them that often. Usually, I had to steal or con them out of someone. A lot of the time if I had the money, I'd let the people know that my grandmother had sent me. I asked for a second pack of matches when I bought the cigarettes for Roy what's-his-name.

Getting back to the boat, I saw Roy was up on the deck so I went up the ladder to give him his Viceroys and a pack of matches. He had a lighter so I asked him if I could have his book of matches. Now I had two books of matches. Always thinking.

He said to me, "You smoke?"

"Yes, sir, whenever I have one."

He gave me one. It seemed like everyone smoked in those days. It wasn't unusual to see kids smoke. Cigarettes became a part of your identity. They became a pointer or a weapon when necessary, or even a friend.

One thing led to another and pretty soon I was helping him bring materials up the ladder and just supporting whatever he was doing. He could see that I knew a little about the tools and that I was comfortable helping him as he put some of the finishing touches on repairing the cabin and getting the boat ready for its test run.

The boat wasn't very big. It reminded me of a tugboat. Whatever it had been, Roy must have been working on it for some time and had converted it to sleep two and made it look like a fun thing to have. I'm struggling to remember the name on the back of the boat, but it's just not coming to me. Roy never knew it, but I slept on it at night. The only one in the boatyard who knew was the dog that stayed there. He was supposed to be watching, but he'd much rather play or sit with me.

Apparently, owning a boat was a dream of Roy's since he was a kid. Roy played the violin for orchestras on the East Coast and had done very well. He was around 60 years old and this was his time to reward himself with the boat and to make his dream come true. I enjoyed watching his excitement and energy as he made his way around the deck taking care of the details aiming to the big launch day. I was surprised at how nimble he was on his legs. I never asked about his leg, but he didn't seem to give it any specific attention.

Any time I was asked questions about myself I knew better than to get into a long explanation about who I was or where I came from. I always kept to the story that I had just moved into the neighborhood. If asked where I lived, my answer was, "I don't remember the name of the street."

"What school do I go to?"

"I don't know yet."

"What kind of work does your father do?"

"Construction."

So when Roy asked me what I was doing in the marina, I told him I didn't get enough allowance money to go to the movies with some friends I had just made. He bought it.

That's all that mattered.

I knew the idea of me working for him wouldn't be long term, but he did say that if I wanted to come around for the next couple of days, he would put me to work with some last minute things he wanted to be sure to get done before putting it in the water. I remember asking if he had put it in the water before he bought it.

"No, but I'm not worried," he said.

The man who ran the marina assured him that it was seaworthy.

I only worked for a couple of hours over the next three days, and he gave me $10. That was a lot of money. With the "'Grandmother-sent-me" story, I was able to buy my own cigarettes for a couple days.

The day for the launching arrived. The workers at the marina took charge of setting the boat up and slowly lowering it in the water. Roy played his violin. He was serenading the whole operation. When it came time for the boat to actually touch the water for the first time, he insisted on getting aboard. That meant me as well. I was excited. The engine had been tested and now was the magic moment.

We got in the water. The music stopped. The engine started. The crew on land applauded. I think I was holding my breath, but we didn't sink . . . another magic moment in my life.

The Chesapeake Bay was a beautiful body of water. The marina was near a town called Ridge, Maryland. In order to get to the Bay you first had to take a smaller waterway that took you into the Chesapeake. Roy was in heaven. Standing there at the wheel with the biggest grin you ever saw, it painted quite a picture. Imagine a man shaped like a barrel, with a nose that looked like a ski ramp, his chin sticking out far enough that a bird could nest on it, smoking a cigarette through a four-inch-holder, wearing a brand new hat with some fishing flies tucked in the rim, and you'd have a pretty good picture of Roy Sea-something. And don't forget the one short leg being propped up on its toes in a street shoe. On the other foot, the right foot, he had the deck shoe.

It took just a few minutes to take the waterway to the Bay. I did notice that the water in the Chesapeake was a little choppy but that was to be expected, I guess. The farther into the water we got, the choppier it became, and the wind was picking up as well. After about 15 or 20 minutes, the grin on Roy's face began to fade as it got choppier. It was becoming more difficult for him to hold onto the wheel and keep his balance. I was OK but I started to get worried about Roy. Pretty soon it became apparent that the choppy water would now have to be declared "little waves" and then "bigger little waves."

Roy was beginning to hold on for dear life when he said, "I think I'm getting seasick."

It was time to turn around and head back. Unbeknownst to either of us, there must be some sort of written correct way to turn around under these conditions. In Roy's mind it was "turn on a dime." Wrong. The second we got parallel to these little waves, one of them slammed into the boat and Roy went flying. He wasn't hurt. The problem was that he couldn't get back to the wheel. His legs just weren't cooperating with his determination. As hard as he tried, he just couldn't get his balance. In the mean time, I grabbed the wheel and got the boat going in the direction from where we came. The water was just too rough, and Roy never did get back to the wheel. He just sat on the deck leaning against a bench until we got close to the marina. I didn't know what depression was, but the moment I looked at Roy's face, I saw it.

We got back and pulled up to a dock. I started yelling for help as we approached the landing. A couple of the men came to our rescue. I threw them a rope and I jumped off as they tied up the boat. Roy got to his feet, picked up his violin and case, got off the boat, walked out of the marina to his car and never said a word or looked back. I have no idea what happened from there. Poor Roy. I never set eyes on the man again. Between the "row the boat, no fishing" incident with One Eye and Poor Roy and the choppy Chesapeake…my attraction to being near water stops with the dream of a warm shower, a hot bath and a soft sponge with Betty trespassing over my entire body.

5

MY FATHER

There weren't many places I went that I didn't wonder if my father might be there. Always in the back of my mind was the thought that I wanted to meet him. As much as my mother would associate me with him from the dark side of her mind, I still wanted my own opportunity to reach the conclusion. Who was my father? Why didn't he care about me? Every new place, I would wonder, "Is he here?"

About 90 percent of the time back then, I got around by either hitchhiking or just bumming a ride. One time, I bummed a ride from Virginia to Florida on the back of a truck. It was about as good a way to get around as any. Whenever the driver stopped, I would hop off. If he didn't offer any food, I would go into the restaurant where he and his partner were eating and offer to wash dishes for a sandwich. It never failed that I would eat. To this day, at my own home or at someone else's, if I have eaten or just had a cup of coffee, I wash up after myself. It just makes sense to me. If I make a mess, I should clean it up. Just by offering to wash dishes, I've had many a good meal in a lot of places whose names I don't even remember. Sometimes I did such a good job that I would be offered a job. After a couple of meals or a couple of days, I always moved on. There were many times I wanted to stick around longer, but it seemed there was always something pushing me to go somewhere else. Only when I found a place with horses and people of a like mind toward horses did I really want to settle in, for a short time anyway. The time I spent at the stables on Lake Erie was one of them.

I spent a couple months at a thoroughbred breeding farm in Virginia that I was reluctant to leave. I had a bed in the bunkhouse with the rest of the stable help. We ate like kings as far as I was concerned, and I didn't have to wash one dish as I remember.

Washing dishes had become a habit with me. It meant that I was erasing my trail. I wasn't leaving footsteps that could trace where I had been. I treated the places I had been pretty much the same way I treated the people I met. Out of sight, out of mind. Keeping my distance and putting up that wall of anger was my security system. I didn't have a desire in my heart to hurt or injure anyone or any animal, but at the same time I knew a rage existed inside of me, and if it were ever turned loose, the damages would be irreversible.

When riding on the back of a truck or on a freight train, one of the great thrills was to pee with the wind. It's like swimming in the nude. It's an incredible feeling of freedom. When I became a father, one of my greatest memories was going out in the backyard with my son Andy, now known only as Drew, and pissing on a tree together. There's magic in those memories.

Imagination and instinct are key ingredients for survival

in this world. A little horse sense doesn't hurt either. One year, after working at the stable along the shore of Lake Erie, I ended up in Chicago looking for the stockyards. I was 15 and I figured that I could probably work there for a while and figure out what I was going to do for the rest of my life. I had reached a place in my mind that told me it was time to come out from hiding, to come off the road. Traveling and surviving by the seat of my pants didn't seem right anymore. The older I got, the more obvious it was to me that I was way behind most everyone I met. Everyone seemed smarter than me and I knew it was because I didn't have an education to speak of. I think I spoke well enough but I didn't have all the words I needed. I couldn't spell very well and when it came to math, I had to either try to count by visualizing my fingers in my head or hide my hands behind my back or in my pockets. Any time I got my hands on some money I would protect it like it was gold. I would count it over and over. I think that helped me in the long run with my arithmetic.

At that point I couldn't tell if I was running away from or toward something. I think it's best to say that I was just spinning my wheels. Somewhere along the way I picked up the habit of reading anything I could get my hands on. That habit turned into a joy. I looked for anything to read—a sign, a wrapper that someone just threw out or a paper of any sort became a kind of education to me. I began to want to go to school. I became more and more curious by the day. I wanted to know all I could know.

When I was still with my mother before she turned me over to Pinky Fingers and One Eye, I went to the first and second grades. I at least knew that one apple and one apple were two apples. I liked coloring books and picture stories with the basic words, but it never amounted to what I would call reading. It was the last day of school in the third grade that I left Pinky's and hopped my first freight. I didn't look back. As far as I was concerned, school was just something I was made to do. I didn't pay any attention to what was going on. All I can remember is that I was going to get through the winter and get the hell out of there and away from everything I hated.

I didn't like anything about Chicago. The train yard was enormous. Time to find something going east. I decided to head for Philadelphia again. Time to start over. I thought that maybe I'd be able to find some kind of a trail my father left and catch up to him. Chicago didn't seem like the kind of place he would land in. Little did I know I was just a mile or so away from him.

I rode the rails, I think, a total of about six or eight times, and I ended up in the postal car a couple times. It wasn't legal for the postman to let me in, but they did and it turned out that there was a cup of coffee and at least half a sandwich offered. So at the far eastern end of the rail yard I got into a postal car that had its door open but no one was in it. I crawled behind some boxes and fell asleep. I woke up when they loaded up the mail. I stayed still, not letting the postman know I was there until we were on our way. That didn't go over well. He was mad as hell. He connected with the engineer and they stopped the train, got me off and into the hands of the yard people. They held me while they got in touch with the federal authorities. When the feds got there, they read me the riot act. I knew I was in big trouble. I had to tell them that I was running away from home. I didn't tell them how long ago I started the run.

The end result was that I had two choices, according to the law. Either I go to jail or I could go home. I chose home. They ended up putting me on a plane and flying me to Philly. They had an agent escort me to my mother. They knocked on the door. She took one look at me and almost passed out. After the formality of turning me over to her, they left. The second the door was shut she said, "Get out."

I looked at her as calm as a rock and said, "I'm staying. If you can't handle it, call those people back who just left me here."

Silence is a great weapon for defense. I used it with great skill to keep my mother out of my life. I did let her know that I wanted to go to school. She was more than happy to get me as far out of her hair as she could. Back then, in the 1950s, people put a lot more value in the spoken word than they do now. In this day and age, trust isn't the first response you get from people. When my mother talked to the school about letting me start there, they didn't go into a whole re-search procedure. They believed her when she said I had been living on a farm in Ohio and was now coming to live with her permanently. Apparently, she gave them some story about my records. They bought it, signed me up and that was that. I left One Eye's the day after I got out of the third grade, and now I was going back to school in the 11th grade. I couldn't spell or count very well, but I wanted to learn. That was the key, wanting to learn. A lot was overlooked because I really wanted to learn. I still have that yearning. There is great joy in learning. Today it's the study of Nichiren Buddhism that turns on that joy, the oneness of human life and the entirety of the universe.

I wish I could remember where I was when I went into a library for the first time. I think I was 10 or 11. I really didn't know anything other than I was going into a building others were going into and coming out of. All those books appeared out of nowhere when I went through that door. I stayed until it closed. I walked up and down every aisle, stunned by the number of books. That's when I found the National Geographic Magazines. It was like finding a gallon of ice cream in the middle of the desert.

That first day back in school was surreal. I was very uncomfortable. I felt like I should sneak around, like I wasn't supposed to be there. The funny part came when a girl came up to me and slapped me on the face. Apparently, I had hit her over the head with a cap pistol when we were in the same class in the third grade. I was back in school with the same people I had gone to school with seven years before. From then on it was OK to be there. What a strange set of circumstances to lead me back to where I started!

The next two years were filled with new beginnings. Relatives I didn't remember, stories from people who had known me. The most important information I got was from my grandmother about my father. Unfortunately, I had grown to dislike my mother even more. Absolutely nothing had changed. Her disdain for me was filled with the same bitterness she would sting me with when I was a child.

The morning after getting my high school diploma, at 17 years old, I looked at my mother, gave her the finger and said, "Nice knowing you."

I left the house with the hope that I would never see her again. In my heart I had not the slightest bit of affection for her. I certainly didn't wish her well. If anything, I hoped she would one day have to come face to face with herself, having no way out of taking responsibility for the hell she created.

During my senior year I found that I had a serious health problem. When I left the house for good, my target was to go to the hospital. I didn't know that at 17 I had to have her signature to be treated. The hospital called and when she arrived, not only was she angry, but I could also see that she was having a hard time accepting that I could have kept this problem from her. I wanted her to have as little involvement with my life as possible. I had been seeing a local doctor once a month, and then once a week, to treat me for a double hydrocele. While playing goalie in a hockey game on the ice of a frozen parking lot, I got hit in the nuts with the puck. The pain was off the scale. I recovered, but over a period of six months my nuts started to swell up, and it made me nervous. It made a lot of the guys in the locker room find their sense of humor. They said I had "balls of fire." By the time track season came around I was the center of attention in the shower. I had to stop a team member from telling the coaches by promising that I would get medical help. But I knew I couldn't tell my mother. I should say I wouldn't.

Walking home from school each day, I passed a house that had a doctor's shingle hanging out front. I went in one day and talked to him. He took a look, knew immediately what it was and recommended tapping in and drawing out the fluid with a hypodermic needle. Not fun.

The doctor thought I was older, and I had been able to

pay him from the money I made working at a local market after school. A lot of the time he didn't charge me anything. Right now I'm trying to figure out how the hospital would be paid. I had no idea. At that time I don't think it ever dawned on me. I think the only thing on my mind was the surgery. Another thing I had on my mind was the word cancer. The doctor at some point had mentioned that word, and then I heard that word again when I heard over the radio that a very popular radio and television star, Arthur Godfrey, had lung cancer. Hearing about it for the first time and learning just how seriously everyone was taking the news of this man's illness was a wake up call for me.

I knew only that this had to be taken care of and there was little or no running away. The problem had become painful and I instinctively knew that if I didn't take care of it, I wouldn't get very far anyway. And I had no horse to ride out of town on.

The details of the surgery aren't that important. It took nine hours, and I had better than 40 stitches in the scrotum. Inside, they removed the two knots that were keeping the fluid from circulating as it should, causing the bag to retain the fluid and head toward having the same appearance as a bull elephant. After I woke up in the hospital and became aware, the first thing I remember was that I wanted a cigarette. There was no nurse standing there, so I tried to get up but found that my entire groin area was taped up, and I had to pee. I don't know if there was a bath in my room, but I knew I had to find one. I mustn't have had an IV in me. When I tried to get out of bed and stand up, I couldn't. It was like I had a cast on my groin that kept me bent over. I got myself out into the hallway, made my way looking for a bathroom and hoping for a cigarette. A nurse spotted the top of my head passing the station's desktop. She immediately got me back to my room, but I was able to tell her I needed to use the men's room. Now I find out it was in my room.

Then she shows me the handheld model of a urinal sitting on the table. She wants me to go back to bed and she'll show me how to use it. I don't think so. I want to go to the bathroom by myself. The nurse must have thought I looked like a turtle as I made my way into the closet bath and closed the door. She said something about the emergency light or something, but I'm alone and I have to pee real bad by now.

This must have been the first time I realized that there didn't seem to be a way to get my dick out. I struggled with the taped girdle and found that the dick was pointed directly at my chin. If I don't do something soon, it's going to be a comedy happening. I had to figure out how I could get the dick headed toward the toilet. If I could somehow stand on my head . . . I opened the door to go get a nurse and she was standing right there. Back in bed and into the handheld.

Later, a Red Cross Gray Lady volunteer was doing her rounds and came into my room. She was wearing a gray and white striped uniform under a crisp white starched nurse's type headdress. I think she really enjoyed being a Gray Lady. She must have asked if I wanted anything. If so, I know I would have said, "A cigarette." She said I couldn't smoke in the room, but I could on the balcony. She smoked. She gave me one. It was a long Pall Mall, no filter, perfect. I did wait until I got on the balcony. All I remember was that first taste of dizziness.

This was 1959. I truly wanted to dump my mother. It's a strange word to use, but that's the way I felt. After my stint in the hospital, I had no choice but to go back to her place to regain my strength. Five days later, though still not recovered, I hitched my way to Wildwood, New Jersey.

I slept on the beach and got little jobs by knocking on doors, offering to sweep floors, wash dishes, anything for a meal and a couple bucks. I ended up with three jobs at once—working at a restaurant cleaning up and eating anything I could get my hands on, a couple hours a day at a hot dog stand on the beach and working at a miniature golf course on Convention Pier. The job on the pier seemed to be the best shot I had to make any money. All I had to do was take the money, give change and make sure the amount of money balanced with the number of times the turnstile counter reported. I was probably on the job for about 10 minutes when I noticed that children didn't want to make the turnstile turn. They wanted to duck under it. I had to make a choice. It was either I called the kids back and made them turn it, tell the parents and let them talk to the children or I could figure another way to make everything work out. There were several ways to go about it. With just a little creative thinking on my part, I made a decision. Just wait for a split second, make sure the kids went under, accept the money from the adults, ring up the money according to the times turned, and put the difference aside for "distribution" later. Made sense to me. And because I didn't have a partner to discuss this procedure with, I just put the money in my pocket for a later discussion with myself.

That summer, from the miniature golf course and other

enterprises I got myself into, I ended up with more than $1,200. I kept track of the total amount I had accumulated over the time I was there. I wonder where it went. Had a nice room for a couple of months and bought myself a car. I should say I bought two cars for $75. Nash Ramblers, made in the 1940s. I didn't have much experience with cars. Bought a battery, installed it, and turned the key, the car started. I had the tires switched around so I had the best on one car. Put a big thick rope in the trunk for whatever reason I don't know, but it sure came in handy later. It was invaluable when I got stuck in the desert sand.

I remember driving a jeep once. To this day I don't know how or when I got a license. It must have been in Jersey. It had to have been on a farm or track. The Ramblers I remember. Neither of them had front seats. I ended up sitting on a box covered with a blanket. In the passenger seat area I put a box that I had found. The only real treasures that went with me in the box were two books. Everything I owned and treasured was sitting next to me.

During the 11th and 12th grades I read a lot of books. This is when I started to learn how to use a dictionary. I began to truly love books and reading. They kept me out of trouble, and they became a screen to stay behind, a wall keeping me from having to communicate with my mother. They nourished my mind and allowed me to travel to places I would never be able to visit. Books also painted dreams that I could live in my heart. Stories about dogs and horses gave me freedom and companionship. The Black Stallion, The Island Stallion and The Return of the Black Stallion were three of my favorites. I hope I didn't steal them but The Black Stallion and The Island Stallion were the treasures in that box. Perhaps I just forgot to give them back to the library. Yeah.

By that time I had already decided that I was going to California. Hollywood, California. I was going to start off as a stuntman and work my way up to acting. It's important to have a well drawn out plan . . . unfortunately, I didn't realize that till much later.

Hard to believe I made it all the way to California in that car. From Wildwood, I drove it to Philadelphia, saw my grandmother and my mother, said "so long" for the last time and took off for California. The stop to see my mother was just to be sure she knew I had no need for her to ever be in my life. It's so easy to be cruel.

Just as I had said "so long" to my mother, I also wanted very much to meet my father. Everything I knew about him came from my mother. None of it was good.

"You're just like him. Neither one of you are worth my time."

And, "You're just like your father. You'll never amount to anything."

I had to find out for myself. There was one person who talked well of him, my grandmother, Nana, my mother's mother. I was able to find out that he probably lived in Chicago, and she gave me the name of the company he had worked for. When I left Wildwood, riding in the trusty Rambler, I had one goal in mind. I was going to find my father. Why hadn't he ever tried to find me?

I was 17, had a pretty serious surgery three months before, was just getting my health back and I was headed for a showdown with my father. It also dawned on me that maybe he wasn't my real father. My mother's hunt for love hadn't subsided. But Nana didn't indicate she had any doubts. Soon, I'd find out for myself.

When I got to Chicago, I went directly to the headquarters of the company Nana thought he worked for and asked for him by the only name I had, Pete. I told them I was his son. It took a while to put everything together before they realized that Pete must have been his nickname from childhood. He was now Mr. Richards, Vice President of something or another. He wasn't in. Today, it would never happen, but back then they gave me his home address. They promised they wouldn't call him. I wanted this to be a surprise . . . a big surprise.

I found my way to his home. It was on a street of row houses. Each house was three stories high. Brownstone I think. I sat in the Rambler. I could feel the emotions building up inside. "I've got to be in control. I can't show excitement. Why not? What do I say? What do I feel?" I don't even know what I was thinking. Forget it. Knock.

A woman came to the door.

"Is Pete here?"

"Who are you?"

"Is Pete here?"

"Are you the paperboy?"

"Is Pete here?"

He had heard the exchange and came around the corner. I didn't hesitate.

"I'm your son."

He wasn't ready for that. I think I must have made his heart stop for a second. The lady looked as shocked as he did. There was an awkward exchange and then the invitation to come in. I knew that my best strategy was to wait until someone else initiated a conversation. My mind was divided into a million thoughts, but my heart was numb. Everything seemed to be in slow motion. He suggested that we go into their spare bedroom and talk. His wife, Mary, seemed nice enough. She wore her hair in a bun with a bleached white streak down the center. I immediately identified her with bars and pubs. People reveal a lot in the way they groom themselves. I had the immediate impression she was comfortable hanging out at a bar. I don't know how she and my father met, but my first bet would be that it was in a bar. Shortly after my father and I went into the room, she came in and took a picture of us. That picture is a treasure to me, and as I'll later explain, it became a ticket to bring us together again 13 years later.

Our conversation was pretty general. "Where are you going?" And, "How did you find me?" The longer we talked the more pissed off I got. It wasn't anything he said or did. I wanted and expected the meeting to be confrontational, but it wasn't. I wanted to take the lead and create a moment that would give me some sort of satisfaction. I wanted to win, but I didn't know what that meant anymore. My anger started to build. He seemed like a nice guy but spending that time with him was getting more difficult. I didn't want to like him. I wanted to hurt him. Why would he let me live my life without finding out how I was? It just wasn't right. I wanted to hate him but I couldn't. I didn't want to like him. This was getting worse by the minute. Then he asked if my mother was alive. Click. That question was like changing channels on the TV.

With my mother being the center of the conversation, it became clear that we had something in common. He spoke very honestly about their relationship. He just couldn't stand to be around her. The only option he had was divorce. He said that there were a couple of times before I was a year old that he tried to see me, but she made it impossible. He chose to ignore the entire situation and stay clear of her, which also meant that he wouldn't be able to see me. He was also very honest when he said that he was very self-centered in those days and having a family wasn't a priority in his life.

We talked for a while. I had calmed down quite a bit and was ready to try to normalize our relationship. My father and I moved into the living room where Mary was waiting for us. Small talk led to suggesting that we go out to dinner.

With all the good manners I could remember I said, "Sounds good to me. Are you going to find a broad for me?"

My father was so offended by my reference to his wife as a "broad" that he rose to his feet to announce his displeasure. I thought he was coming to fight.

I stood up and Mary started saying something that got us both to sit down. We sat. He explained how rude and impolite it was that I had made that reference. I tried to explain that I didn't mean that she was a broad and realized that the only thing to do was to apologize. It was accepted. Dinner was still on.

Their favorite local restaurant was in the neighborhood within walking distance. At some point Mary was trailing behind us as we walked side by side. She came up to us and stated, "There's no mistake about it. You are father and son. You should see yourselves from back here."

We have the same bowed legs and same way of walking. That cleared up a lot of the clutter in my mind. He wasn't Dad, but he was my father.

I don't remember what day of the week it was, but the restaurant was filled with friends from the neighborhood, and my father knew all of them. At first I was uncomfortable as he introduced me to everyone saying, "I want you to meet my son." It didn't take long before I loved it. No way was I going to let him know. "Son." I don't remember anyone calling me son, not even my mother. How strange it seemed and at the same time how welcomed.

"Don't let him know that. Never show that. It's weakness. That's not me. Never."

That night I slept in the spare bedroom. I had made up my mind to leave the next morning. I got up, showered, we had breakfast and I announced I was leaving. My father wanted me to stay at least one more day. He wanted to take me to his office and spend the day together. With controlled reluctance, I agreed. It was becoming more difficult to feel anger towards him. I liked him. When he introduced me to his staff, I sensed a little pride in his manner toward me. Maybe it was just wishful thinking. One thing was clear. He was important to his company. He was one of the vice presidents of DuPont Chemical.

As a matter of fact, that night when we got back to his home, he gave me a sweater which had been made by a research team from the collected fur rubbed off from a rare Llama-type animal that lived in the remote mountains of a small South American country. They were going to try to synthetically reproduce the fur because the quality was so fine and comfortable. They expected it would be an important consumer product. He also told me that he was responsible for another team of researchers whose sole mission was to sit and think. They were provided with a quiet relaxing environment overlooking a lake and a forest of trees. Their objective was to come up with product ideas that would appeal to the buying market. His company would spend millions of dollars developing the ideas and turning them into profit. My father had started out selling paint for this company and now he was a vice president. I may have his bowed legs but I don't have his mind. That night when we got back to his place, he wanted to talk about my future. I avoided any lead into that conversation. I had my own plans, thank you.

The next morning we had breakfast and I hurried to be on my way. I had to go. I had dreams to fulfill. I started to feel that anger come up in my heart. I wanted to get on the road. He began to offer me things. He had a 1953 Mercury that I could have. He wanted to put me through college and give me a place to live next to him. He owned the townhouse he was in and the one next door. I could stay there.

"Stop. I don't want anything from you. Where the hell were you when I needed you?"

I started to get to that place just between rage and tears.

"Fuck you."

I left. It was over. Never would I let someone love me, never. Another level of cruel. I was getting good at it.

I left my father standing there watching me. I couldn't have cared less how he felt . . . at least not for the next couple of miles. How alone can I get? There was some sort of comfort in my hell. This was my private world. Little did I know, it was far from over. That picture his wife had taken was a round trip ticket to my father. Thirteen years later, I met my sister. I didn't know I had one. Shall I go on?

It was 1959 when I first met my father. By 1972, I had been practicing and studying Nichiren Buddhism for almost four years. The lay organization practicing this Buddhism was called Nichiren Shoshu of America (NSA). The name was later changed to Soka Gakkai International (SGI-USA). I was on my way to a study lecture at the NSA Headquarters on Pacific Coast Highway in Santa Monica, California and had stopped to have a cup of coffee and do a little reading of the material before the lecture.

I had been served a cup of coffee when the waitress came back and asked, "Is your name Rick?"

"Yes."

"I'm your sister."

That was one of those moments in life that just doesn't seem possible. How does something like that happen? My father had blown up the picture Mary had taken and hung it on the wall. My sister, Linda, recognized me from that picture.

"Did you know your father is no longer working in Chicago?"

"No."

"Did you know he lost that job and is now living in Atlanta, Georgia selling boats? Did you know he had his left leg amputated last year?"

"No."

"Arteriosclerosis. Did you know he's in the hospital today because they are going to amputate his right leg tomorrow?"

"No."

She gave me the number for her mother, Mary. I called Mary immediately and told her to tell my father that I said for him to chant *Nam-Myoho-Renge-Kyo*. She was about to leave for the hospital and promised to call me back. I gave her my number, said "so long" to the sister and went straight home to chant and wait for the call. The ride home was full of emotion and so many thoughts. The day I left my father in Chicago, I decided that was the end, and I wouldn't keep in touch with him. I had kept my word. With my introduction to Buddhism and the practice of chanting, I would on occasion think of him and even pray for him, as well as have a couple of good thoughts for my mother. To be honest, I wasn't in the realm of compassion very often in those days, but when I was, I kind of liked it and was surprised that I could have good thoughts towards people that in some size or shape had been enemies in my life.

It just couldn't be a coincidence running into my sister. Of all the places I could have been that day. A sister I had never met. My father, scheduled for surgery the next day, all that after I had started to experience the benefits of this Buddhism. How could it be? My father, my sister, me at this moment came together out of nowhere. [2]

As promised, Mary called.

"Your father says he's his own man without any religion."

I got the name of the hospital and immediately sent him a telegram.

"You are your own man with one leg and no religion. Tomorrow you'll be your own man with no legs and no religion. You owe me one. Chant *Nam-Myoho-Renge-Kyo*.

---

[2] The chance meeting with his sister in the coffee shop was Rick's only contact with her. He made no further efforts to see her.

Signed, Your Son," with my phone number.

He was in ICU. They took a phone to him. He called; we talked, cried and chanted together, all this in one day. The next morning I called to find out that his doctor, Dr. Perez, decided not to amputate.

I have three items from my father—the picture of the two of us and two letters. He started off the first letter with, "May I call you Son?" In the next three months we talked several times and would chant together over the phone. I was chanting for him daily from that time on, as well as for my mother. Something was changing inside my heart. Sometimes, I didn't seem like me anymore.

Every day my father would exercise by hopping around the dining room table 100 times on the leg they were going to cut off. He would chant for one hour every day and then turn on the "Mike Douglas Show" in the afternoon. He told me of the benefits that had happened from chanting like solving financial problems, and that the relationship with his wife was better than ever. DuPont arranged for him to have a state-of-the-art artificial leg. They produced some of the components for prostheses. He also said that he felt happier than he could ever remember.

"I really don't know what I'm doing, but I know I'll never stop," he said.

Three months later, having chanted for his hour, he turned on the television, sat on the couch, put his head back, fell asleep and never woke up. The following day, my grandmother, Nana, who had started chanting at the age of 84, passed away as well. Amazingly, she was the one person who spoke well of my father, and she was the one who clued me in as to where I could find him. How remarkable is that?

I've now been practicing and studying Nichiren Buddhism for over 40 years, and I am a member of SGI-USA, an organization for communicating about this Buddhism. One of the basic teachings is that life is eternal. Birth and death are just two of the phases of this life we have. I have no doubts as to the continuation of the lives of my father and grandmother. I can't help but feel that they are near and that we are good friends. Good friends are hard to come by.

6

CHICAGO
To Dogpatch

When I had driven away from my father, leaving him standing there watching me, it was a bassackwards victory. He wanted me to stay. The last thing I would do was give him the satisfaction. I'd rather make him wish he had loved me. I hoped he felt sorry for me.

"Where were you when I needed you? I'll never need you."

And it was all bullshit. I was so confused I didn't know what to think. Words just wouldn't stop running through my mind. I couldn't shut them off. From the deepest part of my heart came a yearning. I wanted so badly to be loved and wanted and needed. Just drive. Drive away from this. It felt like I was falling into a pit. I kept going until the pull backwards and the words racing through my mind were being stretched out and were losing their strength. I don't remember seeing the road. I just looked up and saw the sign. Route 66. How did that happen? My next thought was, "How do you get to Hollywood from here?"

What was I doing? Where did I think I was going? What

can I expect when I get there? Will I make it in this Rambler? I had a lot more questions than answers. I did have a sense of excitement though. I knew I was headed West. All cowboys and horses have got to head west sometime. Imagination is like soap. It can wash away reality. At times it's as if you're in an amusement park without paying the admission fee. Do animals have imagination? Can trees travel in their minds? Is a rock or a mountain or a pile of dirt ever able to see itself in the movies? Don't think so.

It never occurred to me that I should keep a log of that trip. Even if I had, I probably would have torn it up. I almost always throw things away. If I couldn't carry it with me I usually just got rid of it. There's still something inside of me that doesn't want to have too much property. What if I just want to pick up and go? I don't want things and stuff to slow me down. Maybe I'm getting better. Nowadays, I don't want to just throw things away. I want to recycle—great excuse for not letting go of insecurities. It wasn't too long ago that I thought I would never want to own a passenger car again. If I were to own a vehicle, it would have to be one that I could live in.

Something was always making me think I would be back in the street again, and it would be better to have a roof over my head. I think that being able to let go of the mindset that thinks I'm going to be hit unexpectedly and forced into that homeless lifestyle again has a lot to do with the woman I'm married to now.

Her name is Eva, Evangelina. The sound of her name is poetry. Sometimes I call her Evita, and sometimes she is. Sometimes she's Honey. She has an instinct for how we fit together. I read that a wise woman plays about seven different roles in another's life. At all times Eva's love is beyond words. I'll tell you more about her and my *familia* later. Writing these stories and experiences is very exciting. I was born in Philadelphia. I raised myself up-and-down the East Coast. I've got the heart of a cowboy and I'm developing the mind of a Buddhist. Now I'm married to a beautiful Mexican woman, and if you listen closely, I may be getting a Spanish accent. Am I confused? No way. Just flexible.

I'd better get back on Route 66 before I have an accident. Pay attention to the road boy.

Back to 1959, Route 66 and the pursuit of a cloudy dream. Sixty-six kept going south, southwest. As well as enjoying the ride I also liked stopping to get gas. It gave me a sense of being somewhere. Walking around a bit was almost like making a claim on something. "Yeah, I've been there." I wasn't really in a hurry. It felt good to just get out, check the oil and water, stretch out and get a bite of something to eat.

Meeting my father, talking with him, awakened something inside of me that didn't feel very comfortable. I was changing and it made me very nervous. Until that point in time, I had a comfort zone in my anger that made me feel secure and in a strange way at peace. I was in the box that I had built and suddenly it wasn't going to be enough. For all the torment I felt from the rejection by my parents, I hadn't the slightest notion what I was going to do about it. I knew I needed to step out from behind my walls and at the same time I had no idea how to do it without putting myself in harm's way. I was afraid there was no answer for me. I feared that I had become someone who just may be unlovable.

Thinking like that was as if a stranger appeared in my mind. Stop the thinking; just drive.

Sitting on a box with no back support makes things a little uncomfortable at times. The steering wheel became an exercise bar. With very little experience around cars, I would try to strike up a conversation about the Rambler with some-one at the gas stations when I stopped. There was a noise that seemed to come from the wheels. I decided to buy a map and at the same time ask the attendant if he thought I had enough brakes to get me to California. He used his jack, took off one of the wheels and told me:

"I wouldn't try it."

That's great.

"Thank you."

I wasn't going to spend money on brakes. I'll wait until the car won't stop any more. Then I'll get brakes. Always thinking.

Somewhere down the road, I remember it was later in the afternoon, I decided to look at the map. This type of coun-try was new to me. The openness was on a scale I had only seen in films or in magazine pictures. Nature is the great-est of all artists. There were times when I would just sit and look around. There was a fusion that took place with what I saw and what I felt deep within me. Just to experience the movement of the clouds. How many shapes and shades are there? The formations were as if they all danced together, harmony and rhythms . . . silent music . . . the sounds of life. At times these thoughts and feelings inside me meshed with nature like a mother and child. Or at least how I hoped that a mother and son could be. Would I ever know this oneness?

More questions. Who am I?

The map. Stay with the map. It seemed to me that Route 66 was going farther south than I wanted. Then it turned west, then a little north again before swinging west again toward the desert and California. As I looked at the map it seemed clear to me that I could turn west and cut across for maybe 75 miles and get back on 66 again. I wanted to make sure I got to Oklahoma City. My grandmother or mother had told me about someone who was a good friend who lived in Norman, Oklahoma.

"She'll feed you and put you up for the night."

They didn't tell me she was on The World Council of Churches. If they had, I'm sure I wouldn't have looked her up.

It was about time to call it a day. I came across a motel-cafe-gas station that was designed to give the impression you were at a stagecoach depot. I went in to the cafe to get something to eat and asked if it would be all right to sleep in my car out back. Just didn't want to give up money to a motel. The manager said fine. After eating I walked around a bit and climbed in the back of the car.

The next thing I knew, it was morning. I looked at the map again and made a decision. I was going to cut across country and pick up 66 on the other side. But first I went into the little cafe and had breakfast. Walking toward the cafe, I looked around and I realized that I hadn't seen this country before. It was only the night before that the same scenery had mesmerized me, but now in the morning it appeared totally different. It was just as beautiful and exciting but with the change of light and direction of the winds, Mother Nature had revealed her creative instinct in the order of time. All of the appreciation that was coming from within my mind and heart was pretty new to me. Although I was excited by these revelations, at the same time it made me a little nervous. Was it also a little frightening? Maybe. But I don't get frightened do I? Right.

Bacon and scrambled eggs with potatoes and bread—eating in a restaurant was not something I had done very often. My grandmother took me to Horn and Hardart's a couple of times, and I always ordered the vegetable platter. I knew it was the cheapest thing on the menu, and I didn't like her spending money on me.

I wish I could remember the route I used to cut across the country. What I do remember is the farther I went, the narrower the road became and the fewer buildings there were and hardly any other cars. I had plenty of gas and knew I was going in the right direction. When the road turned to dirt I decided to stop and look around. It was the kind of country that Li'l Abner might live in. He lived in Dogpatch, a backwards stone-age community located between two uninteresting hills. I loved it. So did my imagination.

As I write these stories and adventures of mine, it brings back too many memories to put all of them down on paper. By the time I had finished the third grade and hit the road, I had developed a love of reading. I didn't have that many opportunities to get my hands on books so I would read anything. Those two books that I treasured, The Black Stallion and The Island Stallion, both by Walter Farley, I kept with me always. There was always room for those two books. The thing I feel I missed most by not going to school is the ability to spell. I guess I should credit Mr. Farley for some of my education. Dictionaries became good friends, as I would hunt for the meaning of a word and how to spell it. Now I have an educated wife and spell check. Who could ask for more? Even now, I can't go a day without reading something.

These days, 99 percent of the time it's the study of Nichiren Buddhism and lectures or essays by Daisaku Ikeda. The practice and study of this Buddhism has no ceiling. As long as I provide the seeking mind, it never fails to open up my life to the unlimited potential of the universe that exists in my heart. Mr. Ikeda is my mentor, my teacher. For over 40 years I have done my best to live up to his expectations. Those expectations are never dictatorial or authoritative. He only hopes that I will realize my fullest potential and live as humanely as possible. He has the hope and faith that all humanity can live the life of complete freedom that Buddhism promises.

Better get back to Route 66 before I get lost.

That shortcut was no longer a road. It was a path for wagons, tractors or anything that could go off the road. I knew it had to lead to somewhere until I came upon a creek that I had to cross to get to the path that continued on the other side. Now, a few doubts came to mind along with a dream or fantasy. Wouldn't it be wonderful if Dogpatch was near by? And what if Daisy Mae would come out of the bush and want to have her way with me? I hoped Li'l Abner wasn't around.

I got out of the car, laid down at the creek's edge and waited. I must have dozed off because it was mid-afternoon when I woke up. Daisy never showed up, except in that place of imagination. Love that dreamland. Don't need a ticket to get in. Never did pass through Dogpatch.

The creek wasn't deep and it was easy to cross and continue on my way. Before long the path intersected with a more traveled road that led to a paved highway that took me to a little town and a much needed meal. I was very pleased with myself for the day's adventure and dream. There was a very healthy waitress at the diner who would have looked wonderful in a black and white polka dot halter. I decided to sleep in my car that night. I fell asleep with Daisy Mae on my mind. Remember the cutoff shorts Daisy Mae wore? I wonder if Daisy Mae was kin to Daisy Dukes of "The Dukes of Hazzard?" Could be.

7

GETTING LOST
In My Mind

I had to get to Norman, Oklahoma and find this friend of
my mother and grandmother. I remembered that they called
her Aunt Ruth. I also remembered she had been married
to one of the youngest, if not the youngest, president of a
university in the country. Apparently, he was driving to the
school when he hit a section of ice, lost control of the car and
died at the scene. Soon after, she lost her adopted son as well.
He had experienced car trouble that forced him to pull his
car over to the shoulder of the road. He left his pregnant wife
in the car while he went for help. As he walked away, his wife
watched him getting struck by a motorist who drove off and
left him lying by the side of the road. He died at the scene.
How much can one family endure?

As I made it to Norman, nothing of much notice comes to
my mind with the great exception of my amazement at seeing
the vast and colorful nature of our country. Prior to this trip, I
hardly noticed the land changes from one state to another or
even one hour to the next. There was one day and night when
it rained so hard I had to get off the road for not being able

to see six inches in front of me. Pulling off to the side was done as if blindfolded. It was just as dangerous as trying to go forward. I imagined the shoulder of the road falling out from under me as I disappeared into an abyss.

I had a heavy army blanket that I kept folded over the box I sat on when driving. I wrapped myself in it and listened to the variety of rhythms the rain played as it pelted the car. At times the wind would pick up and the rain became waves of water slamming into and rocking the Rambler. There were moments when I wondered if I was going to be in big trouble, but for the most part it was a great joy to experience the moment-to-moment excitement and awe at being a part of nature's ways. Sometimes, when I hear people talk about man-made disasters or Acts of God, I wonder if it ever occurs to them that it may be that we as humans forget that Mother Earth was here long before our footprints ever appeared and that maybe we just haven't developed the wisdom, as of yet, to live with appreciation and respect, united with the nature of life. Perhaps we've encroached on a way of life without much thought about the future and our co-existence. As the very wise man Nichiren said, "If the minds of living beings are impure, their land is also impure, but if their minds are pure, so is their land. There are not two lands, pure or impure in themselves. The difference lies solely in the good or evil of our minds."

I got to Norman, found Aunt Ruth's house and knocked. When the door opened, a very distinguished woman in her 40's welcomed me with open arms. She knew I was coming. My grandmother must have called and let her know I might stop by. At this time in my life I never considered there was a spiritual world, but as I look back, Aunt Ruth was spiritually happy. We talked about the loss of her husband and son, but she must have come to terms with these events in her life and continued to move forward, developing herself. Looking around her home there were several certificates and framed papers in recognition of her work with the World Council of Churches. She was obviously well respected and appreciated for her contributions. She did talk about my mother and remembered when I was born.

At this point I started to become a little uncomfortable. She spoke of my mother in glowing terms. I knew this subject was going to come up. The farther west I went, my mother, my parents, my past, became harder to leave behind. As we talked, it became clear that she and my mother had been very close and shared more than a few very important experiences together. Apparently my mother had been by her side at the time she was grieving over the loss of her husband and son. Aunt Ruth and her husband, Howard, shared many dreams for the future of their family and were very involved with their church. They were active within their community and extended themselves to be of service to their families and neighbors alike. It's very sad that those shared dreams and goals should be shattered so dramatically. Aunt Ruth took hold of her life and directed it to create as much value as she could. I quickly learned to appreciate this woman's strength and determination.

Her praise of my mother was what caught me off guard. Why couldn't my mother have stood side by side with me instead of shipping me off to some strangers who only wanted a body to take out the trash? She made me feel like I was the trash in her life. She ended up putting me out with the garbage.

Ruth offered me dinner and asked me to please stay in the spare bedroom, have breakfast in the morning and get a fresh start on my way to California. I was hoping she would suggest just that and that we would be able to continue our conversation. I wanted to know what she felt and saw when I was a child. Did she know my father? What did she think of him? Did she think my mother loved me at all?

I don't remember what we had for dinner but I do remember our conversation that evening. She started out with, "I'm going to be perfectly honest with you because you must know the truth now or you'll just go through the rest of your life spinning the wheels in your head, and it may interfere with any thoughts in reference to having a family of your own someday. Please understand this is only my opinion."

This is basically what she said, but in my own words: "Your mother was a very attractive woman and she knew it. She relished the attention she got whether walking down the street or having coffee at a diner. Whenever I was with her I knew I was the piece of cheese and she was the meat. She knew how to flash it and did so with regularity. Even in high school she was the one. She was athletic and had a mind as sharp as a whip. She also knew she was one of the upper class, both financially and socially. Your family had the money and the attention that came with it. The interesting thing was that when we were alone or just going about being girls, she was the nicest of all my friends. She didn't show off for me nor did she ever make me feel that I was that piece of cheese. The change came when the attention was put on her.

"When she met your father, something else appeared from

within her. She baited him with looks and moves that I hadn't seen before. She knew how to get men hungry, but she didn't allow them to bite. With your father it was another story. From the time they met it was 'lust at first sight'.

"Your father was a good-looking man. Strong, physically and mentally, and had a look in his eye that gave you the impression he could be trouble. There was also the element of monkey business that seemed to be the aura around him. The missing ingredients in their relationship were the most important, the meeting of the minds, and the meshing of the hearts."

Aunt Ruth wasn't pulling punches as she described her impressions. I appreciated that she spoke to me as an adult. She went on to tell me that their plans for marriage came fast and furious. My mother's family had a large three-story house on the "right" side of town. There were 400 guests at the wedding. I have a picture of my father and mother taken after the ceremony, and they did make a striking couple. Both were dressed in white, and my father looked like he was excited as hell or scared out of his mind. In either case it proved to be the beginning of the end. And then I came along to finish it.

From the start Ruth didn't have much hope that the relationship would work. She felt that my mother was too self-centered, self-righteous and stubborn to ever allow someone, particularly a man, to be her equal. On the other hand, my father was still caught up in conquering the world, and he was not ready to give up his hunt for women. As I listened to her describe both of my parents, I could only think that she was pretty much on the mark based on my experience with them.

I then related a story that my mother had told me just before I turned 8. It was another chance to punish me for my birth into her world. She told me an experience she had with my father. She let me know how much she detested him, as well as how my appearance turned her world upside down and how I removed any chance for her to ever be happy.

She described the night I was conceived. She was asleep when my father came home late one night. He must have come in quietly, undressed, greased himself up and without attempting to wake her up, mounted her before she could stop him.

"He raped me," she screamed.

Her anger built to such a level as she told me this I was afraid she was going to beat me. She went on to describe the pain I caused her during the pregnancy. At 10 pounds I "tore her apart because I was so big." She lost her teeth because "I took all the calcium" from her. There was nothing about me that didn't draw up disgust. Her dream was to become a dancer and actress. Of course I was the "star" of this great disappointment. What had I done to experience such rejection? Why was I born to this family? Why was I even born at all? As a child it didn't make sense.

Fortunately, much later in my life, I was able to turn all this pain of not being wanted, loved or needed into a great treasure in my life. My dream now is that through my behavior and prayer, I will be able to repay my debt of gratitude to my parents. This is what is in my heart now.

Ruth listened intently to the story I told and at times I thought she was going to tear up. When I finished, we both sat in silence for a while. It was awkward for me as I had never told or discussed this with anyone. I also realized that I didn't bring up the subject of the "rape" when I met my father. It never occurred to me then and as I look back, it was probably for the best as it may have ended any relationship. And I am sure the details would never match from the two sides. Ruth broke the silence.

"There was so much about your mother and father I never got to know. I'm sure there is much you don't know either. I think the people you know as your parents were there, but I know that there was also another side of them that we would admire. What I think is most important is that you move forward in your life without spending too much time looking backwards."

At that she began a new discussion. What are your plans? Why California? What's your dream? The change in the conversation was welcomed. I would remember her words "move forward."

I didn't talk about acting but told her I was going to Hollywood to work as a stuntman. I told her of my love for horses and my experience riding Trigger and that I had a talent for taking falls and fights and so on. She encouraged me and suggested that I stop by the ranch of a cowboy from film who lived just out of town by the name of Tim Holt. Great, I'll see a couple horses and maybe get some advice. Git-'em-up, Scout.

A good breakfast, a meaningful good-bye, a hug and I was on my way again. She insisted on giving me a little gas money, which took me right back to having rejected my father's offer of some money. The heart is capable of unimaginable changes. Horses and Tim Holt. My next stop.

8

NORMAN
to the Sea

I found the Tim Holt ranch but was told he wasn't there. He was out of town on business. One of the cowboys working there let me go over to a corral that had about five horses in it. I leaned on the fence and waited to make a new friend or two. Nine times out of 10, with a little patience, humming a little music or whispering, you'll get their attention. Eventually, the one with the most curiosity will come over to see what's up. One did come over and began the introduction ceremony. First he would get close and take in a light breath to identify me, and I would lightly blow in his nostrils. That's usually all it takes to get acquainted. If I don't smell like someone who has abused him in the past, a friend is made. To this day, whenever I'm around horses, I feel a peace and an excitement that very few people or things or places can duplicate. How fortunate I am to have this comfort in my life.

I love the smell of horseshit. Where do these sensory attachments come from? It's one of the great mysteries in life. It amazes me how each of us responds to the environment in totally different ways. We can see, hear, smell, taste or touch the same thing, but each of us reacts differently. And then there's the mind's conclusion as to what we've just experienced.

After about an hour with the horses I left and got back on Route 66, a fresh start with a lot to think about. The time spent with Aunt Ruth stirred up a lot of feelings .. . and even more questions. How much of my personality and character did I inherit from my parents? I really didn't spend that much of my life with either one of them. Only three days, two nights with my father. The time with my mother was random after the first eight years, and I always made the determination that I would never be like her. Once I realized that she would never really love me, I lived with the hope that I would never have to see her again. That was a daily wish. My basic life condition was anger, but that was more for my own protection than a truth in my heart. I built the walls of anger around me so that I would be able to keep people away. It was a lot safer than letting some-one get a foot in my life and kick the hell out of my heart. Nana, my grandmother, was the only one who was never a threat to me. She was the only encouragement I ever got and the only one I could talk to about my dreams. After my conversation with Aunt Ruth, I began to wonder how it was that my mother ended up with the disposition she had when such a gentle woman as Nana had raised her. Could it be that my grandmother presented one side of her person-ality, her character to me, and another side to her daughter? My mother had this quality according to Aunt Ruth.

Driving and thinking was a great way to travel. There

I was, 17 and headed to California in my own car. Sitting next to me was everything I owned. I had a box with fresh clothes that Aunt Ruth had let me wash at her house and a huge sandwich she made for me. She gave me a couple shirts that had been her son's but I never wore them. It just didn't seem right for me to have them. I threw them away at some point but I don't know why. I've never felt comfortable accepting something from anyone. Whether it's a compliment or something tangible, I just don't like it. Perhaps it's because I was always made to believe I didn't deserve anything, I don't know. That is something that hasn't changed after all these years.

When someone would try to pay me a compliment, I became almost defensive. It was very hard for me to see how I could be of much value to anyone. Today when I receive a positive reaction to something I've said or done, I still shy away from taking it as something I deserve, but I am now very grateful for my reaction. I've met and seen too many people who just can't wait for praise. They are mostly concerned with the impression they make on others for the satisfaction of their own ego. They fail to experience the true benefit of helping another cross a bridge from suffering to happiness and fulfillment. I guard myself from ever becoming such a person like those who only live for themselves.

I'm now sure that because I don't seek the light being shined on me, I didn't go after the level of success the artist in me wanted but was contradicted by the other side of me that didn't want the attention. I did want to do the work. I just didn't want the fame or notoriety that went with it.

When I left Aunt Ruth's, she gave me a piece of paper

with the name and address of a relative of my grandmother's who lived in Pasadena, California. She was elderly but Ruth suggested that I look her up if only to know someone out there. I don't know it for a fact but I think she must have called back east, spoken to Nana or my mother and just reported that I had been there and was OK. In her shoes, I probably would have done the same. I also think she kept our conversation confidential.

I began to feel an urgency to get to California. I wanted to be there now, so I decided that I was going to drive as far and as long as I could. I hadn't been driving much at night, but from here on I was going to go non-stop.

I had seen some NoDoz on the counter at a truck stop. Asking about them, I was told that a lot of the truck drivers used them to help stay alert on the road. I bought two boxes thinking that when I started to get tired, I would be able to take a couple and they would help keep me awake and alert. Better get a couple Cokes to take them with and make sure I had cigarettes and matches. That was my survival kit for the day. I still looked pretty young so when I wanted to get a bottle of booze I still used the "My father, my mother or my grandmother sent me" story. Most of the time it worked. If it didn't work at one place, try another.

As I continued to drive and drink and think, I would go back and forth being in awe of the land and the sky and a sense of disbelief that I was actually seeing and experiencing all this. It was as if I were seeing a movie. The road was a pointer. Just go on. Look around; see what you've never seen before. I would catch myself with a big grin on my face. Nothing was funny. It was just so much more than I ever imagined when I was riding with Hoppy or Roy, galloping along side a herd of cattle that had been stampeded by the rustlers. But that was mostly in black and white, and it didn't smell like this. I put my head out the window and could feel the wind whip through my hair. I enjoyed sticking my hand out, pretending it was a bird flying along side. At times I would have a laugh come out of me revealing the joy I was experiencing. I never laughed. What was this? Come back. Look at the road. Pull over at the next gas station just to be safe. Fill it up, check the water. Walk around. Touch the ground with your feet. Make it all real again. The hope I felt inside me was frightening. Is it all right to feel this?

Back on the road, I began to look at the fences. I didn't like them. Burma Shave signs, they didn't fit. They were invaders. It took effort to block them out and see what nature made. Occasionally the fence would have a gate and a long road leading to somewhere. I wanted to go there and see what was at the end of that road. I would hope it was a ranch with cowboys and a bunkhouse and a barn. Maybe I could sleep with the horses again. Maybe I could be with my best friends. My heart cried sometimes when I couldn't be a part of the herd. To put my arms around a neck and let them rest their head on my shoulder. To find that place they couldn't reach and scratch as they quivered with delight because I found the sweet spot. Maybe the next gate will be open, and it will invite me to come in.

Driving and looking and thinking and drinking became a way of life I was really enjoying. I decided that I was going to see if I could drive all night, stop for food and a nap in the morning. The plan was to fill up the tank around dusk, get some food or maybe a sandwich to take with me and go as long as I could keep my eyes open with the NoDoz. Sitting on the box without any back support was beginning to take its toll. I was finding that stopping more often and stretching was becoming a necessity to keep me from cramping up. My back and arms must have been getting stronger by the minute, but I had to shift positions more often trying to find more comfort.

As the day wore on I found I was driving directly into the sun. With no sunglasses and a visor that was so worn out from old age it wouldn't stay in place, I figured it was time to get off the road at the nearest gas station and take a break. It was also a good time to take the NoDoz to give them time to dissolve. I washed them down with a Coke. Again, checking water and oil, topping off the tank and walking around a bit as the glare of the sun faded, I started up a conversation with the attendant. One thing led to another and I told him of my trip to California.

He took a long look at my car and said, "In that?"

Feeling a little insulted, I said, "Yeah."

He slowly walked over to and around the car, looked inside and turned to me. "Someone stole your seat."

"No they didn't. The car didn't come with one."

"Oh." A long pause. "Want one?"

"Yeah." No pause.

He took me around to the back of the station and pointed to a single seat mixed in with parts from wagons or tractors and anything else that moved. It had been sitting there covered with dust for a long time.

"It's yours if we can get it in."

We took it over to the car, moved the box to the passenger side, kept the open end facing the front and slid my possession box inside to hide it from anyone who thought there was anything valuable around, especially my two Black Stallion books. We put my new seat in position and I was ready to go. With a little wire and a coat hanger threaded thru two drainage holes in the floor of the car and wrapped around the frame of the seat, I could lean back and be as happy as a king on his throne. A "Thank you." and I was on my way into the dusk and a great night's drive. Two more NoDoz and I was set.

No more direct sun. I was headed into the night. With that time of day came the adjustment to the light. There was still the light coming over the horizon that gave an incredible backlight to the hills and the roll of the land. The clouds were few, but the color and shades and shapes were all partnered to paint a picture that can never be forgotten. Even now, 51 years later, I see them in my eye-of-dreams and remember them in my heart. My life is filled with the gifts of being human.

One scene would change for another as I traveled this road. It never failed to amaze me how all the sights and sounds and shapes and colors fit like the pieces of a puzzle. A mountain or a cliff cuts into a sea of sand. One minute everything seemed to be veiled in the colors of the sun. The next minute the tints of the moon would envelope the land and a new world would appear, and my heart would sing as if it were a personal gift given to my soul by Mother Nature.

I was going deeper into the night and the headlights revealed another view of the life around me. Now, I was enjoying the view through darkness, but at the same time I kept centered on the road knowing I could easily run into the unexpected. The novelty of the night drive went on for about an hour before I decided to turn on the radio to pick up a local station for news or music or just company. Maybe a minute after finding a country station there was a fpht. The lights went out; the radio died. Whoa . . . What was that? I tried to keep going but that wasn't a good idea, so I pulled over to the shoulder. Everything else seemed to be okay. There wasn't a light in sight. I couldn't go on. I was watching the cars and trucks go by when I got an idea. If I timed it right, when the next 18-wheeler passed with all those lights on it, I'd just floor my car and get back on the road, letting the truck be my guide until we could come upon a gas station. At that point, I'd turn off, see if there's something that can be done and be on my way. I picked out the truck and gave chase. I must have caught my trusty Rambler by surprise. As I put the pedal to the metal it coughed and let out a fart powerful enough to make an elephant smile before taking hold and catching up to our lead that would take me out of the night.

Everything was fine until I noticed the truck was slowing down and that there was another 18-wheeler coming up behind me pretty fast. When it was about one car length behind me and the truck in front of me was slowing down, it dawned on me that I might be in trouble. The driver in the rear got out and came up to me. I explained what happened. The two of us walked up to the lead truck. They had used their CB's and decided to fence me in and check me out. They couldn't have been nicer. Just keep up with them and they'll get me to the next station. As we got close to one, they signaled with their lights for a right turn, slowed down and I peeled off. I blew the horn at them but nothing came out. The fart was the biggest noise of that night. My best way to thank them is to help another when I can. It wasn't until much later in life that I learned that helping others is the best way to live.

The man on duty at the station wasn't a mechanic. When I told him what happened he said, "Check the fuses."

My question was, "Where are they?"

He handed me his flashlight and told me to look for a box under the dashboard. He showed me what a fuse looked like. I found it and fortunately the box was labeled, radio, horn, lights, etc. I popped them out and saw which were blown.

"You must have a short somewhere, but there is nothing I can do about it. You'll have to come back in the morning after 8 a.m. There should be someone who can help you fix it. Or you can buy some fuses and see what happens."

I decided to see what happens. I bought two boxes of 12 each of the two that were blown, replaced them and made my way west with a certain joy at having learned something. I got the lights to come back on. Yay! That joy didn't last too long. I decided not to turn on the radio and see how far I got. Maybe an hour later it was getting a little chilly so I decided to turn on the heater, which turned on the fan, which blew out the lights again. Good thing I smoked in those days. Today I never say anything good about smoking, but matches are another story. I had several packs of matches and needed quite a few to determine which fuse blew this time. I was afraid of running out of matches before I ran out of fuses.

Probably after midnight, being happy with the effect of the NoDoz, I began to think that it would be wise to take a couple more just to be on the safe side. I had taken maybe four or six by then and was enjoying the stimulation. It was also a good time to pull over at the nearest diner or truck stop, have a cup of coffee or two and a piece of pie. I had a half-pint of something hidden under the box so I washed the pills down with the last couple of mouthfuls before going in the diner. Sitting there with my coffee I began to feel a little wired. It was a little uncomfortable but I felt assured that I'd stay awake and be able to continue driving till dawn.

Topped off the gas, checked water and oil and was on my way. I took a couple more NoDoz for good luck. At this point it occurred to me that I wasn't having as good a time driving as before. I was beginning to feel as if I was entering a trance as I concentrated on staring down the road. Switch around in the seat and relax a little. Blow the horn to wake me out of the stupor. Not a good idea. Fphit. No lights. Now no horn, no nothing. I used the key to remove the fuse but now I noticed that my hands were shaking and that this was no fun at all. I dropped the fuses, had a hell of a time finding the matches, and I couldn't get the damn things back in the little tin box. By the time I got back on the road again I was a nervous wreck.

There was only one thing to do, keep going until I couldn't. I held on to that steering wheel like I was climbing a rope to keep from hanging myself. My eyes felt like they were going to pop out and land on the pavement. I have no idea how long or how far I got before I suddenly had to cut to the side of the road to avoid hitting a black and white striped detour sign blocking my lane. It scared the hell out of me. It woke me out of another stupor that I didn't know I was in. I got out of the car and stood there looking at the sign. It may have taken a minute before I realized that I couldn't see the sign. I walked back about a hundred yards and there was no sign. Hold it. What did I see or what did I not see? Was this a delusion or a mirage or what? Then I was thinking, "Am I going out of my mind?" I even thought of waiting until another car came along to see how he handled it. Second thought, get the hell out of here.

Back on the road again.

Just keep alert and I'll be all right. Eat something as soon as possible.

Then it seemed that the gas stations, diners or anything with a light on, were much farther apart. I don't remember seeing a Route 66 sign for a long time.

Have I gotten off track and gotten myself headed for who knows where? At least I know I'm in my car. Other than that, I don't know much else.

There was a truck stop ahead, a local haven for the stranger with kaleidoscope eyes. Maybe they would have a pinball machine. Just what the doctor ordered. Another cup of coffee with a ham and cheese sandwich. A couple more NoDoz. Wash them down with the bottle and hit the road again.

I wasn't happy. Getting back on the road was good for a while until I found myself staring at and counting the broken white lines. I don't remember seeing another car for miles. The trucks have been hiding from me so why not drive down the center of the road and let the line disappear under my car. That was fine for a while until I noticed that I had slowed to a crawl and the lights had blown out again. I was beginning to realize that perhaps, just maybe, the NoDoz and coffee weren't getting along. No more coffee. Way too much caffeine. The loudest horn in the world suddenly blasted me off the road as the lights of a truck went past me like a shot out of a cannon.

The fuses, the fuses, where the hell did I put the fuses?

Matches were gone. By the time I got a fuse in place, got the car and myself in running order, I knew I was borrowing luck. I walked around the car four or five times just to be sure I could. Once back on the road everything seemed to be going well until I noticed something sitting on one of the broken white lines up ahead. It got bigger as I got closer. It was a bird, a huge bird, a huge brown bird. A huge brown parakeet was perched on a broken line in the middle of the road facing my side.

I stepped on the gas with all my might, made sure my window was rolled up tight, and ducked as I passed. I took a peek and it wasn't there. I decided not to stop to check things out. I'm just going to drive and find the light of day. It can't be that far off. Never owned a watch. Couldn't turn on the radio. I was shaking like a leaf but couldn't figure out if I was freezing to death or going nuts. Had no idea where I was and was beginning to question my sanity. I kept my wits about me and continued on my way. Nothing could deter me now. Looking ahead I could see that I was going to be passing under a bridge. There was something dangling down from the overpass, but I was sure I would clear it. The huge brown parakeet had flown ahead and was now hanging upside down from the bridge. Again, pedal to the metal, a fart from the Rambler, I lowered my head a bit and beat the bird before he could get the best of me. This time I did look back. The bridge and the bird were gone. Either they didn't exist or he picked up the bridge and took off with it. I can't be sure.

I made it through the night unscarred. At first light I came across another neon city—motel, cafe and truck stop. I was almost out of gas, the oil was low. Topped off the water and just thanked my lucky stars I made it this far. After a good breakfast I crawled in my car and fell asleep. A night to remember and coming up was a day I could never forget.

I slept for a couple hours, got something to eat and headed up 66 with the determination that I wasn't going to drive at night unless I had to. I was missing too much of the beauty of the trip and the country. The night before took my mind to places I just didn't like. I wanted to get back to thinking about my background, my parents, the puzzle of my life that I wanted to put together, and clear up the picture of who I was.

I was much more at ease now and enjoying myself as I recalled the night before. No more NoDoz. Just seeing this country for the first time was a lot more exhilarating than caffeine. After gassing up, I couldn't find my map. I was sure I had either left Texas or was in New Mexico, but I got confused when I saw a sign reading, "Las Vegas 49 miles." I had made a point of avoiding major cities. I just wasn't interested in seeing any downtowns. Las Vegas was another story. How could I have made it to Nevada already?

It didn't seem to me that I could have gone that far during the night of NoDozing myself silly. What if I was wrong? Did I want to take the chance of missing a look at this oasis in the middle of the desert? There was a bridge at the exit, nothing else.

Forty-nine miles later, I got there. It had a general store with a post office, a gas station and three other buildings. Las Vegas, New Mexico—not Nevada. Leading out of this little town were four roads. Three headed out to somewhere else, the fourth one would take me back to 66. I bought a coke, a half-pint of bourbon, topped off the gas just in case and turned around. On the way back I counted at least 40 jackrabbits. I'm sure they were thinking, "Gotcha."

As I approached the bridge to get back on 66, I slowed a bit and started braking to make the right turn down the incline toward the west. One of the brakes didn't grab and I was going too fast to make the turn. I ended up on the left shoulder of the incline and rolled the car over down the hill, ending up on its passenger side. I wasn't hurt, crawled out through the driver's window and was amazed at the fact that, as this was going on, it was as if everything happened in slow motion which gave me time to brace myself. The windshield had a crack in it, the roof was dented, but the car seemed to be in a lot better shape than one would have expected. The ground was sandy and the hill wasn't very high.

The trunk had popped but there was no gas spilled. The spare tire was still there as was that big thick piece of manila rope. It occurred to me that I had better turn the ignition off. I climbed up on the car, got the key out just as two men in a pickup stopped to see if I needed help. They were Mexican and didn't speak English. With a little help from homemade sign language, they got a rope they had in the truck, tied it to the doorframe of the car and using their truck, pulled the car up on its wheels. I opened the hood, which had been tweaked out of alignment, saw that some oil was spilled but there was plenty of water. Next step was to try and start it, and it did. Don't ask. I don't know. I think the two men were as amazed as I.

Somehow, the communication between us got better after the "Gracias" and the "Thank Yous." It became clear that I could return the favor by giving one of the men a ride down the road. All I knew was he wanted to go to Santa Fe. I was happy to help and we said good-bye to his friend. We had been driving for about 15 minutes when my whole body began to shake like a quake. I realized just how close I had come to killing myself in the accident if not a car fire. I must have scared the hell out of my passenger as he held on to the door and began saying something in Spanish that could only mean that he wanted out. I pulled up. He jumped out before I came to a complete halt. With half a bow he started walking away from the car with a swift gait. I drove away as my hands steadied and my mind now clearer than ever. California watch out. Here I come.

From that point on, the most exciting thing that happened was when I ran into a dust storm. I could see it in front of me from as much as four or five miles away, and then all of a sudden I was in it. All I could do was pull off and wait. The car was rocking from the power of the wind, sand and dirt beating on the car. For a while it made me nervous. Then it turned to amusement. Then it was time to close my eyes and take a nap. When I had rolled it, the doors were knocked out of alignment, creating small gaps. I woke up to find that my car was filled with flies and sand. Where the flies came from and what made them target my car, I have no idea. The storm passed, I rolled down the windows as far as I could and hit the road. Slowly the flies got sucked out of the car. Most of the sand went to California with me. Later I realized the sand had taken off some paint from the car. I'll bet I was somewhere near the Painted Desert. Makes sense to me.

For the rest of the trip, I just cruised along with the wonder of the earth, the mountains and the sky surrounding me and the approaching excitement of Hollywood. I felt privileged to be in Arizona. As the clouds passed under the sun, the changes in the light patterns made the hills and cliffs and mountains dance for my eyes and heart. The colors, shades and shapes were constantly changing. The artists of the earth and sky have a palette of unlimited potential. The artists of the West never fail to take me back to this wonderful trip. I love the art of nature and my imagination would allow me to fuse with it and ride Trigger or The Black into the scene as I sat in the Rambler heading west at 60 miles per hour. Actually, I couldn't go past 55, at which point the car would shake as if it were saying,

"Take it easy. I'm old."

Seeing the sign saying that I had just entered California made me bear down as much as I could. More deserts, more sand, more heat and plenty of road ahead fueled my mind. What was I going to find there? What were the people going to be like? Where's Hollywood?

Route 66 was my lifeline to the future. It was as if I was being pulled toward the unknown. With the history of my past, the excitement of the present and the mystery of the future as my energy, I just darted ahead as best I could. I learned early in my life that there was little value in being afraid of the dark. Fear can be used and converted into courage if you just don't pay much attention to it. Set your target and go for it. There always seems to be something or someone that keeps trying to get you off the track. Let that next target make you stronger as you proceed toward your super goal.

Little did I know that it was the smaller targets that became the great lessons in my life, like blowing out a tire at 55 mph and realizing that when I had bought the Rambler, I hadn't thought of checking to see if I had a jack and lug wrench to go along with the spare tire and rope. The blowout caused me to cut across the highway and end up on the opposite shoulder going the other direction. The Mojave Desert is a great place to live if you can bury yourself in the sand or have no need for neighbors. I needed help and the desert wasn't offering any. After about three hours a police car or highway patrol came by, offered to let me use his jack as he sat in his car while I changed the tire. Those little targets just kept appearing.

The car was settled on the dirt shoulder. Once I figured out how the jack worked and started to put it to use, I discovered the need to put something under it to keep it from sinking in the sand. I asked the officer if he had any suggestions. He got out of his car, walked around mine and came up with the idea of taking my wooden box, tearing it down, putting it under the jack for support and seeing what happens. I learned three more important lessons. One, when you try to jack the car up while on a sandy shoulder that isn't level with the road but pitches downhill a little, the car has a tendency to lean in that direction and fall off the jack, breaking the boards under it as well. The second was don't jack the car up before you learn the third lesson: put the car in gear and pull on the hand brake before trying to loosen the lug nuts. The car pitched forward. Fortunately I got out of the way. More broken boards. The base of the jack got tweaked, the officer got out, examined the situation, got back in his car, which must have had air conditioning, as I with great pride got the tire changed. I returned the jack and wrench to the trunk of the officer's car, thanked him for his consideration, got back in my friend and hit the road again.

At that point, I began to pay attention to the names of the towns as I got closer to Los Angeles—Needles, so many miles, Amboy, Barstow, Los Angeles, 300 and something. I didn't see any signs that said Hollywood.

There had to be a place where I could stop and figure out where I was. I ended up in a downtown L.A. parking lot at 6th and Spring streets. It was exactly 12 noon. The attendant came up to give me a ticket when I asked him, "What's the best paper to get to look for work?"

He asked what kind of a job I was interested in.

I said, "Anything."

He asked if my license was valid. If so, I could work there parking cars starting that night at 5 p.m.

"I'll be here. Can you tell me how to get to Warner Bros. Studios?"

Got the directions, promised to be back by 5 p.m. and took off. All I knew was that just about every western on TV seemed to be made at Warner Bros. Where else would a cowboy go?

As a kid looking for horses and love, I always knew that asking for work never failed to start a conversation. The results were almost always favorable. I found the studio and noticed that there was a drugstore and a coffee shop right next to an entrance to the lot. The store was on a strange corner with just enough room at the front for a door, and it then fanned out toward the back where there were tables for people to sit and eat.

After parking my car, I went into the store and asked the manager, "What's the best paper to get for help wanted?"

"What kind of work you looking for kid?"

"Anything, Sir".

"Go across the street to the driving range and tell them I sent you over. That golf driving range is now the back parking lot of Universal Studios. I did as I was told. The next thing I knew I had a job driving a jeep picking up golf balls. I could park my car in the lot and sleep in it and make a couple extra bucks as the night watchman. I was in Hollywood and already working right next to the studios. I thought it shouldn't take too long before they hire me to do stunts and from there I'll just work my way up to the top. Just like in the movies.

At night I drove the jeep, picked up the balls, washed them for the next day and filled up the buckets, swept out the clubhouse, cleaned the restroom, made sure everything was in place before closing and got paid in cash. I used the bathroom to clean up and I slept in the car with one eye open. It was hard to imagine anyone wanting to steal golf balls. It was my job to see they didn't, and I was already the head of security.

During the day I walked around in circles trying to figure out what the hell I was doing and how I was going to find work in the movies. If you don't have any contacts in Hollywood it's like having a map with no streets. Every time I turned around I was running into a dead end. I hadn't been in California two weeks, and I was already thinking that this wasn't the best idea I ever had. The timing wasn't right. I never got hit in the head with a golf ball but all of a sudden a light bulb went off in my mind. I need to get some lead in my ass. "JOIN THE ARMY." Maybe they still have a Cavalry. I could become a horse soldier or at the very least a glider pilot.

"Sure," they said. "Sure. Sign right here."

First things first. I've got to sell the Rambler. Leaving things behind has never been a problem for me, but this time I wanted some money for my car. And it has some problems. The front right wheel suddenly got twisted on its outside but would straighten out once I got the car going straight forward. I could make right turns okay, as long as I was gentle with the old boy. The problem happened when I was making a U-turn near the Hollywood Bowl, leaving me turned south on Highland headed for Hollywood Boulevard.

Moving like a turtle, I made my way, thinking if I go past the Boulevard at least one block, circle around to the right as much as I can, and I would eventually find something that makes me think I can sell old faithful. It took me a while before I found the spot I figured was as good as any. I pulled into the underground parking at the Hotel Roosevelt and walked up to the attendant and asked if he wanted to buy my car.

He laughed, looked and asked, "How much?"

"$75."

"No. $25."

"Ok."

No good-bye tears but one hell of a memory.

9

MY NEXT THREE YEARS

I was on my way to Fort Ord, California. I had the clothes on my back, a couple of bucks and another chance to leave the past behind. That's like trying to leave town and telling my shadow to stay put. It just doesn't work that way.

My first impression of the army was that I was not going to like it at all. I found out quickly that I did not want anyone telling me what to do. Surviving on my own was a different world. I wasn't ready to have someone put his face in mine and tell me that I had to do this or that. I also had another startling realization: I didn't know how to have a dialogue with someone. My experience with Aunt Ruth was probably the most in-depth conversation I ever had with anyone. Although I didn't spend a lot of time in school, I don't remember talking just for the sake of talking. I do remember that I liked to make people laugh, but that was usually just a one-way exchange.

Most all my life was spent trying to avoid developing relationships. I did not trust people. I kept my distance and made sure they kept theirs by putting up my walls to keep them at bay. Whether I was in a social or work related environment, I was very comfortable to just stay back and watch. I could make myself fade into the environment, thinking that others didn't see me or notice I was there. If I wanted attention, I could get it, but when I didn't, others didn't exist. A lot of people at one time became a great opportunity to hide. I could easily disappear among them, or slip out and no one would know. Another reason to seek out horses. They don't ask questions. Why worry about communication skills?

The army became the schooling I missed as a kid. The teachers were strict but this was just what I needed. It was almost like having an uncle. Uncle Sam. Let's call him that.

By the time I was issued my uniforms and boots, I was in the world of learning. I knew I was not going to get out of this unless I could get them to consider me nuts or a danger to the security of my country. Better to just go along with the program and get as much out of it as I could. I enjoyed the physical training. It was the administration stuff that I had to work hard at.

Around this time something hit me like a rock. I was going to be fed three times a day. I had all new clothes to put on each day. I was going to be paid real money. More money than I had ever had before except what I conned out of the miniature golf job. If I got sick, it would be taken care of for nothing. If I missed work I still got paid. I had it made. Never before did I have it so easy. And they gave me a rifle. If only I had a horse.

Personnel, medical, assignments, where to sleep, keeping everything in order. Shine the boots, police the area, and always be ready for an inspection. KP (Kitchen patrol). Latrine duty. Socks, underwear, uniforms, equipment, everything had to be just so or some smart-ass was going to ream you out and start calling you names, one thing after another. There was nowhere to hide my bad habits. How to cope with all this? Just do it. Then something happened that made it easier to handle. I started to enjoy the training and actually found that much of it made me laugh. At the same time I began to see that I could make opportunities happen if I just kept my wits about me.

The first eight weeks passed quickly. Boot camp, basic eight, then on to specialized training. Ninety-nine percent of the army is regulation and repetition. They want all the soldiers to operate as a well-oiled machine. That's understandable when the objective is to become a united force for the winning of a war. Better to have a flock of men that will follow rather than a tribe of thinkers. Thinkers have a tendency to take time to analyze the situation rather than jump when told, especially when facing an opponent whose purpose is to defeat you at all costs.

The day I signed up, knowing I had a hard time spelling and would get nervous if I had to count the change in my pocket, I decided to volunteer to go to school. The recruiter said I could pick any school from a list he showed me. I chose a 52-week course in Electronic Navigation. I didn't think I was trying to fool anyone. I figured I could learn everything I needed in the school, including how to spell the words and do the math. Besides, the navigation part meant that I would be able to fly. Why not? After the first eight weeks of training, they sent me to another eight weeks preparing me for the training and the job I would be doing for

Uncle Sam. I began to think they had made a mistake when I found that my next assignment would be artillery training at Fort Sill, Oklahoma. When I tried to point out the obvious mistake, I was told not to worry, it would all work out.

By the time I got to Fort Sill, I realized I got screwed. The army did not intend to send me to school. I was assigned to an artillery unit and would soon be pulling a lanyard on a 105mm howitzer cannon. It was time to make some moves. Going through personnel, getting my unit assignment, seeing the people in the paymaster department, it became apparent the army had a lot of other jobs besides carrying around guns, firing cannons, or driving tanks. How did all those people get jobs typing? Maybe I should teach myself to type. I did try to learn in the 11th grade but was kicked out of the class when, in a fit of anger, I picked up the typewriter and dropped it on the floor. Every time I got to the end of a sentence and had to shift down to the next line, the hood would flip open and the damned thing would jam. It had to have been a bad typewriter. Kill it and get another. The school did not agree, so they expelled me for a week. But I was in the army now; give it another try.

You don't get a lot of spare time in the service. Finding a typewriter and the time to practice wasn't too easy until I realized that each company has a company clerk, and each clerk has a typewriter. I ended up getting in a few hours pounding away on the keys. A better way of putting it would be to say I beat on the thing with two fingers while hunting for the next key. Whatever I learned in high school—if anything—never came back to me. This did not seem to be my cup of tea. I did my best, and even asked the company clerk for some advice and pointers. He looked at the paper I was practicing on; asked me to copy something from a memo, examined it, and after watching my performance, sat down at the desk and typed out his advice, "Stick with the cannons."

Not long after, everyone was given the opportunity to volunteer for airborne training. It was time for that move. I raised my hand and that was that. In all honesty, I didn't know what airborne meant, but I was sure it had something to do with flying. They flew us from Fort Ord to Oklahoma. I loved it. Airborne. I didn't know that it meant jumping out of planes. Paratrooper. Once I got a few details, I got excited. It was the landing that made it so unique. Another experience to add to my life. From then on, Fort Sill was just a waiting period. I kept at the typing. Over and over, I typed the same sentence until it seemed like I knew what I was doing. "Now is the time for all good men to…"

Fort Bragg, North Carolina. 82nd Airborne Division. I was excited about jump school. When I asked questions at Fort Sill about parachuting, one person would say they didn't know much about it. Another would say it was the greatest thrill in their life.

Get ready. I'm going to love it; I can feel it in my bones.

Checking in even got exciting. At each department, whether medical, uniforms, finance, barrack assignments, or personnel, I would tell them, "I can type."

Nobody cared. They cared a lot about appearances. Boots had to be spit-shined. No one wore low quarters, street shoes. My uniform and the way I wore it was my identity. Airborne All The Way. All American Airborne. Pants bloused, uniform starched. Everything had to be airborne. Pride, Esprit de Corps.

First thing in the morning, a four-mile run. Exercise, exercise, exercise. Push-ups, sit-ups, pull-ups. Every time I was just a little out of line, I was punished with more exercise. I was punished several times a day with more and more push-ups. It got so bad that I would start smiling or laughing when I had to get down and give them 10 or 20 more. It drove the sergeant nuts but I loved it. After a short while he and I got to be a little friendly, and he started to teach me some of the things about "working" the army. He and I had a couple of things in common. He loved horses and he loved to drink. He helped me find a place to hide a bottle. I kept it in his quarters next to his stuff. He conducted most of the inspections rather than have to stand for them. This taught me to look for opportunities to be in a position where I didn't have to follow like a sheep. As long as I was going to spend the next three years of my life serving my country, I might as well make the best of it and get as much out of it as I put in. After about three weeks of ground training, it was time to start jump school.

For the next five weeks, the training was intense. Every morning started with that four-mile run. Then there was the instruction in class, then the practical application. After that, it could be anything from harnessing up for the jump from the 34-foot tower to more calisthenics. I don't remember the order of things. I just remember that I loved it, especially those extra push-ups. I was having too good a time for some sergeants' liking.

Stopping for lunch always became a special event. We ate like pigs so we would have time for a smoke and a chance to go to the bathroom. One day after eating, I had to take a dump and ended up falling asleep on the toilet. I woke with a start and realized I was going to be late for formation and the afternoon training which started with that wonderful four-mile run again. I rushed out of the mess hall and ran to the formation area. On the way I decided to get as much of a smoke as I could. When I got to the formation, I butted out the cigarette, put the rest in my fatigue jacket, fell in, and immediately had to do 20 push-ups for being late. About a minute into the run, the guy behind me tapped my shoulder.

"You're on fire."

A stream of smoke was rolling over my shoulder. I didn't butt the cigarette all the way out. It burnt a hole in the jacket and the t-shirt. The sergeant in charge heard all the commotion and laughter and jogged over as I scrambled to get the jacket and shirt off. He started laughing so hard he lost his rhythm in the run and had to stop the whole platoon. I dropped down, gave him 20. He didn't have to say a word.

Jump school took five weeks to complete. The training was intense and deliberately designed to put us in a state of mind that would cause us to respond instinctively in a number of given situations if we had a problem with our chute deploying. The training was designed for our safety as well as that of others. All this training has served me well through my life. There have been many times when something would happen that put me or another in danger and the instinct to respond with a clear mind becomes the factor that turns a critical situation into a much better outcome. I really enjoyed the training and have a lot of appreciation for it. It soon was time for the first of five jumps. This is what we were all waiting for. There was one more bit of the training to go through.

125

They called it the "Bear Pit."

Imagine a four-foot deep circular pit lined with sand bags about 18 or 20 feet in diameter. Into it, put a platoon of 30 to 50 men, half in t-shirts, and half without, competing to see which team was the toughest. The one man left in the pit determines the winner. No weapons, no holds barred, no reward. On more than one occasion, bones have been broken and blood spilled, but it was all in the "spirit of the airborne." This game was to be played out only once. The day I went through the Bear Pit was a day a number of visitors came to the jump school. Military brass from Washington liked to bring their wives and friends to show off the rough and ready airborne. Celebrities were also brought to the school as a form of entertainment for the troops. This particular day Wayde Preston, the star of a new Warner Brothers show "Colt 45," was one of the visitors. They came through different times of the day so we were made to go through this "exercise" five times. Unfortunately, one solider was unable to keep his feet under him and fell to the bottom of the pit. He was trampled on and seriously hurt. His injuries were bad. I was told he received a medical discharge. This happened in front of some of those wives. It was the last day ever for the Bear Pit. Apparently, one of the objectives of the Bear Pit was to see if there was something in the character of a soldier that would reveal a fear of combat. If that were the case, they would receive a different assignment. That type of fear could cause all kinds of trouble and be the cause of injury or even the death of other soldiers. Other means had to be used for that kind of evaluation from then on.

Finally, it was time for the jump of a lifetime. Every step

of the training was leading to that day. At 1,250 feet we would leap into the back draft of the props of a C-130 cargo plane at the end of a 15-foot static-line cord that pulled out and deployed our parachutes. First, we would look up to see that our chute was fully deployed. Then it was a ride from heaven to the ground. While feeling suspended in air, a sense of well being came over me unlike anything I had ever known or experienced before.

In the plane, the noise is deafening. Then after taking that long step out, there seems to be dead silence. Nothing ever came close to that experience of the first jump. It was as if I was being suspended in space. Not just with my body but with my life itself. After what seemed like forever, I began to notice the earth coming toward me a little faster than I expected. The training for the landing comes naturally and I rolled into the "parachute landing fall" and felt like I had just been given the gift of life. I almost felt reborn. I knew that I had an addition to my life that I would always consider to be a reward. That first jump is often the one most remembered as the best. It was for me, but not for everyone.

After the fifth jump with the school program, we were certified as graduates and then assigned to the company where we would be serving according to our duties and responsibilities. Our next jump was with that specific company and platoon that we would be living with during the remainder of our time at Fort Bragg.

That jump, our sixth, was called, "The Cherry Jump." That was the jump that got under our skin before we left the aircraft. That was the airborne tradition that came as close as we got to college hazing. The members of the company who had already had six or more jumps were ready to give us reason to think that we might not make it through.

"You may not break your 'cherry.' You may break your neck."

Besides the verbal scare tactics, there was always the possibility that the jumper behind us had done something to our harness to make it difficult for our chute to open properly. Or maybe stuffed something like a bottle of beer, roll of toilet paper or a pair of a women's panties in our pack. When the chute opened we never knew what might come flying out.

On one occasion, I was in the fourth position from the door as we were standing in preparation for the green light to signal it was time to file out. The light came on, the soldier in the door, who had been in that position for a few minutes, froze. The jumpmaster tapped him on the shoulder a few times but he refused to go. He went involuntarily with the help of the jumpmaster's boot. He was soon transferred out of the airborne and became a cook's helper. There was one man I went through the school with who got hung up when his chute didn't open because the static line got wrapped around his harness. He dangled at the end of the 15-foot cord while in flight. The C-130 had been adapted with a wench that was able to bring him back in the plane. On his very next jump the same thing happened. It affected him enough that he was encouraged to seek psychiatric counseling or a discharge. He went home.

During training, we were made aware of this kind of potential problem and what action to take. Not all the planes had the wench to bring us back in the aircraft. If we were conscious when this happened, we were trained to place one hand on our helmet and one hand on the D-ring of the reserve chute. The jumpmaster would then cut you loose. You'd pull on the D-ring, opening the reserve and descend to the ground. If we were unconscious and unable to put our hand on our helmet, it was another story. I never witnessed the "no wench" situation, but while at Bragg, a film was being shot with just that story line. The actor-stuntman was lowered onto a runway that had been sprayed with foam to protect him from the concrete. At the right moment the cord was cut and the plane accelerated its flight. The bad part about this alternative was that there was a good possibility that the dangling jumper could drown in the foam.

Jumping from a helicopter was a change of pace. Instead of jumping into the back draft of a prop engine, we came out under a down draft, and it took a couple seconds longer for the chute to deploy. Four of us were attached to D-rings on the floor of the chopper and went out from one door in rotation. I was second out the door. While looking up, checking my chute, I got a good chance to see the last two men go out. Just as the third man's chute began to deploy the fourth jumped. This was a great opportunity to watch the deployment from an angle that would allow me to see all the action up close. It was more than I expected. As I watched, the man's parachute began to wrap around itself like a rolled cigarette. He passed me trying to get his reserve to blossom but didn't have time as he headed for the drop zone. This man had incredible good fortune. It had rained the day before and there were several places on the ground where the water had gathered but hadn't sunk in the earth. He landed in one of them. By the time I landed he was up on his feet and had begun to gather up his chute. He walked off the field and was later given the option to be discharged for medical reasons.

Once in a while families were invited to witness a jump by several companies of men. It was a kind of show and tell. One soldier's wife and two young children were there to watch him jump and then to celebrate with a weekend pass. Neither his main chute nor reserve opened and he died on impact. I can't imagine the hell they must have experienced.

I'm not sure what in my past might have prepared me for the responses I had to incidents like this, but they made me realize that the future was unpredictable. They also made me realize that the most important thing I could do was to always keep my wits about me and not to take anything for granted. Most of my life I had spent living and sleeping with at least one eye open. And even now as I head for 70 years of age, I still have a very difficult time getting a good night's deep, solid sleep.

All this time, during jump school training, I would practice my typing whenever possible. The company clerk let me use the office typewriter for practice. I knew the jump training was good for me physically and I needed the discipline. What I wanted was mental training as well. It didn't make sense to me to spend the rest of my time in the army running around with a rifle and waiting for the next jump. But I didn't know what action to take to get the chance to better myself. When someone would ask me if I could ride horses, I would always say, "You'll have to tell me." Now I needed to talk to someone, but who?

Just about every officer I saw looked like they were cardboard cutouts. Neat as a pin and straight as an arrow, except for this one I saw coming out of an office building one day. This soldier looked like he had been sleeping in his uniform for a week. His sleeves were rolled up, his hat was cocked off to the side and his boots hadn't been spit on for a month. I don't think he was tall enough for the minimum height of a jumper, but that would never be his problem. He didn't become an officer in a school. He was a field grade full Colonel. I made sure I got into a position where I could salute him. The closer we got, I could see a face filled with experience. I gave him the sharpest salute I had. He flipped a salute back and was continuing on his way when I immediately saluted him again. "Soldier! Who taught you to salute like that?"

"I want to ask you a question, Sir. I would like your advice."

He gave me his full attention as he listened to me explain that I needed direction about my future. I made sure that he knew I could type. That was a good thing. When I finished he said, "Come with me."

I followed him into another building with a sign out front that said Support Group. He told me to wait while he went into the Adjutant General's Office.

Today, I can't remember that Colonel's name. Even then, I couldn't pronounce it correctly. Let's call him Col. P. Before I knew what was going on I was sent to personnel to change my status to clerk typist and assigned to the typing pool that was necessary for all the paper work needed to run the 82nd Airborne. About three days after being assigned my desk and given work to do, Col. P stopped by to see me. It seems that my typing didn't reach or even come close to their standards.

I was really fast in practice but not so good when it came to typing anything other than, "Now is the time for all good men to come to the aid of their country." I probably should have said something about my spelling as well. I didn't lie. I just didn't tell the holy truth. Col. P seemed to take it all in stride. It was the captain who got bent out of shape. If he saw me coming, he would just look away so he didn't have to acknowledge my presence.

It just so happened the colonel needed a driver, and he got me assigned to his office which just happened to be on the second floor above the captain's office. I was now a part of the Division Logistical Operations Center (DLOC). The colonel was the perfect man for the job. He had jumped during the Normandy invasion and had been commissioned in the field. Formality didn't get his full attention. It was the preparation for battle that kept his heart and mind sharp and his love for the soldiers and country. In his life, there was nothing more important than protecting The United States of America. That spirit was his lifeblood.

In 1962 after my discharge, I drove to Chicago to see my father for what would be the last time. I mentioned that I served in the airborne, and my father told me so had he. During the war he was a member of the 501st Airborne Division, part of the 101st Airborne Division during World War II and the Vietnam War—the same unit I was in. A bullet from friendly fire hit him in the left knee and it became the reason for his discharge. How odd that I became a jumper and also served in the airborne? Unknowingly, to some degree, we shared the same path in life.

Working at the DLOC required me to apply for and

receive a Top-Secret clearance. I was given an interim clearance immediately and permitted to report to work. I liked my job, I liked the colonel and when I could, I continued to try to learn how to type. I never got to the point the captain and army expected, but I never gave up until the day I got discharged. After that I never told anyone I could type. I still don't, but I haven't given up. Still can't spell either. During the approximately six months that I worked with Col. P, a lot changed, not just my lifestyle in the army but how I viewed my life and its purpose.

The activities of the DLOC didn't fall into any balanced rhythm. There was always something to be attended to, both day and night. The tension between the Soviet Union, Cuba and the United States had escalated quickly. President Kennedy was in office and was being challenged daily by the Soviet Union and Cuba. It was at this time Col. P—while I drove him to a meeting—asked me to pull over and park the jeep. He pulled a piece of paper out of his pocket, handed it to me, asked me to read it and waited for my response. Unexpectedly, this was a major turning point in my life.

The paper was a request from the Department of Defense for me to transfer to McDill Air Force Base, Tampa, Florida. "Request" was used, rather than "ordered" because when I volunteered for airborne and became certified as a parachutist, I had the option of saying "no" to any request if it could possibly take me off jump status.

I didn't know what to think. The Colonel informed me that it was he who had recommended me for this opportunity. Somehow, I had impressed him with my work ethic, my efforts to always do my best at whatever I was told to do.

And in this particular situation, he knew I could be depended upon to keep my mouth shut when I became knowledgeable about top-secret information. No one had ever had this kind of faith in me before. His words hit me deeply and caused something to stir inside my heart that had never occurred before. We laughed when he recommended, "Don't tell anyone you can type. Just do what you can, when and if you have to."

It didn't take time to make my decision. "Thank you, Sir. I will do my best".

10

THE LAST OF THREE

For the next year I kept my word, and I did do my best. Flying down to McDill with four other enlisted men and about a dozen officers made me realize that this was indeed going to be a special assignment as well as a hell of a challenge personally. With eyes wide open, I looked forward to digging into my new job. As we approached the air base we came in over Tampa Bay. It seemed we were going to skim the water on the landing approach. Disembarking the aircraft, I caught the salt air in my lungs and felt like I had landed in a new world. Immediately we were processed onto the base, assigned our quarters and introduced to personnel who had already logged in and had been placed at their work location.

When I got to my operations office, I was told the sergeant major was expecting me but was taking a shower at the time. The general's driver suggested I go to the restroom and introduce myself. Suddenly, it seemed I was out of the Army. It was more like being a new member of an exclusive club of some sort. The sergeant major was shaving a face that looked like he was about 22 years old. The truth was he was almost 50 and had served during the Korean War—with honors. He was awarded his stripes in the field. This man had the courage of a lion in battle, became a master administrator during peacetime but had a real serious drinking problem. Otherwise, I think he would have been an officer by this time. He and I became friends as well as teammates at work. Both of us took our jobs very seriously, and we fit together like a pitcher and catcher. The mutual support between us is another great learning experience for my life. We also liked spending off hours drinking together. It was at this time I got to the highest amount of booze I could put away on a good night. A fifth of Johnny Walker Black suited me just fine. It never stopped me from working, never gave me a hang-over or reason to think I had a problem. My sergeant major, however, had a lot of problems. He never got to work on time, and I became his work-related caretaker. Once he got there, his performance level wasn't affected. At this point in my life, I didn't see the alcohol as a poison; it was just a part of the routine and ritual of living my life. My drinking prob-lem didn't become a challenge until much later in life when it dawned on me in 1990 that I wasn't drinking the drink anymore, the drink was drinking me. The problem was solved with tough love. Details later.

I was able to keep my jump status. The very first assign-ment was to check out every possible drop zone in the lower half of Florida. If and when the time came for physically notifying Cuba and the Soviet Union of our readiness and our level of alert, we would be able to bring in a company or more of the 82nd Airborne. Even though the airborne was considered obsolete after their first jump in World War II, they always posed a threat as long as they were in the air. As soon as they left the plane, their effectiveness was diminished. You then knew where they would be. The mystery was over.

My basic responsibility, once I was settled in operations, was logging in and keeping track of all lines of communication. Twenty-four hours a day there was constant sharing or conveying of information with every Commander in Chief of Operations in every region of this planet. We were on the brink of a world war. It was vital for the unity of all services to be on the same page with the White House, Department of Defense and the Joint Chiefs of Staff. My boss was the former director of operations at the Pentagon. I was at work each morning by 4 a.m. to prepare the reading file and all its references.

The most outstanding lesson I learned during this stage of my life was the value of actual proof. President Kennedy was determined to show the American public evidence of the Soviet Union's intent to install and position missile launch pads in Cuba. To take aggressive action before confirming the existence of these pads would be unconstitutional. With the actual proof, any action would be defensive and legal. When the photographs were released and shown to the American public, it became a standard for behavior that should be practiced at all times. It has passed over the heads of too many since then. Rumors are the cause of a lot of bloodshed. I don't believe the holy truth is the only option, but rumors are and can be deadly.

The planning and construction of The Strike Command had been going on for some time before I got there. One entire floor of the headquarters consisted of a map that was able to electronically track every sea, land and air vehicle of our armed forces as well as those that would be inclined to cross our path. It knew the personnel, fuel capacity, armament and speed of each piece of transportation. There was also a war room where the department heads and staff would meet every morning for an update and briefing. This was a world I never even imagined existed. Oh, I did have a typewriter. Did I try to type? And, uh, no.

I felt very fortunate to be there, to do a little something for my country. It also helped me develop those much needed communication skills. There were a lot of brilliant minds working there, and I got to see them operate. There were a lot of other opportunities like flying in a jet fighter when my general invited me to go along with him as he flew for his proficiency ratings. I got to serve as a bartender for the officers when they would have their private parties. It made me flash back to the Friendly Tavern. Even those times became a source of good training.

There were about 50 female government workers serving as executive secretaries. That was another good thing. My communication skills were always being sharpened on several levels with the help of these women. That year was forever going to be a good influence in my life. The only negative was that the entire experience in the army honed my nature and skills of anger. The service for my country didn't encourage concentration on becoming compassionate, forgiving or kind and considerate. That wasn't its purpose. But it did provide a training ground for self-confidence. I awakened to the fact that there were some things I was good at or could become so. For that I am grateful. My mother's words, "You'll never amount to anything," or, "You're pathetic," might not be completely true after all.

Just about everyone I met, especially during that last year, was encouraging me to extend my service and consider going to Officer Candidate School. I think I would have made a good officer and a career in the army would have been a good move if it weren't for the fact that my heart was in acting. I was grateful for the direction they were trying to get me to consider, but I knew I had to follow my heart. There was no alternative in my mind. I had no doubt.

There wasn't much time for partying but when the time came, I did take advantage of it. One night my sergeant major and his wife decided to have some friends over for a little food and a lot of drink. My body could absorb a lot of booze before it began to lose its coordination. That night my feet seemed to have developed a mind of their own and even decided to go in a different direction than the rest of my body. The sergeant major and I discovered that everyone had either left or had crashed on the floor throughout the house. At the same time we became aware that the scotch, bourbon, vodka and whatever else was gone. We both knew we couldn't go out, but he remembered that there might be a bottle of vermouth stashed under the sink in the kitchen. On our hands and knees we found it, got to our feet, filled up two glasses and put it away. The last thing I remember was when those feet of mine tried to slide on a white throw rug across the oak floor. I came down on my back, causing me to up-chuck in the air and have it come down on the rug and me. Good night.

On one other occasion I went out to a diner or coffee shop with a friend who was going to meet a woman he had met on the base. The woman brought a friend with her and we hit it off. My friend and his girlfriend kept their conversation pretty much to themselves while the other woman, let's call her Carol, and I were having a good old time talking about anything that came to our minds. We liked each other and at one point I mentioned that maybe we could go out sometime and go to a movie or just hang out. She said she would like that. She also said that she had two children and had to work. I asked what she did for a living and she responded, "I go on pay dates." I wasn't clear what that meant so she explained she went on dates with men for money. Got it.

I told her that I liked her too much to think about paying for a date with her and let it go at that. I knew exactly what she was saying, but I really did like her and didn't want her to think I was judging her in any way whatsoever. She picked up on that and later on asked if she could have my number on the base. I gave it to her and at the end of the evening she kissed me goodnight saying, "I hope to see you again sometime."

It must have been three or four days later, she called and asked if I would like to go to the carnival with her and help her win some toys for her children. We hooked up, went to the carnival and won so many stuffed toys it was almost impossible to find room for us to get back in her car, a Corvair. We had a great time. She drove me back to McDill and we had a hard time saying "so long." It wasn't anything more than holding on to each other. There was a lot of loneliness between the two of us.

A couple nights later she picked me up and took me to

a motel she had obviously been to many times before. Why she felt she had to tell me the manager was her uncle, I don't know, but I wasn't going to ask questions. She had obviously decided to share herself with me that night.

With riding Trigger at the top of the list, that night with Carol is right up there in the unforgettable category. We were together for almost two hours that night and not only did I spend that time with one of the greatest artists of lovemaking, I ended up feeling like I was King of the World. I had been serviced by a woman who knew what she was doing. I also witnessed what it was like to float in the air. I think I may have been completely dehydrated by this woman.

I felt as if someone had filled my balls with helium, and I was floating high above the clouds. Unforgettable was she. A few days later she called and cried while telling me how much she enjoyed our time together. I didn't have to ask. She told me her husband had just been discharged from the Navy and she was going to try to be the best wife ever. Thank you, Carol.

11

DAD . . .
a New Word

About a month before I was to be discharged, I wrote a letter to an actor named Terry Wilson in care of the Screen Actors Guild. Terry Wilson was at that time working on a TV series called "Wagon Train." His character's name was Bill Hawks. He had a long list of credits, including work as both a stuntman and actor in a number of films directed by John Ford. I was surprised when I got a reply. The guild had forwarded it to Mr. Wilson and he quickly responded. In my mind the shortest way to becoming a working actor was to start out doing stunts.

I figured that stuntmen work more often than actors and I had that love for horses, was very athletic by nature and it just seemed the best way to go. I also had a crazy streak in me, and through the years had managed to love making people think I had hurt myself by doing something like running in front of cars and getting hit, falling down stairs, just about anything I could come up with. I asked him for advice, what would he suggest as a good first step? He said he would think about it, but in the meantime he gave me his phone number and told me to call him when I got to L.A. Whoa! What more could a cowboy expect?

I was honorably discharged from the Army with a lot of hope for the future. I had purchased a 1955 Ford Crown Victoria, filled up the tank and headed north. Something was drawing me to want to see my father again on my way to California. Over the last three years there were a number of times I would wonder what my life would have been like if he and I had been together. What if I could have played catch with him? Maybe he could have taught me to drive. I spent a hell of a lot of time trying to get knots out of my shoelaces. He could have taught me how to tie my shoes. Maybe I could have asked him to help me with math or taught me how to use a dictionary. Did he like horses as much as I do? Did he like movies? Could we have gone together? What would it be like to experience being a son? His son. The draw to go to Chicago to see him wasn't because I missed him. The real reason was to confront him again. This time would be with a little more intelligence and a hell of a lot more muscle.

I left Florida in good health, money from saved up leave time and a determination to get to California. As I made my way to see my father, my mind was spinning as to what I was going to say to him. The trip started out with the objective of getting everything in my mind out on the table to let him know just how much I resented the fact that he abandoned me. Then something strange began to happen as I headed for the showdown.

Once I got to North Carolina, I decided to take a route through Virginia and the Appalachian Mountains to Kentucky then Ohio, Indiana and Illinois. Just as the beauty of the country overwhelmed me on my first trip west at 17 years old, at 21 it was even more so with this part of the country. The strange part was, as the appreciation for this experience of fusing with the beauty of nature increased, so did the gratitude for the opportunity. I even thought that if my life had been any different, I would have missed this great adventure. It dawned on me that my father was partially responsible. By the time I got to his front door I had lost the desire for the showdown. I just wanted to see him. Mother Nature sure has a way about her.

I came out of the Army with a new sense of identity and broader outlook on the existence of life. Many of the limitations I had felt about myself were off to the side of my mind now. Although many of the thoughts and memories of my childhood were still there, I had a sense that if I just kept going forward, I would be able to move fast enough to leave them behind. Maybe I can outrun them, leave them so far behind they'll give up and get lost. My mind began to paint pictures of the future without chains to the past. No more mother, no more people with dark hearts. Just keep dreaming and it will all go away. Not yet, not ever, they just won't go away. Sit, shadow, sit. It doesn't do what I want until I do what I must.

I got to Chicago mid-afternoon, called my father's office, got him on the phone and told him I was on my way to California and wanted to stop by to say hello. He left work and we met at his home. I got there before him and waited in the car. Sitting there, I realized I had lost my reason for being there. We just didn't have anything to discuss. Leaving Florida with a plan for a war of words got lost somewhere in

Virginia or Kentucky. Now it seemed our connection which was based on abandonment and bitterness was mute. I didn't want to get into issues or what could have been. I just wanted to be on my way. He must have parked his car behind his home and gone in the house expecting to find me talking with his wife, not realizing I was in my car on the street. He eventually came to his front door and saw a 1955 Crown Victoria painted Florida Pink.

I still don't know what caused me to buy a car of this color unless Johnnie Walker Black influenced me. While still in Florida, Johnnie Walker got me to drive this very car at about 60 mph on the beach, and he decided that I could take it up to the top of a water ski ramp that had been pulled up onto the sand at waters edge. As I approached the ramp I think Johnnie put his hand over one eye. It was Mr. Walker's fault that I missed the ramp by one half the width of the car and ended up landing on the passenger side. Some other friends, with their friends, Bourbon, Scotch, Beer and Vodka, helped Johnnie and me get Pink back on her wheels. From that day on, with the help of a coat hanger keeping the door closed, the missing window became the passengers' entrance and exit. The rollover in the Rambler three years earlier was without help from Johnnie. Maybe it was just me.

I noticed his bowed legs as my father came down the steps from his front door and approached my car. He had a big smile on his face and was dressed in a suit and tie. He looked like a very successful man from a foreign world of business. He had a very strong presence. I wasn't ready for this but as far as I was concerned, I had no intention of paying compliments. I hadn't gotten to that place yet.

I got out, we shook hands and he started to hug me. I stiffened up and he took notice but said nothing. Not ready, not yet, not ever. These responses were a surprise to me and put a fence up between us. There was something deep in my heart that was dark and was not going to change at this point in my life. I wasn't aware that these walls were this thick and this high. It hurt him when I reacted as I did.

We went inside for a while. Mary, his wife, wouldn't be home until much later. He suggested we go out to dinner, asked me to wait while he changed clothes. As I waited for him, I walked around looking at pictures and generally checking the place out. I went into the spare bedroom I had stayed in the first time I met my father. On the wall was a picture of us. The photo his wife took three years before was enlarged to about 8 x 10 and framed. Looking at it wasn't easy. My father came into the room asking if I wanted a copy of it. He gave me a wallet-sized photo, which many years later, I had copied and enlarged and it now hangs in my home next to a photo I took of my Grandmother, Nana.

Conversation was very uncomfortable. Small talk about my service time and he told me about his days with the 82nd during the war. How strange to find out my father and I were both jumpers with the 82nd Airborne Division. I realized we were alike in many ways. We went out to dinner, had a couple of drinks, went back to his place and had a couple more. He was drinking as I would drink. It wasn't social; it was a habit. When the glass is empty you fill it up. I think we shared the same bad habits. Bowed legs, drink too much and get a little heated when a subject comes up that seems to be nobody else's business. Conversations with my father were stiff and formal. We really didn't have much to say to each other.

In whatever daydreams I had about my father, I always wished I could call him Dad. As he and I spent these last few hours together, it was on my mind the whole time. I just couldn't bring myself to say it. Throughout my life, I've wished to be able to say, "Hi, Dad." Now when my children say something like, "Dad, how are you feeling?" or "It's good to see you, Dad," a chill goes through me. It's a real treasure to hear that word "Dad." I wish I could have just once said, "Thanks, Dad."

The next morning Mary made breakfast. My father said he would take the day off and we could hang out together. I was too uncomfortable and felt emptiness inside. I just wanted to be on my way. In a sense, I wished I hadn't gone to see him but had headed straight for California. I think he was disappointed. I caught a look between him and his wife that said to me, "Let him go." I got out of there soon after. He walked me to the car.

"Please let me do something for you."

He was starting to choke up. I knew this would be the last time I would ever see him. The emptiness in my heart was now a knot of emotion that made me think I was choking. I looked at him.

"How much money do your have in your pocket?"

I didn't need it or even want it. I just didn't know what to say. He pulled out $62 and handed it to me. That was it. It was over.

"So long." And I drove off. This is one of those moments I wish I could take back. I didn't say, "Thanks, Dad."

12

MY FIRST SET
of Spurs

The entire trip back to California is almost a blank. Other than thinking that I had something tangible to accomplish when I got there, I can honestly say I don't remember much of anything about the trip itself. I don't remember stopping to sleep or eat. I don't remember being moved by the beauty of the land this time other than it was a welcomed background for this next step in my life.

Following Terry Wilson's advice, having talked to him the day I got back to California, I called second unit director Cliff Lyons. He was preparing to leave for Israel to make a feature called "Cast a Giant Shadow." When he got back he would meet with me, but in the meantime I should go out to a place called Corriganville and introduce myself to Ray "Crash" Corrigan. Tell him Cliff sent me, and get advice from him. What Cliff didn't know was that Crash and I go way back.

Back to when I was eight years old, living with One Eye and Pinky Finger with the inch-long nails used for cleaning ears and turning on her husband, making me sit on a stool watching them eat was one of their favorite punishment games. My game was to shift the stool into position to watch the television in the mirror. *"The Three Mesquiteers"* starring Ray "Crash" Corrigan, John Wayne, Max Terhune, his dummy, Elmer, and just about every western film from the 30's and 40's played every night on Frontier Playhouse. Don't play games with me, One Eye.

Trigger was there too. Long before the silver saddle and Dale Evans, Trigger caught my heart. I was in love. The films were in black and white, but Trigger showed the true color of his heart and skill as an athlete. What an animal. Better stop now and get to Corriganville.

Corriganville was a 22-acre piece of land in Simi Valley, California that "Crash" got for a great price back in the 30's. He developed a permanent western town with a hotel that served as a sound stage. There was the western street and the Mexican street. The bank, the blacksmith shop, the livery stable, the general store and of course, the bar, The Silver Dollar Saloon. All this provided the background for better than 4, 000 films, TV shows and commercials. The back lot of Corriganville had hundreds of trails and rocks that could be filmed from any number of angles. Riding back there was like going to cowboy heaven. If you listened real close, you could hear the hoof beats of a thousand horses echoing through the canyon or crossing the old wooden bridge. Behind any rock you might run into Hoppy or Buster Crabbe and Fuzzy St. John, Lash LaRue or Bob Steele. How many posses passed this way? The stagecoach that was robbed after a long chase happened just about anywhere around here. Fort Apache was built there for John Ford and served as the home base for Rin Tin Tin. The Lone Ranger and Tonto, Silver and Scout, when was the last time they came to town?

By the time I got there in late 1962, the market for western films and television productions was fading. Roy and Trigger, Gene and Champ weren't coming into town and stopping by the sheriff's office or the Silver Dollar Saloon, but Crash was. He was hosting the public that would come out on Saturday and Sunday to witness how the West was really won. The great West was open for people to come and watch live action shows. Gunfights, hangings, cowboys beating up on each other and roof falls were performed six times a day. Sunday's featured "The Gunfight at the OK Corral." Each Gunfight at the OK had a guest star. Sunset Carson, Nick Adams, Rory Calhoun, Tim McCoy, Rod Cameron, were just some of the actors who would come out on a Sunday and step into the character of Wyatt Earp.

I got to the ranch on a Saturday morning and found Crash having breakfast in the Cafe. I went over to his table.

"Excuse me, sir. When you finish eating, may I talk to you?"

He pointed to a chair, signaling me to sit down.

"Let's talk now."

When I mentioned Cliff Lyons had told me to get in touch with him, he warmed up and I told him about my dream.

Mr. Corrigan, "Call me Crash," listened to my story and suggested that I should think about working here at the ranch, get some training in stunt work and also get used to working in front of a crowd. That way I would be better prepared when Cliff returned from location with his picture. It sounded like a good idea. Crash walked me around, showed me the town, told me a few stories and introduced me to some of the stunt people who worked the shows. One of the members of the cast conducted classes on fighting and falls. Insurance prohibited the more dangerous stunts like stirrup drags or saddle falls. Between watching a couple of the shows, listening to Crash tell me his experience starting out as a physical trainer at MGM, doubling Johnny Weissmuller, getting his acting start in a 15-reeler, to starring in over 100 westerns, this could be a good start for me. How lucky can a cowboy get?

Those 15-reelers, also called cliffhangers or serials, with each reel or chapter ending with the hero or maybe his horse about to get killed, drove me nuts. As a kid, when I would sneak into a theater to try and catch a Roy Rogers feature, they would almost always have one of those cliffhangers as well. I never was around by the next week for the next chapter to see what happened.

After that first day at Corriganville, I went out that night and bought myself a .45 caliber Italian made replica of a Colt revolver, a holster, used thrift store jeans and shirts, a pair of rough-out boots, that I scuffed up immediately and a great old hat. With the attitude of a man working in Hollywood, I reported for work the next morning. I was the first one there and took the tour again with just my imagination and my dreams. I was ready to work. Work? Nobody "works" in Hollywood when you're in love with the day.

The shows were narrated stories with a little history thrown in. All you had to do was sync the action with the storyteller. Each tale was an account of real facts told with a Corriganville twist. My first day's work centered on either walking, standing or sitting in the background while the story unfolded. When the action began, I would be drawn to the sounds of yelling or screaming or maybe gunfire. My response would be to run toward or from the disturbance, hide behind a building or disappear down the street. By my second weekend at Corriganville, I was shot two times and got to throw a punch at the bad guy. The third week was a really big bump when I was cast to ride the horse out of town.

Speaking of the horse, his name was Flash. Except for one of the six shows in a day, his job was to be tied to a hitching post in front of the Silver Dollar Saloon while the children and adults would walk up and pet him. I think Crash told me he was about 20 years old and loved the attention the public gave him. That may be true but there was the one day when Flash just got fed up with the children groping him, stepped back, broke the rein that was tied to the hitching post and walked out of town. When Crash found out, he walked out of town, trailed Flash to the dried up Robin Hood Lake and led the horse back to the same spot he left. Crash closed his fist, pulled his arm back and hit that animal right across the top of his nose. Poor Flash went down as if hit by Rocky Balboa. Crash got him back on his feet, tied him to the hitching post and went to the cafe for a late lunch.

I went over to the horse and stroked him for a couple of minutes. I don't believe in that kind of treatment toward an animal. In the meantime Max Terhune, Crash's partner in most of his films, was sitting on a bench not far from the horse. I walked over, sat down and asked if that happened very often. Max must have been 70 or 75.

"That ain't nothin'," he said. "Go in the saloon and get me a phone book."

I went in, asked for a phonebook and the bartender pointed to a pile of them and I took one out to Max.

He said, "Feel my arm."

It was like trying to squeeze a river rock. He took the phone book, about 4 inches thick, and tore it in half.

"If that horse was a buffalo, Crash probably would have asked me to do it."

Max started to laugh and that was a signal to me that these two men were lifelong friends who liked each other a lot.

By maybe the third or fourth weekend at Corriganville, I was gaining a lot of confidence in both my concentration on character and the ability to pull off the stunts without looking as if they were staged but happened in the moment. There weren't a lot of clues as to the nature of the person I was portraying, so it gave me a great amount of freedom to create the personality and nature as I wished. The stunts were no problem. Anxiety or fear never entered the picture. I just kept inside myself, found my rhythm and danced through whatever the obstacle was. Later on, when I started working professionally in film, I did come across a few challenges when I realized one mistake could be my last.

I was beginning to get comfortable doing the shows and getting more involved with the characters and action. I did my best to make everything as real as possible and make the shows as believable as I could. Sunday's were always the biggest draw primarily because of the appearance of the guest star. Nick Adams starred in the TV series "The Rebel" as Johnny Yuma. He had been the guest star a couple times before I got there. I had my picture taken with him just before the OK Corral show. During the enactment, he used a martial arts move and knocked one of the actors on his ass. Of course, he apologized but there weren't too many of the cast who believed him. I didn't realize it at the time, but it was going to be my last show for a while.

The next morning my grandmother called and practically begged me to come back east; she needed me. This was my Nana, the one person in my life who used the word "love" toward me. There was no second thought or hesitation. I took off for Philadelphia the next day. The pink Crown Victoria and I were headed east. It was January of 1963. Ever been in Flagstaff, Arizona when the wind-chill factor registers 30 degrees below zero?

When I bought the pink car from another soldier, I wasn't concerned that it didn't have a firewall. In Florida it didn't hurt to have the extra ventilation. The fact that the ski ramp stunt broke the glass wing vent on the passenger side didn't bother me either. But when it got to be minus-30 degrees and I was driving at 60 mph, I had a tendency to think I might freeze to death. With a lot of tape and cardboard, I covered the open window. I found an Army-Navy Supply Store, bought a jacket, a blanket and didn't look back. I was afraid that if I did look back I would turn around and head toward California, but Nana had called.

The entire trip east was as if I was going downhill. This wasn't the direction I wanted to go. I felt like I was going from light to dark. I knew I was going somewhere I didn't want to be. Against the pull not to go was the love I felt for my Nana. I couldn't refuse her. No one other than my Nana had ever said "I love you," to me. My mind was split into pieces during this trip: disdain for my mother, confusion about my father and love for my grandmother. All the facts of my relationships with all of them, mixed with my thoughts and imagination, played so heavily on my mind that other than knowing I was headed to a war with myself, I don't remember much about the trip until I crossed the Mississippi River in Missouri. My car was running a little rough, the money was getting low and my heart was getting darker as I headed for Kentucky and West Virginia. It was just about 30 miles east of the Mississippi when I realized I had to make an important stop. There was a noise coming from the engine that sounded something like fingernails being drawn down a chalkboard. The problem got a little more noticeable when it began to sound like two and then three hands of nails dragging on the chalkboard. By the time I got to a gas station, the noise was so loud that the people at the station were covering their ears and ducking behind anything for protection. They thought I was going to blow up like a bomb. A fine mess, yeah.

The "car doctor" came over with the grin on his face of a man about to haul in a big one.

"Does ya think ya have a problem?"

I was looking into the face of a man who had more blackheads than I had hairs on my head. He was also a gambler.

"I'll make a bet ya blew the rear main oil seal; I bet cha."

He put the Pink up on the rack with one little remark.

"The last time we had a pink car come through here, the driver got arrested for indecent exposure. He lost a hubcap and his nuts was a-showing."

Have you ever heard a jackass laugh? I think this man must have choked on a sparkplug. His voice sounded like what you might expect if a tank could talk. He knew his business though. And I knew I couldn't spend $200 to have the seal replaced. Now what?

Without oil, I was going nowhere. The car doctor came up with an idea. He scooped out a couple quarts of sludge oil from a 50-gallon barrel. Using a funnel he put the sludge in my car and told me to start it up after he covered the concrete surface under the car. The old oil came out exactly as he thought it would. The next idea was to give me five gallons of the sludge in an old gas can, fashion a funnel out of a cardboard display from some old promotion gimmick his supplier gave him years ago, put five quarts in the car and send me on my way. I left there with my car sounding as pretty as a hummingbird. Within about 10 or 15 miles it started again, that blackboard-fingernails-to-make-your-skin-crawl sound, and I stopped to fill it up again. Overall, I think I must have filled up the five-gallon can 15 times before I got to Philly. But I did get there, well almost. Somewhere near Lansdowne or maybe Upper Darby I had to cross a couple sets of railroad tracks. I didn't make it. The two rear tires blew at the same time. I got the car off the street, into an alley way, took off the license plate, put everything in the duffle bag and left the Pink sitting there.

With my pistol and holster on my hip, boots on my feet, hat on my head, duffel bag over my shoulder, I made it to Nana's and knocked on the door. She took one look at me and had to sit down. She was afraid she was going to wet herself. Laughing at a cowboy doesn't always get a loving response. Didn't stop her though. She let out a couple short farts and we were both laughing so hard it was like being in the monkey house at the zoo.

13

NANA'S
Wish

Grandmothers and grandfathers are a very special breed. What I've heard most often is that they have the better of two worlds. First, they get to spend time with the children of their own children but they're not chained to them for the rest of their lives…except in their hearts. The little cute adorable kiddies go home. The responsibilities of the grandparents are part time. And of course grandparents get to spoil the kids by offering an opportunity to have the wonderful time that they, the grandparents, wish they could have had with their own children.

Flip the coin and the grandchildren get the treatment and affection they wish they could have had with their parents. That was certainly the case with me. In my world, through the first eight years, my grandmother was an oasis of joy in my hell. She was the love. She was the person I looked forward to seeing. From my Nana, I had the hope that my life might one day have a niceness to it. My father was no more. My mother was just darkness. Nana once said to me, "You're so aristocratic." I had no idea what that meant, but the way she said it made me think I had something worthwhile in me. I have no idea what caused her to have that impression. I was, in my mind, unworthy. But she was the one I wanted to run to when my heart hurt. And she could fix it with a hug and a kiss on my forehead.

How could she have been my mother's mother? From Nana's mouth came words of praise, from my mother's, words of disdain. Could my grandmother have two opposite personalities? After my visit with Aunt Ruth in Norman, Oklahoma, many differing thoughts came to mind about all the people, the so-called family, in my life. The biggest puzzle was how did all this come about with me in the middle? It seemed that I was the one factor or piece that didn't fit. If I weren't around, maybe everyone would be happier. I think my mother had the same idea. She took action; she dumped me. I don't think she was ever happy.

So there I was, 3,000 miles from where I wanted to be because my grandmother wanted to see me for something so important she couldn't tell me on the phone.

"So, Nana, why am I here?"

It didn't take long before the reason became clear. She wanted my help with her daughter...my mother. What she thought I could do, I don't know. I do know that if it was her intention for me to be a good influence on my mother, she was barking up the wrong tree. But Nana had a plan.

"Please stay here, with your Mother, for one year. Try to mend your relationship. If at the end of a year nothing improves, I'll never bring up the subject again. Do you want to play Canasta?"

Twist my arm, nail me to a cross but don't ask me to

move in. Please. But that's what she wanted and that's what she got…almost. I did move in. I loved my grandmother, hated Canasta. I won. I never played Canasta again.

The welcome mat was very small, but it was there. They must have had some very interesting conversations before I got there. It became clear this plan was coming from both of them. How they expected that the effect on me from all the experiences of the past was going to vanish and that I was going to become kind, considerate and sweet was beyond even my rich imagination. And I truly don't know why I decided to give it a try. It's another piece of the family puzzle that doesn't fit. Whatever Nana wants, Nana gets.

That first night I stayed with my grandmother with the promise that she wouldn't call my mother until the next day. I just didn't want to talk to her yet. Tomorrow would be soon enough. Nana gave me the rundown on what was going on. My mother had a nice two-bedroom apartment not far from there. She worked for an executive of a large grocery store chain, was dating a lot of different men, and she was still as mean-spirited as ever.

"Then why would you want me to have to go through all this again? I don't need this."

Nana started to cry,

"I can't take the way she talks to me and treats me any-more. I need your help. Please just try. Just try. She's still my daughter."

Sometimes you just don't have a choice. "Just move forward," Aunt Ruth said. Can you do that when you feel like you're going backwards?

The next morning I called and caught my mother just as

she was leaving for work. She would call the manager and ask them to let me in the apartment. She would be home around 5:30 p.m. That was good. It would give me time to figure out which was my room and generally check out the building and the immediate surroundings.

I made my way to the apartment. The manager came to the door with a wide smile and great teeth. I was immediately aware this could be an opportunity to hone my communication skills. She was at least 12 years my senior and had a 13-year-old daughter she had just dropped off at school. If she had a nickname it could have been Frisky. Frisky offered me coffee and conversation. Let me just say that if Frisky and I became friends, it would make the prospect of living with my mother for a year seem a little easier to swallow.

Frisky and I did become friends—not good friends, just intimate friends. I immediately felt that she had a history. The kind of history I wanted to explore. From that first time we met I instinctively knew there was a curiosity between us. I really liked the fact she was older and that instinct told me that her history would be mine to enjoy and learn from. She seemed to drip sexuality.

When my mother got home that first evening and came in the door, it felt like two people were at the opposite ends of the street and we were going to see who was the quickest on the draw. Slowly we approached each other and very slowly we hugged…kind of. The distance between us was huge. So was my dislike for the word mother. I don't remember ever calling her mother when I was a child. I thought the word in my mind but I don't remember ever saying it. It didn't fit. Mom never entered my mind. I did think of calling her Jean at some point, but that didn't last long. She just wasn't a mother in my mind. She was someone who was forced on me. There we were, knowing one of us had to say something, and for my part I just couldn't say, "Hello, Mother." And I didn't. She spoke first.

"Hello Dick."

I hated being called Dick and she knew it. She knew it from the day I went to school for the first time and sat in the assembly when I was either in kindergarten or the first grade and they called out everyone's name: William, Joe; Brown, Bill; Washington, Carl and then Richards, Dick. You're laughing. It's not funny. From that day on it was Rick. You can call me most anything but not Dick. She never wavered, not even once, in her entire life. I wavered. I called her mother but that comes much later. Everyone has secrets. I'm going to confess one of mine. With great affection, sometimes Nana would call me Dickie Boy. I let it go. Not one word, please.

That first night was like drinking out of a glass with a crack in it. Great caution, each word thought out before spoken, both of us trying not to step on the toes of the other. But we made it. One thing became very clear. At the slightest leaning toward bringing up anything from the past, a red flag would appear in her eyes and I knew immediately there would be fireworks. I pulled back each time. Where I was getting this control from I don't know, but I realized that the present and the future were the only time periods we could discuss. I was determined that we would spend this time as peacefully as possible. This was Nana's wish. She wanted and needed her daughter's love and kindness. That was much more important to me than settling accounts. As the days and weeks became months, whatever controls my mother was using slowly began to slip away and the mean spiritedness began to raise its ugly head. As that happened, the desire to fill my Nana's wish began to fade. I began to think about getting out of there.

I had been there for about three or four days when I started working the midnight shift in the warehouse, unloading box cars for the same grocery chain where my mother worked. Frisky happened to be checking the mail near the entrance to the building when I came home. Her mouth, her teeth and that bra-less blouse of hers greeted me with a welcome that not only warmed my heart but also seemed to invite me in for more than coffee.

Frisky didn't beat around the bush for very long. I went into her apartment and before we could even get into small talk, we were brushing against each other and getting used to our scents. It was like two animals getting to know each other as the heat got turned on between them. At her suggestion, I went upstairs to my mother's apartment to take a shower. I was to leave the door unlocked and she would be up in a few minutes.

I don't remember much about the shower other than by the time I was done she was in the bathroom waiting for me to step out. She took a towel and began to slowly pat me dry. Frisky then asked me to sit on the lid of the commode and lean back as she toweled off my feet and legs. She was kneeling before me when out of nowhere I think she mistook me for a Popsicle.

There are some things in life that happen that you have to struggle to remember, and there are others you can't get out of your mind. It's the ones that bring back a total recall that you lock up in your memory, and each and every time you bring them to the surface, you relive them with complete delight. This was one of them.

From that day until almost the day I left for California, Frisky and I carried on as if this was the only purpose of life. If you can name it, I think we did it. Other than this form of entertainment, I don't remember anything else we had in common. Our conversations usually didn't go outside of primal grunts and groans.

I worked in the warehouse unloading one freight car after another of foods. Canned foods are the heaviest, so of course that's where the new kid started. I liked it though. Each case weighed about 54 pounds. Great exercise for the arms, back and shoulders. I kept to myself and did my job. I worked the third shift so I didn't have to spend much time alone with my mother. By the time I got home in the morning she was gone.

I'd just take a shower, climb in bed and wait for Frisky. I may have bolted out of this situation sooner if it wasn't for the things I was learning from Frisky. She knew I was going back to California in the near future and we would not be seeing each other after that. I had made that perfectly clear. What I didn't know was that she and my mother were working out a plan. And of course Nana was a big part of the strategy.

For the most part, the relationship between my mother and Nana was better than it had been for some time. Weekends were mostly centered on the three of us spending time together as a so-called family. Poor Frisky was left out in the cold. If she had hung out with us it would have been very awkward. Our relationship fell into the category of games. When the time came for me to leave, the games got called off. Frisky didn't want to stop playing. I refused to play anymore. One of the games was that I would go to the movies sometimes without telling her. Frisky started to think I had a girlfriend on the side. It put another dimension in our relationship. A little spice you might say. Seasoning can turn a boring meal into something unexpected.

I had been working on my own plans for some time. I needed a car. I didn't have any credit, but I did have a plan so I could buy the car with cash. I didn't spend a lot of money on entertainment during this construction of family ties. Didn't need to. I had Frisky. But I did need more money than I was saving. Warehouses have a lot of opportunities if you just think about it for a while.

The door that was used to back the freight cars to the unloading dock is square at the top. There was a cement block wall along one side of the car and on the other is the warehouse. The top of the freight car is about a foot below the door but the car isn't square like the door. It's curved so that there is quite a bit of room at the edge of the car. I hope you can picture this. It was an important part of my plan to get a vehicle to return to California.

The physical work was great for my body, but at the same time it gave me too much room for my mind to work in its most comfortable manner. Naturally, the comfortable thought that ran through this uneducated brain of mine was, "How could I do the least to acquire the most?" Cigarettes are a big ticket item for the grocery stores. Each carton comes into the warehouse in a large cardboard box, 144 of the smaller cartons. Usually, an entire freight car would be stuffed with the huge cartons. How could they miss one or two or maybe three of these boxes?

All I needed was a plan, a man with a crooked mind like mine who had a truck, another keeping his eyes open while I crawled under the car, got to the door by the wall, broke the seal and pulled out three boxes of 144 cartons of cigarettes. The seal was easy to duplicate with a little piece of thin sheet metal and wax from a candy with liquid in it that you chewed. The red cherry flavored liquid would mix with the wax and become soft. I'd roll it into a ball and press it between my thumb and finger with the metal in between. Timing is important as well. And don't do the same thing more than three times.

Then it was the struggle to get up the ladder to the top of the car, pull up the boxes with the pre-made sling, stash them on the edge and wait till the end of the shift when the cars were taken out and switched with the new loads to be worked by the next crew. The man with the truck and I would bide our time looking for just the right opportunity, quickly lower the boxes and be on our way. We already knew an owner of a chain of smaller stores who would be very happy to take them off our hands, pay cash and he let it be known he was in the market for anything we needed to get rid of. Bicycles anyone, pots and pans, utensils? Along with a couple of other methods of making—that's the wrong word—putting money in my pocket, I was able to buy a used VW Bug for cash. Of course, I thought I was getting away with something because I never got caught. What I didn't know was that the Universe was watching. It's that cause-

and-effect thing. Every time I wanted, or I should say, needed someone to help me execute one of these plans, I always attracted someone just like me. If hindsight came before payback, I might have been a wealthy man by now, but no.

I've spent a lot of time trying to figure out why my mind always went in the direction that would have to be called negative when it came to filling needs on a material scale. It wasn't because I was lazy or didn't want to work. I came to the conclusion that I didn't think I deserved the opportunities for building a foundation that was solid enough to support the dreams I had. It probably can be traced to my first years as a child, and I also have to acknowledge the character that was mine alone. My parents certainly left their prints on me but as I began to experience my life not just through their eyes but also through my own, I became aware of the self that was uniquely mine. In some ways, I began to become my own best friend. Can a man with a "monkey business" mind really be your "best friend?" Don't think so.

California was calling me. I took Nana out to dinner and we had a long, wonderful conversation. She was happy with the way the relationship with her daughter was developing and was grateful for my having come back east. She was also ready for me to leave again. It was time. It was also time to break off the relationship with Frisky. She seemed to understand and didn't offer any real argument. It was just as easy with my mother. We both understood that our spending this time together was as if borrowed. I felt good about having come back, but I felt better about leaving. Not too many words were wasted. "Good-bye." That was it.

Do you ever talk out loud to your car?

"With the speed of light, and a hearty Hi-Yo Bug. California, here we come…again."

I decided not to go up to Chicago to see my father but to head straight across country on the southern route. It was a beautiful trip. This was late September, early October, 1963, and the eastern part of the country was changing color minute-by-minute. While going east seemed as if I was going slowly into hell, going west felt as if I was being drawn up toward the sun. This trip was unlike any other in that I felt a freedom in my heart I hadn't felt before. Much of the relationship with my mother that I held on to with revenge or with a desire for vindication was missing. There still was nothing I could describe as love, but I was no longer in the claws of hate. I was no longer drawn toward my father. I didn't see any possibility or reason to make it any more than it was. In both cases, with both of my parents, I saw no future. Of course I couldn't see the back of my head or the nose on my face either.

Another change in me was the attitude I had going back to California. It was the seriousness I felt toward acting. All the romantic thoughts about working in film were still there, but something had changed from the images of riding Trigger across the open range to wanting to study the art of the actor. During this trip to Philly I began to take the making of movies to a different level. When I was much younger and would sneak into the theatres to see westerns, I also would sneak in to see other films as well. During this trip east I saw a lot of films. I knew I could do that.

Certain actors took me with them through these stories of the lives of the characters they were playing. There wasn't a moment I didn't believe Montgomery Clift in "Red River." I understood what he was going through. I saw him as an example of the art I wanted to master. Marlon Brando was being torn apart between truth and loyalty. He didn't have a chance but neither did he have a choice. His heart dictated his mind. "On the Waterfront" forever etched in my mind the need to tell the stories of these human activities, to believe truth can exist in the circumstances of film. I can do this. I can finally direct myself toward a dream that I can make become real. I have never seen acting as anything other than art.

One day around the time I was in Philadelphia and had either met or was going to meet my friend, Tony, I snuck into another theatre and they were showing a film called "The Great Caruso" with Mario Lanza. Never before had I heard such music. Opera. I had never even heard of opera let alone seen one. I was blown away by the sound of this man's voice and by the intensity he revealed as he sang. That was my first real experience with music. Of course, Roy could sing but this was from a different world. I'm not attached to music per se, but a certain song or performance or voice will stay with me forever. Music in film is subliminal with its suggestions to my subconscious, just as John Ford would frame each scene as if painted by Frederic Remington or Charles Russell. I was caught in a trap that I had no desire to get out of.

Not unlike the inborn love for horses that set my heart to beating with the passion of love, movies gave me a sense of purpose. There wasn't the slightest doubt in my mind that I wouldn't succeed and become a part of the pictures that movies painted. What I didn't know, I felt I could learn. All

I needed was the opportunity and the training. That was the light that shined so brightly as I headed for California. Don't even think I won't make it. As soon as I got there I put on my boots and hat, strapped on the .45 and headed for Corriganville. It wasn't like I had another choice as far as my heart and mind were concerned.

14

HONDA . . .KINDA

Back in the 1960's after Corriganville, I had started a
career doing commercials, episodic TV and some print work.
Honda was just making its way into the United States with
its first motorcycles and cars. Grey Advertising Agency
decided to shoot one of their first ads at an Encino Tennis
Club. It was the beginning of their campaign, "You Meet the
Nicest People on a Honda." I was sitting with a friend at a
table when the agency said they would pay for all our drinks
if we would stay seated and provide background while they
got their shot. Shortly after, I got a tap on my shoulder,

"Can you ride a motorcycle?"

I had ridden a little but not enough to brag about, but
without hesitation, "Yes. Of course."

The actor they hired couldn't get the front wheel of
the bike to hit its mark at exactly 7 mph. That was what
they needed to get the spokes to reveal that the bike was
actually moving. Hal Adams was the photographer. They
gave me a test around the tennis court, put a good-looking
woman on the back and before I knew it, I was doing their

ads for the next year.

That first shot came out as a two-page center spread in the June 18, 1965 issue of LIFE Magazine. It just so happened that issue of LIFE had 16 pages of color pictures: 'The First Space Walk." It had to be one of their biggest distributions ever. And that same shot became a billboard across the country. Don't drive and try to look at yourself on a billboard on Sunset Boulevard. It could be fatal. I enjoyed the work and the bragging rights. I was one of "the nicest people on a Honda."

Now skip to July, 2005. I went on a commercial interview for Ameriprise Financial. First interview, "What are your hobbies?"

I answered, "Horses and sculpting."

Two weeks later they called me back.

"Do you ride motorcycles?"

I answered, "Yes, I was under contract with Honda for a year."

"We're looking for someone to ride an old Triumph at around 25mph down a residential street. Can you handle that?"

"Yes, of course."

About a week later they booked me and set up a wardrobe fitting.

"Just bring in some old cowboy boots and jeans. We'll find you an old beat up leather jacket. Your part of the story takes place in the Sixties."

Perfect.

I went in for the wardrobe fitting and all went well. The story line has people during the 1960s with their dreams. Then they flash forward and they're in their 60s, and their dreams have come true, with the right financial guidance of course. We found a great old leather jacket and a great hat. On my way out, one of the producers' stopped me to look at some pictures of riders on some pretty big, powerful bikes.

"You were under contract with Honda, right? Do you think you can handle something like this?"

No hesitation,

"Yes, of course."

"OK, thank you for coming in."

I left there very grateful for the job and at the same time wondering exactly what the job entailed. About two days later I got a call from New York.

"Mr. Richards, what qualifies you to think you can handle a bike of this magnitude?" Oh boy!

I said, "First of all I haven't been told what the magnitude is and secondly I'm 3,000 miles from you and I'm a very good actor. I've done a lot of riding in my life, and have found that motorcycles and horses are very much alike. Each has their own nature and character. Each has their own capability and it's up to the riders to bring out the very best in either case. Given the right cues, you ask them to perform at their highest level. The biggest difference is that bikes have two wheels and horses have four legs. Now tell me, what magnitude of bike you're talking about?"

After a pause, "You'll be riding a 2004 BMW 1150. Mr. Richards, thank you, we'll call you with another wardrobe fitting for the upgrade."

"You're welcome. Thank you, and don't worry."

Maybe I should worry. Hanging up I was thinking that they're having some serious doubts about whether they had hired the right man. I may have gotten myself into another tight squeeze.

Back in 1976, I was hired to work in a commercial for AAA. The ad's character, Charlie, never saw anything that represented danger or an obstacle to his life. The storyline called for Charlie to walk down the street with his wife, Cassandra, beside him doing her needlepoint as he read a newspaper ad from AAA about the benefits of life insurance. He accidentally stepped onto a stack of ¾ inch plywood that was being craned 110 feet up in the air to the top of a steel skeleton for a hospital under construction. Charlie then stepped off the plywood onto an 8-inch wide steel girder. In Charlie's world, he's still on the street, not a problem in sight.

The day after I was cast to do the job we went to Western Costume, picked out the clothes, and went by the location, which upon completion became the Veterans Hospital off Wilshire Boulevard. Standing there at the top of this 110-foot frame with the director, I knew I was in for a big day. When they asked if I wanted to walk through it, I politely said, "I don't have the right shoes on."

When I got home my wife took one look at me and said, "What's wrong?"

I replied, "I think I could die tomorrow." But the show must go on right?

The next morning I was there, ready willing and maybe able. Everything was going great until we got to the top of the 110 feet and it was time to step off the plywood onto the 8-inch girder. I had a big problem. I couldn't see the girder as I stepped off the plywood. It was very important that I didn't change the position of the newspaper I was reading from to Cassandra. The camera angle didn't give me the slightest chance to cheat. Stunt friends told me that there was no way to get air bags or a cable or any protective equipment to catch me; if I made a mistake, end of story. We got the shot but not without some anxiety on my part. Need life. Stepping off the wood onto the girder was done with a great deal of faith. As I took that first step on to the girder, I pushed the plywood away from me causing it to then swing back towards me, hitting me in the back of the knees, knocking me down on the girder. Take two was called and it was fine. I made my way across and through the hospital on the girders before stepping off the building on the opposite side onto a stack of 2 x 12s that carried me down to the street, back to walking side-by-side with my wife. I then declared, "I probably don't need insurance." The shot went to freeze frame as I was about to fall into a manhole as we crossed the street. We won a Clio Award that year, and I filmed around 10 or 11 more commercials. "Of course I can do it".

The BMW 1150, however, was way beyond my experience. I knew I had better get to work and make this opportunity happen by getting a little practice. All I needed to do was screw this up, and I would never work for the advertising company or the production company and certainly never again be seen by the casting agency. First, find dealerships that sell the bike. I found two, visited them to only find out that their insurance prohibits test drives. That's great. One had the same model in for maintenance. And "yes," it would be all right to just sit on it for a minute to get a feel for the size and weight. It was then that I discovered that I couldn't balance the bike because my feet couldn't reach the floor. The seat was 35 ½ inches off the ground. My inseam is 33 inches. The plot got thicker. Sitting still, I would never be able to keep the bike from leaning and probably falling on one side or the other. The bike was too heavy to keep it up with one foot on the ground. And, of course, there's the issue of knowing what steps had to be taken to get this machine to start. I had better get this down in my mind or just hang myself. Get it right and I would be OK. Get it wrong and the results added up to a ride out of town—a reputation I'll never shed and no residuals.

The salesperson was nice enough to talk me through the procedure. The moment I got to my car I wrote it down. I studied that so intently it almost became a mantra. If I got it wrong it would have been one of the few mantras that lead straight to hell.

What's next, the wardrobe fitting to complement the BMW 1150? I learned a lot more about the commercial and its intent. Through a series of short stories we would see people 40 years ago pursuing the hobbies that became their dreams. Of course it was Ameriprise that enabled these dreams to come true. My dream? Cross the Ethiopian desert on a motorcycle. Little did I know the Ethiopian desert was just outside Palmdale, California in a dry lakebed in the Mojave Desert.

I got fitted with the right outfit from the helmet to the steel tipped boots. Everything a man could want to look good and be protected for the trip. The wardrobe people were wonderful. At the same time I felt a little distance or distrust from them as we tried everything on. I sensed they were a little uncomfortable with the fact that I was studying the outfit I was trying on. The motorcycle clothing was as important as the bike I would be riding. It was a professional piece of equipment, and it didn't appear to them that I was too familiar with how to get everything to work together and how to adjust it. No one said anything until I was finished and one of the production assistants was walking me to my car.

"You seemed a little nervous in there. Are you sure you'll be all right for the shoot?"

I wondered if he had been asked to feel me out.

"I'm fine. My bird died yesterday and I can't get it off my mind. He broke the mirror in the cage and he thought he had killed his wife. It must have broken his heart."

Sometimes, I can't remember how to spell imagination… but I do have one. After a slight pause, "Oh, sorry to hear that. I'll see you on location."

I had converted to Nichiren Buddhism in 1968 and by 2005, I'd had many experiences to cause me to have a lot of faith in this religion. I knew I had to truly rely on that faith to get me through this latest adventure.

I had already been feeling the anxiety build, but with this new evidence of skepticism it started to feel a little like a rope was going around my neck. I would go home and with each little obstacle mounting on my back I would tell my wife what was going on, and we would first shake our heads, laugh at how ridiculous all this was and then chant like we were trying to get blood out of a rock.

In my mind, the commercial was wrapped and looked great. But that was the day before we shot it. The next step was to follow the directions and appear at the location on the lakebed in the Mojave at 8 a.m. on August 5. I got there all right, with the rope around my neck getting tighter. By the time I arrived, I had determined I just had to do my job and not to let anything—like the cost of screwing up this production—enter my mind. Just go ahead, get dressed and take the next step. At 100 degrees or more, it was already hotter than hell. By the time I was suited up and ready to see the bike for the first time, I was sweating like a pig. The pants were already sticking to me like glue, and the pits of both my arms and crotch were beginning to feel like two pancakes in a bucket of syrup.

The bike was being lowered off a truck by lift. If it had been a horse, I'm sure it would have been just as nervous as me, sensing for the first time who would be on its back. I only wished I could go up to it and give it a hug of love, but that would be another commercial. They positioned the bike on its side stand and handed me the keys. It's getting hotter by the minute and the pants are getting to the point that I know I needn't even think about getting my leg to swing over the bike. Only one thing to do, pull the bike back onto its rear stand and get on that animal like Roy Rogers would. It's called a Cooper Mount. I vaulted myself on to the bike. Follow the plan, started the thing, jerked it forward off the stand and head for Ethiopia.

Seconds later, I felt like I was flying through heaven. That bike responded like Trigger. We circled that whole lakebed like we had been partnered together for years. The rope was cut and the anxiety turned into a cold shower. I was a kid again and happier than a monkey in love.

I took at least two good spins around the lake, came back to the truck, pulled up to the director and asked, "Did you have any reservations about me being able to do my job?"

Without skipping a beat he replied, "No, no. Not at all."

Another good thing: those steel-tipped boots gave me just what I needed to barely touch the ground and keep the bike balanced when standing still.

The obstacles weren't over yet. By the time we were ready for the first shot, the temperature had gotten at least 20 degrees hotter and I had drunk about four bottles of water. Now they tell me that I will not be able to wear either goggles or a shield over my face. They needed to be able to see me when I got close to the camera and identify the same face for the close-ups later. It became apparent that I was getting myself deeper in trouble as the day progressed because at times during the shoot, I had to catch up to the camera and reach speeds of 60 mph. In the meantime, my eyes were burning up. During the lunch break, I took a look in a mirror and my entire face was as red as a beet. My eyes looked like paintballs on their way to becoming the logo for the Target stores.

By the time we finished lunch and got back on the bike I had drunk around 10 bottles of water, but not once did I have the slightest desire to go to the bathroom. The water was coming out my pores faster than I could replenish it, and I was beginning to think that I really was in Ethiopia. The production had hired a man with a donkey pulling a small wagon to be part of the background. The temperature must have been at least 135 by 2 p.m., and I was ready to go into LaLa Land. For a split second, on one of the last passes in front of the donkey and wagon, I swear it was a 7-Eleven.

That commercial must have been cut in five different

ways. Friends keep telling me about different versions they saw. It was a great experience. Perhaps I should have said something to them like, "My Honda adventure took place 40 years ago," and "I only did their print work." But then, I love the fact that as an actor, I can call on my life's experience to bring a character to life, and in the Ameriprise commercial I did just that. I made a dream come true, just as the storyline called for. Only in Hollywood. Or maybe it really was Ethiopia. I'm not sure anymore.

15

MO' HORSES

With all the love I have for horses you would think that when I began to work in the film business, I would naturally get many opportunities to work with them. It didn't happen. I never got to work in a western movie. But I did have a couple commercials that were challenging. I was on an interview for a beer commercial when I spotted an actor wearing a hat that just spoke to me.

"Take me home, Cowboy. Take me home." I had to have that hat.

If I remember correctly, the commercial's principal actor was a farmer. I had a couple hats that would work. I picked a beat-up old straw hat that could have been half a meal for a goat. It was ugly but it was perfect for the job. Staring at the actor's hat got his attention, and we said, "Hello."

After a little bullshit, I said to him, "Try my hat on. I'm going to be honest with you. I think you would look great in my hat."

I took a little pause. He tried it on, took a look in the mirror, and looked over at me.

"Perfect. I was right. I'll let you wear it when you go in. Just let me have it back when you come out."

He went in to see the casting people and came out with a little grin.

"I think you might have made a mistake lending me your hat. I think they liked me."

I took another thoughtful actor's pause.

"You may be right. I had better not wear my hat in there. Let me wear yours. If they see me in the same hat, it'll make me look like I borrowed it, and I don't have my own stuff."

He understood that well enough. I went on the interview wearing his (best looking cowboy hat in the whole wild, entire, complete world) hat, and made sure I came out with a little disappointment painted on this face of mine.

"Well, that's over…but I was thinking, 'What if they call you back and one of the reasons they want to see you again is because you look good in that hat of mine?'"

A short pause. He's thinking.

"Here, hold on to my hat and I'll keep yours for ya just in case I need one. What do you think? Or maybe we could or should just trade. I think my old hat should be your old hat. I'm serious. It looks great on you."

I love my new hat.

That must have been in the early 1970s. My new hat has been talking to me for a long time now. And I talk to it. I put that hat on and I become a new man whose heart and eyes are a couple hundred years old and have been on a horse every day in their life. The horse, the hat, the man are one as they live with the earth, sky and wind. As long as they are together, all is well. No matter what happens in a day, a month, a year or ten, they do it together. And now they are old, they are tired, they have shared hell and heaven in this one life and on this earth, and they are intent on going on forever… together.

I never got a chance to play that character on film. But I am that man in the quiet of my mind.

I had a wonderful experience doing a commercial for the foreign market. It was a Carling Black Label Beer ad. The storyline was about a bunch of cowboys herding about 50 wild horses across the Mojave Desert to a ranch. The herd was rented from a company that supplied bucking horses for rodeos. The storyboard said, "We herded, then penned the animals, unsaddled and fed our horses and headed for the beer that was waiting for us in the barrel of ice."

We spent four days getting the herding scenes and another getting the slow-motion shots of the cowboys going over to the beer, tossing bottles in the air over the backs of the horses as one of the cowboys catches a wet one in midair. The next shot has to show him as he uses his belt buckle to open his beer while he strolls over to another cowboy leaning against the corral. That other cowboy was me. Shooting this commercial, herding horses out in the open range for four days, was as if someone had handed me a dream. It was like living in cowboy heaven for a week.

Because it was going to be sold in Europe, it had to be 6-point beer. That meant it had twice as much alcohol as allowed in the United States. It sounded simple enough until we got to the wrangler they had chosen to open the bottle on his buckle and take a big thirsty hit.

The cowboy they picked had the look of a man who just

got thrown from a bull and landed on his face. He looked and was tough. But he wasn't comfortable with himself on camera. He was very stiff and when he tried walking across the corral toward me, as sketched on the storyboard, he looked like he was forcing himself to look relaxed. The director came up to me and asked if I could help him. As we began another take, I yelled over to him, "Make sure you drink that whole bottle before you get over here." It took his mind off the camera and he was as casual and natural as you would want. It was a long walk.

After three more takes he began to relax a little more than expected. By the sixth take and the sixth bottle, the beer and a long day in the sun was beginning to take over. That shot was everything they hoped for. The last shot of the day would be the close up on the opening of the bottle on the cowboy's belt buckle.

It was starting to get dark. We were beginning to lose the light, so they had to come in close with the reflectors and camera, and it was becoming difficult to keep the bottles looking as wet and as cold as necessary. This was the money shot. They had run out of the glycerin that was being sprayed on the bottles to give them that wet look they needed. One of the crew had to go to a truck to fill the spritz bottle. The entire crew was French and many of the production assistants were pretty young ladies. To their surprise, our wrangler decided to help by pulling his "hoss" out and spraying the bottles. He was hung like a pony. They got their shot and a hell of a story to tell back home. The next morning, it may have just been my imagination, but I swear I think our cowboy had a French accent and that two of the girls were bowlegged.

Back in the 1960s there was a hair product called Score. Apparently, their sales were doing very well and so they decided to bring out another product, banking on the popularity of the hair crème. I don't know the whole story, but they apparently thought Score Underarm Deodorant should be on the shelves and advertised on television as soon as possible.

My agent called. I went on an interview and a week later got a callback to see if I could ride and rope a calf, tie it off, walk over to a fence, reach up and lift a beautiful actress, who would be cast at just the right height for me, down to my side and then put my arm around her shoulder.

"Of course I can. I've been working with horses, one way or another, all my life."

I went home, and about three hours later I got the call. I booked the job. This is going to be great. There was only one little problem. I had never gotten far enough along practicing my "cowboy ways" that I had actually done any real roping. I had better do something about this now. The "got it" call came on a Thursday, and I was to fly out of L.A. Sunday. A couple phone calls to stunt friends, and I was all set.

I arranged to learn the basics on the ground with an old cowboy who would show me everything I needed to know. He let me rope from foot, a calf made out of a barrel with horns. That was Friday. I was also able to get a hold of an ex-bull rider who would take me out Saturday to a ranch in Malibu Canyon where a lot of the West Coast cowboys meet to rodeo and compete for jackpots to keep up their proficiency. This would be my only chance to get the practice I needed.

The work on the ground went well. I felt confident I could rope well enough to give the production what it needed.

The next step was to do as well from horseback with a live calf doing everything it can to get the hell away from me and a horse that looks like it wants to climb on its back. In my mind's eye it was working out very well, but it was the reality I had to work on. I was excited about that Saturday, not just because I would get the practice in, but I was excited to just be able to be around the horses and other people who loved them as much as I did.

The ranch, the horses, the calves, the cowboys, all were icing on the cake. And then there were the bulls, the Brahmas, and Larry, the cowboy who invited me to come out to the ranch. He had been a professional bull rider but had to give it up after getting gored pretty bad while competing. He became an actor/stuntman. He had set it up for me to be able to ride one of his friend's trained roping horses and to take a couple runs at bringing a calf down and tying it off. He had forgotten to mention that there was an initiation type thing I had to do first.

I had to ride a bull. That's the deal agreed upon by the boys. Ride the bull and they'll let me practice roping. Half the cowboys there were actors as well. Westerns were still going strong in Hollywood and many of these guys were trying to make a living doing the hard riding, action stunts or supporting roles. This was a time when the Marlboro Man was still doing cigarette commercials on television. Many of the boys were a packaged deal because they would also hire out their horses as well. The cowboy was in.

I made the deal. As I prepared for the ride, the butterflies began to stir inside my belly. It's amazing what you have to do to get ready. The equipment is one thing; nerves are another. Just looking at these bulls up close made me think I was nuts. I had been married for a year or two. I'm sure that watching me prepare to ride one of these bulls certainly didn't strengthen my wife's confidence that she was living with the sanest man on the planet. I was getting excited. It was like the first time jumping from a plane. Or perhaps a better analogy would be making love with a new partner for the first time. There aren't too many things more exciting than having sex with a stranger.

Back to the bulls. Larry let me use his equipment, little belts to keep my boots from being torn off during the ride. The bull's skin is so thick that it will shift from side to side during the eight-second ride. The spurs are made at a 15-degree angle to give you a better chance of staying in control when the bull moves and the skin shifts one way or the other. The glove was tied to my wrist; the harness that goes around the bull is called a bull rope and pad. Slowly I got ready, all the time looking over at the bulls and then to my wife Lynn. The look on her face was like reading a bad comic book. I think she thought I was out of my mind. Use the rosin; work the rope. It was time to climb up the fence and get on board. Sit down, wrap the rope twice through the hand, hold on for all you're worth and nod your head. It was slow-motion time again as the gate opened and out I came, thinking I was going to be launched into the next county. But no, I stayed on board for the full eight seconds.

For all the build up and excitement and anticipation, I think that bull jumped maybe five times and then only about three inches in the air. I was really disappointed. But Larry and his friends weren't going to let me get hurt. They just wanted to scare the hell out of me to see if I would back down. They were probably right. You can't make a commercial roping a calf if you're injured and not well enough to peel a banana.

The next morning I was on my way to The Three Forks Ranch in Texas. This ranch had been the location for a number of Marlboro cigarette commercials and print advertisements. They picked me up at the airport, put me up at a hotel for the night and the next morning we drove an hour and a half to the ranch location. The first news I got was that I wouldn't be able to do my own roping because a couple "Hollywood Cowboys" had been so rough on the horses they tore their mouths with their John Wayne impersonations of what it means to be the master of these animals.

The horses used before that were handled so badly, and the horse I was to ride and rope from were the working horses of the ranch. These animals were not only raised and trained on the ranch but were the personal property and pets of the cowboys and their families. They were partners for life and for work.

When it was time to start shooting, a decision was made to start with me chasing after a calf in the open field. I was to get right up on his tail, get to the point where I was just about to throw and release the rope at the calf and stop. They told me not to throw, and the actual roping would be done on a long shot with one of the ranch hands dressed in my outfit. Then we would cut back to me going up to the calf and tying it off.

After two takes of the first shot, the director came up to me and said that the ranch foreman could tell that I was handling the horse like I knew what I was doing and suggested that we could go ahead and try for the actual roping. Perfect. That's exactly what I wanted.

Let me tell you one thing. That horse they put me on was like riding on a cloud. He was on that calf like a shadow on a wall. His nose was close enough to that calf's tail that I could count the hairs. There was no way I could miss. We got it on the first try. We did two more for safety's sake. The tie-off went great. The last scene was to pick the cowgirl off the fence and put my arm around her.

I never saw Score Underarm Deodorant on any store shelf anywhere. I was told that they had shot a total of four commercials with the same message they ended my commercial with. I also heard that when they viewed the commercials at a preview house in New York, each one got the same response.

After the roping and tying-off of the calf, when the girl is down and I put my arm around her, she turns to me with her nose in my pit and says, "I love the smell of a working man."

They booed. They hissed. They were pissed. They left the theatre. How sad. Too bad. I got paid. Thank you. Love those horses.

16

SURPRISE! SURPRISE! SURPRISE!

Now it was time to get serious. I needed a job. I was going to find an apartment and enroll in a good school for the training and practice I needed as an actor. I actually had money saved from the warehouse work. Work? I don't think so. When I left the Army I had two letters from two generals I worked for and worked with while stationed at McDill Air Force Base. I also had very high clearances due to the classified communications I was required to handle.

The letters were very complimentary in reference to my character and work habits. That was a first. Usually, when I parted company with anyone, it had a "good luck, good-bye, and good riddance" feeling to go with it.

The classifieds were filled with want ads looking for people to work in the aerospace industry. With my letter and a cocky attitude, I ended up working for the Aerospace Corporation. My security clearances were all I really needed. I went to work in their security department at the ground level with the promise that I would soon be elevated to a higher station as soon as I became familiar with their operations.

I got an apartment near the Los Angeles International Airport. Work was close by. The apartment was furnished with just about everything but the sheets, towels, toothpaste and tail-tape.

The next thing on my list was to find an acting school. I didn't have the slightest idea where to look so I went to the L.A. Times classified under the acting category. I made two phone calls and decided on the one who said he would charge me $10 per hour for private lessons. What have I got to lose? I made an appointment and drove to Hollywood, the Argyle Hotel to be exact. A disappointing surprise was in order.

I knocked on the door and a squeaky little old man answered. He invited me in. You know that feeling you get in the pit of your stomach when someone takes off his or her shoes and a sour aroma begins to make its way up to your nose? That's how I felt with his shoes still on his feet. It must have been a while since he opened a window or cleaned up the place.

First, we sat for a minute or two while names were exchanged. Then came the tour of the walls of his tiny apart- ment. There were a couple pictures of him in various poses in different clothes, but it was obvious they had been taken in the apartment, all at the same time by someone with a Mickey Mouse camera. Then there were two or three shots of him from work he had done on the "Superman" television series with George Reeves. That was it. The tour is over and it's time for the lesson, all this for $10.

I'm going to get as close as I can to the words he used to introduce me to his method of acting.

"The whole idea is to fool the audience into thinking that

what they see you doing is really happening, but you have got to make them believe that you believe it's happening even though you know it isn't. For example, I want you to walk over to that table and pretend to open the drawer as if no one else is in the room. Go ahead."

I did it.

"Good. Now, do it again as if there is an audience watching."

Is he serious?

I asked, "What do you mean?"

He said he would explain in detail during the next lesson, but in the meantime, just do it.

"Do what?"

"Do it knowing there is an audience watching."

He is serious.

"I just did it knowing there was an audience watching. You're the audience, fool."

We were at about the halfway point with my first lesson when I came up with a "not for discussion" suggestion.

"Give me $5 and you keep the other five. And do yourself a favor, don't argue with me."

My anger has a wonderful quiet intensity about it. It would be very difficult to misunderstand my intention.

"Pretend there is no one looking, and give me the five. Good-bye."

This was just one of the many important lessons to be learned in and about Hollywood. It is saturated with bullshit. The search for a school continued with the good results that led me to the Beverly Hills Playhouse.

Getting involved with a great actors' workshop at the

Playhouse was a really wonderful experience. It was filled with professionals who knew what they were doing as well as being staffed by very skilled and talented teachers. The second great lesson came when I had been to class for the second time.

There was an actor there who I mistakenly thought was someone else. I thought he was the man who starred in the series, "Mr. Lucky." He was friendly and invited me out for a cup of coffee after class. I was anxious to listen to and talk to someone who was a working actor. Perhaps I could pick his brain. That's exactly what was happening until he made a statement that started taking the conversation in a different direction.

"One of the most important skills an actor must work on is getting in touch with his feminine side."

He said something to the effect that Laurence Olivier had arrived at this conclusion.

"The great actors, artists, must have the freedom to explore all sides of life's possibilities."

I asked him, "What do you mean?"

He went on to explain that many of the stars, the great actors in Hollywood, are gay even though you would never know it.

"Like who for instance?"

He started to give me a list of those he thought or knew were gay, or those who some of his friends knew were gay, and one by one there didn't seem to be many, or any, who weren't gay, according to him. I let him go on until he must have realized I was just waiting for him to finish.

"May I ask you a question?" I said.

"Of course."

Truthfully, I don't think I had ever heard the word "gay" used to describe someone's sexual preference. I knew what queer meant. I knew what a homosexual was, but not gay.

So I asked him, "Are you a faggot?"

Boy did I hit a nerve. He turned as red as a beet, and I think he held his breath for half a minute.

"No, I'm bi-sexual."

"How bi-sexual are you?"

That's enough about that story.

Lesson learned. Rumors are just that, rumors. I do my best to not listen to rumors or gossip. It's a killer. Many people have been deeply damaged because someone starts spreading unfounded stories. What others call a fact of life could be the biggest lie of all. This actor I mentioned, the not Mr. Lucky man, was given a contract at a major studio and a couple starring roles in movies. He had the looks of a Sean Connery but not the talent, and he ended up with nothing but an unwanted reputation. Someone began talking about his "insane" sex life and Hollywood listened. He was a star unborn.

Back to Corriganville. Crash welcomed me back, with open arms and I immediately felt like I had never left. The cast I had known the year before had pretty much gone. It wasn't long before I was able to play some of the main characters and was doing some of the more exciting stunts, like falling off a two-story barn. Most importantly, I was exercising my craft. A side effect of working at Corriganville was that I could use the audience to help me with my concentration. I imagined what it would be like on a major studio set and how important it was to remain removed from any influence from the environ-ment and to stay within myself. When working on a film or movie there would be anywhere up to a hundred people or more involved in the day's work. It could be an influence that could hinder me from doing my best in character if I let it.

Corriganville was a permanent western set. The buildings had foundations, electrical and plumbing. I remember during one show, after successfully completing a roof fall and ly-ing on the ground as if dead waiting for the tape to play out, someone poked me on the leg to see if I would react. I didn't respond until the show was finished and then jumped up in anger, ready to knock someone's head off, only to find a very attractive woman who was a friend of one of the cast mem-bers. She had snuck behind the buildings to do exactly what she did. One look at her and there was no anger left. I told her she needed a spanking and she agreed. I took her over to the Silver Dollar Saloon, bought her a beer, and took her for a tour behind the rocks out by Robin Hood Lake. She told me she was a special investigator for the DA's office. This woman had a big appetite for love and affection. We saw quite a bit of each other after that. I had a good job. I was studying at the Beverly Hills Playhouse. I had a hungry woman, and I got to play cowboy every weekend. A pretty good life if I do say so myself.

The future looked bright until a phone call from my mother.

"I'm in Huntington Beach. Frisky and I got here this afternoon. Here, talk to Frisky."

Please, no, please, please, don't let this be true. Too many surprises can throw a man way off track.

The best and shortest way to tell this story is to say that they had been cooking up this scheme almost from the day I got to Philadelphia. And Nana was included from the beginning. I listened until Frisky started telling me how much she missed me and then I let loose with a voice that had no reverse in it.

"You've made a big mistake coming out here and not listening to me when I made it perfectly clear that there was not going to be a relationship between us after I left for California."

I wanted to hang up but instead, "Put my mother on the phone."

While making it clear to my mother that this was her worst idea yet, I could hear Frisky crying and yelling in the background. I told my mother that she had better come up with another plan quickly, but don't include me in it. I told her she needed to call Nana and let her know she's not to come out.

"Keep out of my life."

For the next couple of days I couldn't stop my mind from wondering what was going on. I could only hope they were headed back east. Poor Nana, she must have been going nuts with this entire mess while she sat and waited for some news or some sense of direction in her life. This woman never worked a day in her life. Now she lived on a small monthly allotment she received from the merciful hearts of the lawyers who had represented her father. She had inherited big money from her father, E. W. Saybolt, who was in business with Standard Oil of New Jersey. As best I can figure out, he was involved with or had designed a refining process for the oil company and was entitled to, at the very least, a lifetime payment of royalties. A series of letters I now have reveal that she was led to believe that she would be taken good care of financially for the rest of her life. All the while she was slowly having her rights to the fortune slipped out from under her. Now she sits in Philadelphia waiting to hear from her daughter.

California is where my mother's dreams lived. Her dreams of dance were going to get her to her dreamland. All I remember from when I was a kid was that I destroyed that dream. I came along and killed the dream.

Later on during one of our peaceful meetings, we had a great conversation about her ambitions as a young woman. Hollywood and the lights and the camera. She wanted to be a star. She told me she dreamed about falling at the feet of Tyrone Power to get his attention. I didn't have a problem believing that. That wouldn't have been the first time she laid down for a man.

Another call from my Mother,

"Your friend took off in the middle of the night with all my money and the car we bought together for the trip. I'm stranded. What am I going to do?"

What's she going to do? What the hell am I going to do?

You couldn't have paid me to say what I said, but I did say it.

"Stay there. I'll come get you in the morning."

What is this thing, this unbreakable connection, children have with their parents? It seems that no matter how ridiculous, how negative the relationship is, it's always there. Out of sight, out of mind…never.

I don't think the human mind can perspire, but there may be exceptions. My imagination was so scrambled I wanted to scatter it in the wind. The end result of all this thinking was that I went and got her, moved her into my apartment and introduced her to The Aerospace Corporation for a job interview.

Frisky had cleaned her out of everything but one suitcase and her purse. The money was gone, the station wagon was gone, as was whatever odds and ends she brought with her. They were on their way back east or maybe in a trashcan. This had really shaken her up. I was as reassuring as I could be, telling her I'll do whatever I could to help her get settled until she made up her mind what she wanted to do. Where did this willingness to help her come from? I felt like a contradiction with all the anger and disdain I felt in my heart towards her.

She got the bedroom; I took the couch. Aerospace loved her, offered her a job, which became a problem for me because two people from the same family weren't permitted to work at the same facility. Security was the top priority in the jobs that required clearances. They offered her an interim clearance and she could start immediately but I would have to move on. That sounded fine to me. The last thing I wanted was to work side-by-side with my mother. I was also anxious to get out of the apartment as soon as possible. I wasn't ready for all this family stuff. I gave her enough money to see her through until her first check, paid for the next month's rent and got myself out of there. All this happened as fast I could get it moving. Within a month she had decided she wanted to stay in California and as soon as she could, she was going to bring Nana out. Nuts. I was beginning to understand how an animal would feel locked in a cage. I was not happy by any stretch of my mind. There was no way out.

It was a long time coming but in my later years I realized that even stronger than her desire to be in California was her desire to be at least in the same state as me. That attachment to my mother that I couldn't seem to break apparently was just as strong on her side of this relationship. What could have been? What if? It doesn't do much good to spend too much time looking backwards. If I continue to look back, I'm liable to run into something I should have been keeping my eye out for in the future.

My money was running out. I decided that I didn't want to live near the airport. I wanted to live near the studios. I also decided that I didn't want to be a part of the space revolution. I wanted to work in the film industry. Corriganville was the fresh air I needed. Crash still had his horse Flash there. A whiff of horseshit never hurt me either.

I got a couple of odd jobs, was very happy and excited to be involved with the actors workshop at the Beverly Hills Playhouse, had a couple of girlfriends, and on a good day I would drive by a film or commercial shoot on a city street.

A woman with a young son had started coming to Corriganville on the weekends. She got her kid to ask me for an autograph, tagged after me between shows, and toward the end of the day, the mother told me her ride was going to be very late picking her up. She lived in the Valley.

"Could you drop me off at the bus stop?"

Of course, I said yes, but that was easier than saying no. This was like having to eat too many vegetables at once. I loved my freedom and didn't find it difficult to say good-bye when things got too thick. Although I enjoyed their company, the woman with the kid was out of my life within a week. I had a mean streak in my heart that I used to my advantage when I wanted to. That last time I saw her I told her that I didn't think she had a muscle in her body.

"Sleeping with you is like sleeping with a water balloon."

The special investigator made the mistake of saying she loved me in front of others. She was gone that day. I made the determination that I would only sleep with strangers, but not for more than a day. You can't have too many friends, but you can have too many at once.

I called my mother once in a while to see how she was doing and to find out what was happening with my grandmother. She loved Aerospace and was looking for another apartment more to her liking. We had a middle of the road relationship. She knew not to cross onto my side, and I knew better than to step onto hers. It would be almost a year before we would see each other again. That was on the occasion when we went to the airport together to welcome Nana to California. They were going to live together for as long as it took for them to find a place for my grandmother. Nana looked good and I was actually happy she was out here. I don't know all the ingredients that are in the formula for love, but if glue was a part of the recipe, I had very little for family except in the case of Nana.

Surprises can be a good thing but there are consequences in those unexpected events, which can slowly alter your life. Corriganville was like going to a park. Each day was fun and there weren't any real responsibilities attached to it. It was quite a different story with the actors' workshop. The training directed the actor to dig deeper and deeper into his own inner potential and reveal even the most hidden of emotions and lower conditions of life. I began to recognize that I had a dark side that I would rather be without, but I had no idea what to do about it. Left alone with myself, I didn't find me to be in very good company.

I had been back at Corriganville for a month or so. One day while sitting in the sheriffs' office, which also served as the center for all the activities, one of the cast members called me over to look out the door and down the street at a girl. I stuck my head out the door, saw who he was talking about and said, "Give me a break. She's a Bubble Gummer."

Apparently Crash had met her and her parents the day before when they came as spectators. He offered her a job and overnight her mother made her a pretty blue frontier type dress. That Bubble Gummer was just 16 years old, as cute as a button, and had a head of bleached-blond hair that reached down to the middle of her back. She had to have used enough hair spray to make an elephant stand still. She looked great and would make the shows look 10 times better.

It must have been the next weekend when I noticed her running down the street between shows and racing into to the ladies room. Less than a minute later, she frantically ran to the Silver Dollar Saloon. In another minute she was running to the cafe. At that point I stopped her, "What's wrong?"

"Nothing."

She ran again.

She headed to the bank building. Then I thought I knew. As she started in another direction I stopped her again.

"Now tell me what's wrong."

This was difficult for her. "None of the tampon machines work."

"Come with me."

I took her hand, we got in my Bug and I drove, quickly to a little market just off the Corriganville property and bought her a big box of Super Kotex.

From that time on she began to feel comfortable with me as her friend. Over the weekends, we would spend time talking between the shows. She began telling me stories about her life that were very sad and even traumatic. I felt very protective toward her.

Apparently, Corriganville agreed with her. She began to find creative ways to add to the enactments of the stories and even did stunts. She became quite good at it and seemed to enjoy this new way of expressing herself. It was also apparent that she lived most of her life quietly inside her mind. It was very difficult for her to have a conversation, particularly about what was going on in her heart.

I began to notice that either one or both of her parents would always be there. Most of their time was spent in the saloon drinking and mixing with the cast. Both drank a lot. At the Silver Dollar Saloon the "Special" was always a beer and a baloney sandwich with a pickle for a nickel. Beer was never my drink of choice, and I was a solitary drinker anyway. I kept my bottle out of sight. Her father was in the construction business and was a very nice man. The mother was overly pleasant. She also seemed to be tanked most of the time. It was very difficult to be around them. Their daughter must have had a very difficult time growing up in that environment. The daughter's name was Lynn and she became an important part of my life. She was much more than a Bubble Gummer.

The so-called wild-west weekend was a game; studying acting was real. I was exploring a world I felt in my heart but wanted to experience with my entire life. The man who conducted the classes was brilliant. His name was Sherman Marks. I studied there for over four years. By the end of three years, I was so confused I didn't know what to do.

Sherman's background was the New York stage, The Actor's Studio and live TV. He directed "Playhouse 90," "Studio One," etc. His schooling was grounded on the so-called "Method." I thought he was a genius. I spent as much time as possible there just to pick up anything I could that would lead me toward being able to experience truth under the guise of art. At one point I realized I had been there almost continuously for nine days while putting on a production. Scene study, cold reading, rehearsals, doing one acts, it was all good.

At the same time, I found myself wanting to explore new avenues of my mind. Others were trying to interest me in trying "this and that." I began to enjoy the alterations that took place in my head when I smoked dope or dropped "this and that." I liked the effect of smoking grass but not the other drugs. I tried everything from coke to heroin to reds and just about any other color pill that came along. Other than the grass, I didn't like the experiences I had. The grass gave me another wall to hide behind. Somehow, it was a camouflage I enjoyed because I found that it gave me the feeling that no one knew I was there. I loved watching people with the feeling they didn't know I was watching. Even though I no longer smoke dope, I have maintained that ability to feel as if no one knows I'm around. The drinking, the dope and I became a trio of who rode alone.

Back at the ranch on weekends, I would be playing the cowboy and looking out for Lynn. As she opened up to me more and more, it became apparent just how troubled she was. I became more determined to help her. Romance was the farthest thing from my mind. I had my hands full with an actress or two from class, and Lynn just didn't appeal to me like that. I decided I was going to spend Saturday nights renting a room at a local hotel rather than going to my place and driving all the way back the next morning for the Sunday shows.

I had gotten to know Lynn's folks by this time. One Saturday they invited me over for dinner. Not a great idea but I accepted. Seeing the whole family as a unit, Lynn had two brothers, the picture became clear. Dysfunctional wasn't a word I was familiar with, but by today's standards I think it would be a pretty accurate description of what I saw. It also became clear that although the circumstances were unique, I too was a member of the dysfunctional. That may have been the most common ground in our relationship.

One Saturday afternoon as the shows were closing down for the day, I mentioned that I was going to go to the movies, and I invited Lynn to go along. She said yes but that I would have to ask her mother. Never had to do that before, haven't done that since. I asked,

"Would you have any reservations if Lynn was to go with me to a movie?"

The mother said, "OK."

The father had no problem. It was sometime soon after that the mother accused me of statutory rape. That I remember well. It never even dawned on me to sleep with this girl, let alone rape her. Lynn was mortified and I became even more protective. Corriganville was no longer a great place to go. It had pretty much served its purpose in my mind, but was now becoming a place I didn't wanted to go back to. Then there was Lynn. What was I going to do about her? Way too many surprises.

The acting workshop was another story. I wish I could describe the experience I had as an actor when either in a scene or rehearsal or even some sense memory exercises, it would all come together and that magic moment happened when art and reality became one. When there is no fantasy; there is no dialogue. Time and space become one within your heart and mind. All this art becomes, not a combination of imagination and skill, but a fusion of person and place that has lifeblood of its own. It doesn't happen often but when it does, it's almost otherworldly. And when you come out of that realm of art, it becomes something you strive for not only with performance in mind but also with the desire to achieve that feeling in all activities of life. In my case, not being very wise, I began to seek answers from the outside. Then that harsh voice from my past would appear in my mind. *"You'll never amount to anything. You are pathetic."*

What if she's right? Have a drink, smoke another, look for love and find a horse. Prayer never worked. What the hell am I going to do?

Go west young man. Go back to Corriganville. A strange

set of circumstances began to unfold. Lynn and I were standing together talking when a couple of Japanese people came by and asked if we would pose for pictures. They were going to go home with evidence that they had been on a real western movie set and here are a couple of the actors. They took quite a few pictures with different backgrounds. At one point they asked us to hug and kiss. I should have said no. Instead, we did a little kiss and that was that. I must admit I was feeling more affection for the girl, but not to the degree that I wanted to call it romantic.

Soon after that we were asked to pose for a cover of a mobile trailer magazine. I don't remember how it came about, but later on we were two characters in an ad for the Opel Automobile. People must have thought we looked good together. It didn't dawn on me that we were an item until one day after I had left her family's phone number with a woman I was rehearsing with at the workshop. The actress had been hired for one of the lead characters for a new western television series and recommended me for one of the male leads. She called to say the casting agent wanted to see me as soon as possible. All I know is that Lynn got real upset thinking I was seeing someone. I was, but I didn't expect her reaction. I missed the interview. Things seemed to be getting out of hand.

My feelings of wanting to protect Lynn were genuine, but going steady or whatever they called it in those days wasn't in my mind or even my vocabulary. I was very concerned for her. As I saw it, this was one troubled lady. We needed to have a serious talk, but first I needed to think. Way too many questions were floating around in my mind. Going back and forth between Corriganville and the actors' workshop was a good thing. It was like traveling between heaven and hell. A little of each was in each place. The interesting part was that it all existed inside me. My life was a puzzle. A lot of the pieces didn't seem to fit together. Where did all this concern for someone come from? It was as if a stranger was coming out of somewhere inside me and homesteading.

Never before had I thought of hooking up with someone for life. It just wasn't a part of my dream. I wanted to make films in Hollywood, have a place in Montana or thereabouts, raise horses and go into town once a week, find a good looking stranger for my hormones over a night or two and go home alone. I did not want marriage, kids and any of the so-called responsibilities of being a family man. There was no example of that in my life that gave me the impression there was happiness in all that.

I did some serious thinking and after a week of going from wanting to disappear or just walking away from the whole situation I decided to put it out there that I wasn't going to just abandon the girl. I decided to change my direction in life and see if she wanted to come along.

It must have been the following weekend that we went for a walk and had our talk. Basically, I told her what my plans were for the future. I was determined to succeed as an actor. I don't remember saying, "Will you marry me," but that's what I meant. The idea of marriage wasn't very sacred to me.

Guess what? We got married about a year later...I think. The dates are a little fuzzy now. That whole time in my life was a little blurry. Too much was happening that was beyond anything I could identify with. Too many surprises were coming my way without notification.

We got married at the Glass Church in Portuguese Bend on the Palos Verdes Peninsula. What a beautiful place to get married. Who the hell came up with the idea that people should get married in the first place? Never mind. I remember that I had to drive myself there and the closer I got to the chapel, the closer I got to being very confused as to not only why I was doing this but who the hell was I? Period! I just didn't make any sense to me any more. What the hell was I doing?

I came to the point where I had to turn up the drive to the chapel. And I stopped. I decided I couldn't go through with this. I put the car in gear and took off. I think I drove another four or five miles past the chapel when I saw a florist. It reminded me that I was supposed to pick up a corsage for Lynn's grandmother. I stopped, bought the flowers and went back to the chapel. Don't ask me why I stopped.

Everyone was there. Many of the cast from Corriganville and all of Lynn's family and their friends filled up half the chapel. On my side were my mother and grandmother and a couple drunks I drank with. Then everything went blank. I think my mind left me but I guess I couldn't convince my body to go. The next thing I remember was the moment while I was standing at the altar. Lynn came through the chapel door with her father. With the sun at her back she was stunning. She looked beautiful and that vision brought me back in touch with reality. There was a reception at the Van Nuys Airport and we then took off for a cabin at Mammoth Mountain.

We got an apartment; I got a job trying to sell term-life insurance to families in Watts. They gave me $200 a week during the probation. I sold nothing. Every time I went into someone's home, I could see that they needed food a lot more than they needed insurance. I'd give them the knife set and wish them "good luck." I just couldn't do it.

Within a week and a half I knew I had made the biggest mistake in my life so far. In my mind the most I could do was be there and do my best to get my career going so I could take care of her or at the very least be able to see that she got whatever help she needed to be happy. What I did know was that this wasn't going to work out, and at the same time I knew I couldn't leave her. It was also apparent that any aspirations I had for a successful career as an actor were not going to be shared with my wife.

For the next three years we managed to survive. I drove a taxi, sold pens, pencils and copy toner on the phone. I tried selling "equal opportunity" space in a magazine and became a nightshift telephone operator at an answering service. I continued my studies at the workshop, but by this time I let Corriganville become an adventure I could only talk about. It's very hard to find anything that will really get me depressed and even feel hopeless, but that was what coming up from within my heart.

One of the common threads we did share was we knew what it meant to be alone. Communicating with another person on the level of a partner in life has got to be one of the major problems we have in the world today. If we could all have the freedom to speak and write the words of our greatest desires in life, we would probably find that we have a lot more in common than what we don't know about each other. Don't we want a peaceful secure life? I think so, but in those days of our marriage, my bone-headedness was focused on the outside, and I didn't have a clue how to truly help Lynn.

It must have been in the spring of 1967. We had moved into a duplex in West Hollywood. One of the first things I remember about our new place was when a young man came into our space and was trying to convince me that I should go to a Buddhist meeting and chant. He was a member of SGI-USA and said it would help me to become happy. I wasn't about to stand around talking about religion, so I raised my voice, made a face that would scare a wolf and ran him out into the street. I was beginning to work both as an actor and a model. The last thing I needed was to become a Buddhist.

I worked in a couple episodes of "Mission Impossible," the television series. I was under contract to do print ads for Honda of America, and I had three or four national commercials running.

There was a little money in the bank and it seemed that this would be the "now or never" time to move on. I knew I would be deserting the marriage, but I would still do everything I could to protect her. I had to get out from under the dark cloud.

We just weren't ever going to be on the same page. Our communication broke down on all levels. Then the Ouija Board appeared. I'm not a believer but Lynn seemed to have sensitivity toward the mystical. Let us play.

17

OUIJA
Toward Tomorrow

If I remember correctly, it must have been the summer of 1967, probably on a Sunday, when Lynn and I decided to bring out the Ouija Board. What the spoken purpose was, I don't know, but her intention became to channel her grandfather. I had never seen a Ouija Board before this day, but I went along with the idea thinking that with no faith there wasn't any value in it. I don't know if this board fell into the category of a game or a way of telling fortunes or predicting the future, but I played.

I think you're supposed to ask a question and each person lightly places their fingers on a piece of the board that gently slides over a letter or number or a "Yes" or a "No." And when it stops, that is the answer or a direction in response to the question. After settling on the position that indicated a response, which showed the channeling or connection with her grandfather had occurred, I slowly brought the questioning around to where we began to ask questions about the future of our marriage. By this time I was pretty comfortable with the board, and I was also aware that it didn't take much to get the slide to go in the direction you wanted. It may be that Lynn and I were on the same channel because when asked how long our marriage would last, I remember the slide landed on the number four. We determined that was the response her grandfather channeled. Four what? Four years? Four weeks? Maybe four days. Well, if it was going to end in four something, I suggested that today being Sunday, Thursday would be four days from then. Maybe that would be a good time for me to leave. I don't remember Lynn disagreeing with me, so that's what I did.

If you were to ask me today if this was the most honorable thing for me to do, I would probably have to say, "No, it wasn't." At that time with the way I felt about the prospect of a better future and with the general shape of my mind, I had little or no hope our marriage was going to get any better or that either of us was going to be happy together. At that time I did what I felt I had to do. Today I would not do the same thing, but today's mind and heart wasn't there.

I had an army footlocker we kept at the foot of the bed. By Thursday, I had packed it with my clothes, put it on my shoulder, said "Good-Bye," and walked to a studio apartment I rented above the Sunset Strip. A part of me felt like celebrating and the other part didn't like what was happening at all. When I married Lynn, I truly believed I would be able to help her become happy. The opposite happened. I became less happy day-by-day. There is nothing in my heart that puts the responsibility for my failure to help her on Lynn. If anything, I would never have separated had I had any hope that I would be able to be a good influence and support her as she climbed out of her sadness. I felt that I must have been contributing to her gloom. Perhaps I would help by just being a good friend. Good friends are hard to come by. Ultimate friends, the kind who will never desert you no matter what, are as rare as catching a falling star. In my heart and mind I have never deserted her, no matter how much distance separates us spiritually or physically. To this day, the one common thread of communication has always been toward the welfare of our children. I want my children's mother to be happy. Period.

It didn't take much to get settled in my new place. I was getting residuals from a number of national commercials. Joy Detergent, Gulf Tires, Jergens Hand Lotion, McDonald's Hamburgers and Kentucky Fried Chicken were some of the eight that were playing. I was also doing quite a lot of print work for Honda and several others. I was giving Lynn money and she moved and got herself an apartment in the hills and was beginning to get out and about. I had left the car, a newer VW bug, with her.

This marriage was the biggest event in my life up until then, and the failure to make it work hit me very hard. I felt depressed and went deeper into my own personal hell. The entirety of my relationships with the idea of family never gave me a feeling of joy, only sadness, loneliness and failure. What's wrong with me? Again, I could hear my mother's voice.

"You'll never amount to anything."

I had moved into an older Spanish style apartment complex with a courtyard and lots of trees with plenty of fresh air above Sunset Boulevard. Interesting neighbors as well. There was one lady who had a dog named Monkey. They lived across the courtyard from me and she never put up blinds or curtains. She worked at an upscale shoe store on the strip and would come home at lunch to sunbathe on her little porch. She was an aspiring actress and wanted that all-over natural tan. Her dog and I got to know each other first. One evening a knock on my door became an introduction to this neighbor. She had watched me play with Monkey one day as she bathed on her little sun porch. That was nice. The next night around dinnertime she knocked again, this time with a pot of an herbal rice dish she had just made and a stash of clean grass wrapped in aluminum foil.

"Welcome to the neighborhood. By the way, would you help me change a light bulb?"

I was happy to do anything to help a neighbor. I had a little taste of the rice dish and followed her to her place. I had to stand on her bed to get to the bulb. Before I knew it she stuck a joint in my mouth and was having a little taste of me. Screwing in the bulb didn't take much time at all. Turning on the light was another matter. I had another friend. This one was in need of a "handyman."

Around this time a couple of interesting things happened. Lynn had gotten in an accident coming out of a club in West Hollywood. She had been struck by a woman running a red light and was knocked around inside the Bug. The force of the impact threw her so violently that there were scuff marks from her shoes on the interior roof of the car. She was in pain for quite a while and even moved back with her parents during her recovery. That brought us back in communication again. I hated to see her in pain. I tried to be a good friend. She got back on her feet but has had back problems ever since. Another accident with me driving, many years later, didn't help. I had been drinking and lost control of a 280Z in the tunnel going onto Pacific Coast Highway. Didn't help that back of hers at all.

At about the same time as her accident in the VW Bug, I was standing on a corner waiting for a light to change when a guy on a motorcycle pulled up in front of me and asked if I ever heard of chanting *Nam-Myoho-Renge-Kyo*. He wanted me to go to a Buddhist meeting. Don't try to shove religion on me. I kicked his bike over and crossed the street. He picked it up and drove on. I think he got the idea that he'd better leave well enough alone. That was the second time someone got me mad trying to talk to me about Buddhism.

Probably a year had passed since the time Lynn and I separated. I continued to study and was developing my art. I also got involved with a couple ladies and was just tripping along, riding on the clouds of dreams. Lynn and I talked often. On one occasion we were together talking about going ahead and getting divorced when, coming out of a liquor store, having bought cigarettes, I saw someone coming toward us who I knew, but not very well. His name was Travis. We said Hello and were about to go on our way when he asked, "Have you ever heard about Buddhism?"

I could have said something nasty but I didn't. I'm sure it was because I barely knew him that I didn't stop him from talking. I told him, "Others have tried to get me interested, but I just didn't want to get into it." This was the 25th or 26th of June, 1968. I was 26 years old and my world was about to take a spin in an entirely different direction.

18

HOW THE HELL
Did That Happen?

"I live around the corner. I'll make you a cup of coffee."

Why I said yes I don't know, but something told me to go with this man and at least I'll be able to tell the next person who wants to talk about Buddhism, "I know all about it, and I'm not interested."

We got to his house and the first thing I noticed was an altar with a scroll enshrined in it. While he made the coffee, Lynn and I sat asking each other quietly, "What the hell are we doing here?" I was surprisingly comfortable and Lynn seemed intrigued. Travis brought the coffee to the front room and started to explain the practice of Nichiren Buddhism.

He gave a very clear and direct explanation. Chanting *Nam-Myoho-Renge-Kyo* was the primary practice. Chant with a target or goal in mind. He suggested that having many objectives would give us the best opportunity to see this Buddhism at work. Study was another part of the practice that was important so that we didn't think it was magic or just luck when our wishes or prayers were answered. It would not only confirm what I would be experiencing but would also give me an idea about what to expect in the future. I never had a prayer answered in my entire life, so at 26 years old, this would be a very interesting phenomenon—having a prayer answered.

As a child I was forced into going to a Bible class while living with One Eye and Pinky Finger. By the end of that one session, they were told not to bring me back. I was a troublemaker, and I got the others in the class to think out of line. Today they would have to admit that I got them to think out of the box. I just couldn't understand how I was to believe in someone I couldn't and wouldn't ever be able to see or hear. I was to believe what one person said about what someone else said. What Jesus said didn't mean much to me because I never heard him say it.

I did come out of that church with one thought. Pray. Pray for something to happen that would give me reason to believe. That sounded reasonable enough. So I did pray. I didn't know what I was praying to, but I did try. Over the next five or maybe ten years I prayed a number of times. Nothing. Nothing happened, I saw nothing that gave me reason to believe my prayer was being answered. I prayed for things I needed in my daily life to get out of many a circum-stance I found myself in. Not once can I say that a prayer was answered, not once. Now why should I continue praying if there is no result? It didn't make any sense to me.

And now I'm sitting with my soon to be ex-wife, listening to a man tell me that if I chanted, I would see actual proof that my prayers were bringing results. Another important part of Buddhism was faith.

Faith, from the standpoint of Nichiren Buddhism, was

at first expectation and later would be an accumulation of experience. The topper to all this was the ultimate goal of Buddhism—a world of peace. World peace not based on politics or military might or waiting for the appearance of someone who was going to appear out of the heavens and save all mankind, but a peace that was caused by a change in the human condition. Travis called it a human revolution that took place in the deepest recesses of the human heart. A change from expecting the world to change, to becoming the change yourself, an inner transformation. Never had I looked at life from this perspective. Could my anger be the reason the world always seemed to be against me? He also said that the spread of this Buddhism throughout the world was the correct path to this peace. Telling others was also a part of the practice and would become very natural as time passed. Want to bet? Me no shove religion down anyone's throat. And that's that.

After the coffee, Travis invited us to attend a discussion meeting at his home the following evening. He wanted us to hear the experiences of some of the members so we would have a better understanding about Nichiren Buddhism. When he said "members," the hair on the back of my neck stood up. I hated the thought of organized religion. I made up my mind I wasn't going to go…but changed it the next day. They say that curiosity killed the cat, but satisfaction brought him back. I decided to go back for the discussion for just that reason. Curiosity. The biggest surprise in this conversation with Travis about this Buddhism was an involuntary statement I made.

"It sounds like something I could do."

Lynn looked at me, astonished that I would say such a thing. It just popped out.

By this time Lynn and I had been living apart for at least nine months. Her back was much better, and she was going on with her life. I had the VW Bug she had been in the accident with. She had an older Chevy that looked like it had been tail ended about 20 times. The Bug had a blown engine and was parked on a very steep street where I lived above The Strip.

The next evening I made it to the meeting. I don't remember if Lynn and I met and went together, but at 7 p.m. the meeting began with about 20 or more people chanting. When they finished there were introductions, some kind of explanation of the practice and then people started raising their hands wanting to give experiences.

There must have been five or six people talking about the benefits they had from the chanting. One person said they chanted, and their cat came back. Another chanted for phonograph records and someone gave her a box of 100. One after another, people got food, coats, whatever. I spent enough time on my own fighting for everything I could get my hands on. And from dealing with a tremendous variety of people, I had developed a little street smarts. What impressed me about these experiences was that the people were not lying. That's all I knew. They were telling the truth and were genuinely surprised when the things they were chanting for actually happened. After everyone gave his or her experience, it was time for the question and answer period. I raised my hand as high as it would go.

"If I were to chant to this scroll, according to the Bible, I'm on my way to hell, right?"

The man leading the meeting took a short pause, and then answered, "Gee, I don't know, but you should try it and find out."

Dynamite has a fuse, I don't. The anger in me came up like a perfect storm, but I held back. I don't remember the second question, but I know it was along the same line and I got the same answer. I had enough of that. I stood up in the middle of the meeting and loudly said,

"You people are full of shit."

I stormed out of there with the speed of lightning. I've been angry many times, but this was coming out of me like an explosion and I had no target to strike.

Before going into the meeting everyone had taken off their shoes to make it more comfortable while sitting on the floor. There weren't enough chairs for everyone. When I stormed out of that meeting, looking for some way to let this anger out, the shoes were staring me in the face. First of all, I couldn't find mine, so I kicked a few out of the way and that developed into throwing the rest of them in the street, up on the roof and into the neighbor's yard. When I got to my shoes, I stopped the tantrum and walked home. I totally forgot about Lynn. All the way home I was thinking that this had been the dumbest thing I had ever done. At the same time I couldn't get it out of my mind that the people who gave their experiences were telling the truth. I found myself chanting as I made my way home. So I decided to go back the next evening. I wanted to get the scroll, the Gohonzon, and chant for myself to see what would happen. Fortunately, I talked to Lynn; she was going back the next night as well. I found out the meeting was going to take place at a different location.

My life had taken some radical turns before, but this was a complete about-face as they say in the Army. In my mind, religion was about the control of masses of people, with fear and guilt being the tools to restrain individual growth. The strategy seemed to be that if people became dependent on some external deity, you could keep them controlled and in line. What the hell was I thinking? To enter into a religious path was the most dangerous thing a person could do. What if the path wasn't the complete truth? What if the philosophy wasn't leading toward fulfillment, but had the opposite effect?

It's tough enough trying to figure what's the next step you should take in your life that will lead to happiness, but to think religion was going to point me in the right direction? Forget it. I didn't have much to refer to for guidance from my mother or father if I was looking for words of wisdom. My best bet was to follow my instinct. It was this instinct, this curiosity, that told me to look into this Buddhism. Skepticism was my protection. Trusting in others wasn't going to work for me.

Now it was either the 26th or 27th of June, and I went to my second meeting. In my mind today, I celebrate the 26th as the beginning of my new life. On that day, as I approached the meeting house, my life didn't appear to be so new. A young lady named Wendy was standing on the porch. As I got closer to the house, I heard her say something like, "Oh shit, he's back."

Any welcome was worn out with the flying shoes. Oddly enough, not too much was said about that, but I did get a few cold shoulders.

The meeting started with chanting and then what was described as their evening prayers. They were reciting something out of a book. Later I found out it was the companion or supplement to chanting. A different person was leading the meeting, but I recognized a man sitting off to the side in a supporting position as the same person sitting in the same position the night before. His name was Guy McCloskey. This man did not look like a Buddhist to me. I immediately sensed he had a nature not too dissimilar to mine. What does a Buddhist look like anyway? He had the face of a man who had lost a few arguments. His nose looked liked it had been used to open more than just a few cans of beer. Later I found out it had been broken seven times on the streets of Chicago. I had the feeling he was as boneheaded as me. I was right. Most importantly, I sensed he wasn't someone who was going to be duped by false claims from some religion that had been dreamed up 14 days ago by someone in a rowboat.

The same distaste I had in the first meeting came back, but this time I kept control, gritted my teeth and patiently waited for the meeting to end so I could find out what it took to learn how to chant *Nam-Myoho-Renge-Kyo* and to receive the Gohonzon. That's all I wanted. I didn't want to join anything and I didn't want people calling me. After the meeting I filled out an application to receive the Gohonzon, signed it on the trunk of Guy McCloskey's Chevy Nova, and he drove others and me to an old abandoned Post Office in downtown Los Angeles that the organization, SGI-USA, was renting as their headquarters.[3]

On the way, I got to ask a few questions of Guy and got

[3] When Rick signed the application in 1968, SGI-USA was then known as NSA. The name change took place in 1990.

answers that led me to believe that there was a history and theory and documentation behind all this. My interest was getting responses that were intriguing at least. We also were chanting in the car for a while which helped me find the rhythm. I enjoyed the chanting and was anxious to do more. Something felt very right about all this. I also knew that in some ways this was going to be a hard pill for me to swallow. I was too solitary to even imagine being involved in any type of organization, let alone a religious one. I had to figure out another way to find out about Nichiren Buddhism besides being a "member."

Lynn received her Gohonzon that evening as well. That night I waited until I got back to my place and I chanted. I was sure I was screwing it up with my pronunciation but that didn't stop me. I chanted to the best of my ability. I wanted proof now. I wasn't going to wait to see proof three days before I died. If something didn't happen soon, I wasn't going to continue. What to chant for? I didn't have a cold to chant away, I had no idea what spirituality was and I wanted something tangible I could see and touch. I didn't have a TV. I wanted a TV, so I chanted for a TV. After chanting for a while I smoked a joint, had a glass of wine and went to bed realizing I had no grass for the next day, so I had to get some in the morning.

I woke up, took a shower, ate an avocado, pine nut, and mayonnaise sandwich and chanted for about 15 minutes. First thing I did was to make my way down Doheny Drive to see a friend and get some dope to smoke. About halfway down the block, I saw a man standing in his driveway with his garage door open.

As I started to pass he called out to me, "Hey, you want a TV?"

That scared the hell out of me. He was cleaning out his garage, and I was standing there thinking this is the strangest coincidence in my entire life. Or the Antichrist got me. Or maybe the chanting worked. Anyway you look at it, it happened. I thanked the man for the television, put it on my shoulder and carried it back to my place. I learned another great lesson that day. Be clear about what you're chanting for.

I plugged it in. The 19-inch Zenith worked but the picture was only three inches high. And it was black and white. Nuts! Forgot to think color and for it to work. But It did work—the chanting did work. If it was the Antichrist, he made a mistake because I forgot all about the grass. As a matter of fact, I went from someone who liked to smoke 24 hours a day to just a little late at night, and within about a week or so, to not wanting dope at all.

It took about four days before I could get someone to come over and enshrine the Gohonzon for me. I had the feeling they weren't too excited about having me around. I wasn't interested in participating in any ceremony.

"Just do what you have to do and leave me alone."

It was Guy McCloskey and a woman who appeared to be about 20 months pregnant. Her name was Barbara Efner and she turned out to be one of the nicest people I would ever meet. But in those days I just wasn't interested in any type of social religious gathering. I wanted to chant and that was that.

The enshrining ceremony wasn't the holiest event happening in the world that day. I gave them a rough time. McCloskey started moving things around to make room for the altar the Gohonzon was going to be displayed in. It's not a good thing to start moving my stuff around in my home without asking my permission.

"If you touch another thing of mine without telling me why and what you're doing, you're on your way out."

Guy's a tough old bird and how he held back I don't know, but between Barbara's demeanor, his reservation of anger and my just being an ass, we got it done. When they finished they wanted me to chant for a couple minutes with them.

"Just do what you've got to do and get out of here."

If I said Guy gave me a gesture that wouldn't be allowed in church, I could be wrong, but it was written all over this man's face. They left and I sat down and started chanting. I haven't stopped yet.

Between the time I went to the Buddhist meeting, to the day they enshrined the Gohonzon, I had moved a couple of blocks west to a street called Hillsdale. My lady friend with the dog called Monkey seemed to get it in her head that if she put up curtains, I would be around more. She got it backwards. The curtains gave me the idea that I had to move immediately. It must have been a couple days after the en-shrining that she came over to my new place and caught me in the middle of my morning prayers. I was struggling with pronouncing the words in the book. I later found out it was called *Gongyo*. She looked at me like she had seen the moon fall out of the sky. I told her I wasn't going to be available any longer, but I wanted her to be happy. That was like telling a bear to shave. First tears, then anger, then a broken screen door. Monkey wasn't with her so I didn't get to say good-bye to him. One less friend.

It seemed only natural to find out how this Buddhism worked toward finding women. I started chanting for them. I knew what I wanted: a woman with big lips, a maternal instinct, an appetite for affection and a natural wisdom concerning the wants and needs of a man. I loved sleeping with strangers. I'd chant and go out on the Strip looking for the right one to pop up. I ran into Lynn. Not once or twice but over and over. I'd go back to the Gohonzon thinking it just doesn't understand. "Not her."

This happened way too many times not to think there was a lot to learn about the difference between wants and needs. Was I getting something I needed rather than what I wanted? Made me a little nervous to think so.

For the next two months, one thing after another would keep me on my toes wondering, How the hell did that happen? I would chant every morning and evening and sometimes during the day. I'd had athlete's foot for about nine years. Powders, sprays, creams, anything I could get my hands on to stop the itching. Nothing worked. It would go away for a day or two then come back…with an attitude. So one day it dawned on me to chant for it to go away. Two days later, it was gone. It did come back a couple of times, but I noticed that it was when I was pissed off at someone. I'd chant and it would go away again. Then it was gone forever.

One of my heroes in life was an actor, horseman by the name of Ben Johnson. Watching him ride was better than going to heaven. I was chanting one afternoon, planning what I was going to do that evening, when it occurred to me to chant to meet Ben Johnson. It was like a throwaway prayer. Of course I wanted to meet him, but I honestly wasn't depending on the chanting to make it happen. How silly of me. This had to be within the first two weeks of my chanting. It wasn't that big of a deal, but I chanted for it anyway. Down at the corner of Hillsdale and Sunset was the old Hamburger Hamlet.

As I walked by on my way to find that "woman," coming out of the side door was Ben Johnson. I stopped in my tracks, put out my hand and said, "If I don't say hello, I'll kick myself forever."

We spoke for a minute or two about a horse named Steele he used in film sometimes, and that was that. How the Hell Did That Happen?

I chanted for a guitar and ended up with two people asking me if I wanted one. I chanted for all kinds of things. One day early in the morning I chanted for $500 because someone had told me that the Buddhist organization, then called NSA, was going to have a convention in Hawaii around the middle of August. For $250 everything was covered for the four-day trip. I decided to chant for the money. The VW Bug had a blown engine and was parked on the street across from my place. Hillsdale is a very steep street. You have to park your car nosed into the curb or you might lose it to gravity. I was chanting that morning when I heard a god-awful crash that sounded like a train wreck.

A city trash truck had lost its brakes and plowed into and over my poor dead Bug. Within one hour I had accepted a check for $500. Why I didn't ask for more, I don't know, but I was shocked by the "coincidence." Actually, I think I had just about stopped even thinking that coincidence was a word that applied to anything that was happening to me at this time in my life.

Slowly something was stirring up inside my life that was alien to me. I had always lived my life from a point of a low level of humanity. When alone, sometimes I would sense or experience feelings that were of a higher world, but for the most part anger was where I was most comfortable. Chanting in the morning was always the best time for me. It set my day in a more rhythmical pattern, and my mind started off on a clearer path.

One morning as I finished chanting, I started to cry. I sat there and cried for about a half hour. And I couldn't come up with even one thing that would have triggered this. It came out of nowhere, but it was completely within me. And I knew my chanting caused it. It was as if I was wringing out a gallon of poison from my system. Where did that come from? What caused this to occur? Why? What was next? This was totally unexpected, but after collecting myself and taking time to recover from this sudden burst of emotion, I realized I felt different. The rage that fed my anger was gone. I felt lighter and clean. Most importantly I felt like there was room inside my heart for more than anger. I wanted to talk to someone about this, but who? I'd already separated myself from the organization. I was sure that no one would want to talk to me because of the attitude I had toward them.

Then I remembered that Lynn had maintained a relationship with some of the members. Perhaps I can get to someone through her. I called and arranged to go with her to a meeting. Not having a car, I told her I would meet her at a coffee shop or somewhere and we would go together. It was a long walk to the location we picked. A strange thing happened on the way.

The crying episode had left me with a void or emptiness. The different times in my life when I felt rage, it came from the same place that was now hollow. As I started walking toward meeting up with Lynn, I had a very peculiar set of thoughts come to me. I could fill up this cavity in my heart with love and affection. That was what was missing in my marriage.

For the first time I began to feel what it might be like to be in love with someone. As I walked, I began to lengthen my stride and move a little faster. Maybe I should tell her. Maybe I should say, "I can love you." No, better not. What if I'm wrong? Do I really love her, or do I just think I can? The closer I got to where we were going to meet, the more confused and excited I became. I've got to get a hold of myself. Slow down the walking and slow down my mind. I began to chant to the rhythm of my walk.

Almost there and I can see her car approaching. Hold it. Who's that driving and why is she sitting in the middle next to him? Out of nowhere it was as if someone dropped a rock on my head from 1,000 feet up. I was stunned. I felt like someone kicked me in the heart. I turned around and went home. How the Hell Did That Happen? More importantly, why did that happen?

19

WHAT'S NEXT?

Toward Tomorrow

When I was a kid looking for love and horses, I spent some time at a thoroughbred breeding farm in Florida. I remember that it was the first time I heard the expression "mucking the stalls." It was upscale language that translated to "shoveling horse shit." I had thought that I might be able to love Lynn and that love could fill up the anger space that was now vacant in my heart. Losing that possibility was an emotional roller coaster ride. I felt as if I had just taken a 100-foot nosedive into a bucket of the "muck." I needed to get back to me, myself and I. I determined that Lynn was a devil in my life and that I had to stay away from her.

But after a couple of weeks, I had to speak to Lynn on the phone because I had broken my own cardinal rule. I told someone about chanting and they wanted to find out more about it. I had to take them to a meeting simply because I didn't know enough to answer the questions. And if they wanted to practice, I had no way of getting them a Gohonzon. I got the address of a meeting and took my friend. I decided to pay the $250 for that trip to Hawaii. At the same time,

I offered Lynn the money for her to be able to go as well. There went the $500.

The meeting I went to wasn't designed for introducing someone to Buddhism. Its intent was to promote the Hawaii convention. I spoke up when I realized they weren't going to pay attention to my guest.

"I have a guest here. Will someone talk to him about chanting? He has questions."

The response was, "Not today. We're going to visit members and promote the convention."

That was enough for me. I turned to my friend, "Don't you ever come back to this place. They have no idea what they're doing."

I made my way home, determined to never go back as well. It was later that I remembered I had given them the $250. I did go back. Lynn had paid her money as well. Here we go again.

Actors have a hell of a time finding ways to hone their craft. If you're not employed or a member of a theatrical company or at least in a workshop, it's very difficult to practice your craft. A writer can write if he has a pencil. Singers can sing even if just in a closet. If a sculptor has clay or a rock he can usually find a way to turn it into something. Musicians with an instrument need only a place to stand and happily reveal the sounds of their minds. But if an actor wants to create a character and accomplish an objective, he might very well get arrested for applying his trade outside the box. I enjoyed going into grocery stores with an attitude and maybe a limp. It was always a great exercise to go into a department store trying to keep out of the sight of someone following me. If I did it really well, I would draw the attention of security and then get them to help me find the "bad guy."

To this day I still receive anywhere from $6 to $9 dollars about four times a year from residuals for stunt work I did on the first feature film I worked on in 1967, "Planet of The Apes." That was before Buddhism. After I started chanting, more opportunities began to come my way. I came close to a good job in John Wayne's "Undefeated." Paul Scofield was on board to do a film at Universal, and I was interviewed to play a young soldier who was the object of his attention. His character was a latent homosexual. This storyline had been filmed a couple years earlier in a John Huston film, "Reflections in a Golden Eye," with Marlon Brando. That may be the reason the project was dropped. Still it was remarkable to me that I was being given consideration for roles of this importance. A series called "Iron Horse" with Dale Robertson was in its last year, and they were looking for a young man to be a regular and bring in a more youthful audience. According to my agent, I "just missed." Lucky me. I was still too attached to the idea that booze, women, monkey business and seclusion were the correct paths to happiness. If I would have scored in any of those projects and gotten any type of fame or fortune, I would have been dead long ago.

It came time for the Buddhist convention and I was anxious to go for two reasons. One, spending four days in Hawaii, all expenses included, seemed like a good deal. The second was the theme or purpose of the convention. Simply put, it was to tell as many people about Nichiren Buddhism as possible. Chanting at this point had become pretty central in my mind. This would be August of 1968. The objective of world peace seemed plausible based on the changes that had happened in my life in this very short period of time. The tangible, and even the physical results were wonderful to experience, but it was what was happening in my mind and heart that really got my attention. If these changes continued, if I were able to continue to polish myself, it didn't seem to me there would be any real problem getting this religion, this philosophy, to spread and blanket the world. I may sound like an empty dreamer, but after more than 40 years of practicing and studying the Buddhism of Nichiren Daishonin, I have no doubts left. This is my truth. But in1968 I was at war—a war with myself.

In order to make this trip to Hawaii, I had no choice but to go along with the organization. No easy task for this angry loner. When I had turned in my money, I let it be known I was a vegetarian. What made me become a vegetarian is another one of the mysteries of my life. I have no idea. But it must have seemed like a good idea at the time. Not too orthodox, but I was trying. Of course, I made sure there would be food I could eat.

"No problem. You'll see. Just get in line, get on the plane and follow the leader."

Whoa! I couldn't do that very well in the Army. Now they wanted me to be a "good boy" and join in with the other sheep?

I tried, honestly. When they started singing songs on the plane, I froze my mind. When they asked me to take off my sunglasses so they could film the departure from the plane, I did it...right after I gave the camera the finger. They didn't like that. Fine, cut it. When I found out that we wouldn't be staying in a hotel but in a converted warehouse used for unloading ships, I kept my mouth shut even then. I think there had to have been 5,000 cots and maybe ten portable toilets in the whole place. But when I found that the closest thing to food for a vegetarian was a two-day-old tuna fish sandwich on white bread and a glass of Dole Pineapple juice, I hit the ceiling.

"I will not eat this crap. You better do something about it or I am out of here."

Someone had named the warehouse "The Waterfront Hilton." All I could think of was, Where's the world peace going to take place? Certainly not here."

And then there was poor Lynn. I looked over and realized she must be wondering,

"What the hell has he gotten me into this time?"

I had already gotten her into a bad marriage, started her smoking dope, shown her what rage was, and we even moved at one point to a guesthouse in Laurel Canyon that had no roof. In my mind, every struggling artist lives in a place with no roof. Besides, Laurel Canyon, in those days, was called Reefer Hill—the perfect place to explore the recesses of your mind. Now the poor girl was in Hawaii, everyone's paradise, scheduled to sleep near the toilets and with nothing to eat. And her soon to be ex-husband was making the "best of friends" with everyone he met.

Food has always presented itself as a problem to me. With my Mother it was, "Eat everything on your plate or it'll be your last meal."

Living with One Eye and Pinky Finger, my going without eating was their favorite way to punish me. I fell in love with raw potatoes, which I'd skin and eat from the bin in their basement. In the Army a smartass decided he was going to eat something off my tray. As he reached for it, I stabbed him in the back of his hand with my fork. Even today, I don't look forward to eating. It just doesn't cross my mind until my stomach starts to growl, make demands and call out for help.

In Hawaii a couple of people, young leaders, I think Larry Shaw was one of them, tried to talk to me, but I wasn't listening to anyone who didn't show me where the food was. I was told to wait for a minute and they would get me someone who could help. I noticed I had drawn the attention of a local newspaper looking for a story about the "herd of Buddhists" that came to town. I was about to give him something to write about when a man came over and was introduced as Mr. Kikumura.

He walked up to me and said, "What's your problem, buddy?"

One look at this guy and my first thought was, "He can't be a leader."

This man just didn't have the appearance of religion in any way, shape or form. He looked more like someone you just didn't want to meet outside of your own turf. He looked too sharp, too clever. He wore a pinky ring. He dressed like he was a gambler, and I had the feeling that my problem wasn't the only thing on his mind. I figured he must have been part of the Japanese Mafia at some point. He had all his fingers so he must have been at the top of his game.

The Waterfront Hilton warehouse extended from the coast out into the sea. It had four large freight doors, two on each side and one at each end. Mr. Kikumura listened to my story and casually said to me, "Can't eat the food? OK, come with me."

We slowly walked toward the landside freight door of the warehouse. Hawaii is truly one of the world's most beautiful places. As we approached the door, I could see the beautiful hills colored with what must have been a thousand shades of green. We got to the door and stopped.

He paused for a second and says, "You see that mountain over there?"

I looked, "Yeah."

Another short pause. "Go find yourself a damn banana."

I've spaced out before but this was the best ever. It's like magic when your mind just isn't there. I felt like someone had stolen my thinker. When this man said, "Go find yourself a damn banana," my mind went into outer space.

Then, "Are you kidding? It's OK to just leave?"

It was OK. He reminded me that we would be leaving in three days, and he slowly walked back into the warehouse. I stood there dumbfounded for a minute, and then I went to find Lynn to say I was going to take off and find something to eat. She decided to go with me, and we began our little side trip, which ended up having huge results.

We found a health food store and bought a pound of shelled Sunflower seeds. I think we even went to a restaurant and had bacon and eggs. Vegetarian…right. I remember lying on the beach one day and we heard the sound of a choir chanting *Nam-Myoho-Renge-Kyo*. That was truly mysterious. We wondered if there was such a thing as an official, legal, Buddhist wedding ceremony.

We hitchhiked everywhere we were going and would tell

anyone we met about this Buddhism. At one point, we were picked up by a young couple and began to share our experience when Lynn said, "...and he's changed so much I could even marry him again."

Again my brain left for places unknown, with my mind following close behind. I really didn't believe what I heard but she repeated it. I didn't know how to spell numb or dumb, but I was. She scared the hell out of me. I couldn't imagine why she said that, let alone imagine what about me had changed so much that she would even think that way. This was ridiculous. This Buddhism was becoming a lot more than just "freaky." It was taking center stage in my life. I wasn't sure this was what I wanted, but I was sure I wanted to find out a lot more about it. It was time to get back to the Waterfront Hilton.

"Would you mind being a witness at a wedding?"

Lynn and I had just gotten back when someone came up to me and asked that question. How strange that we had wondered about Buddhist weddings when we were talking on the beach. It was even more bizarre when Lynn got back to her cot and sleeping area and a different person came up and asked her the same question. We both volunteered and attended the wedding. All of this was very unsettling for me. Although fascinated by everything that was happening, to think it was occurring because of this prayer, this chanting was beyond my imagination.

"How the Hell Could All This Be Happening?"

That night, there was the big meeting to conclude the convention. It was intended to introduce all the people of Hawaii who had been told of the wonder of this Buddhism.

Made sense to me. That was the purpose of the meeting and it was scheduled to begin at 7 p.m. on the nose. By 7:45, I was ready to tear the building down. Anyone who even resembled a guest had left and everyone else was either freaking out or singing songs that sounded like they had been written by a third-grader just before being sent to the principal's office. On the stage were about a half dozen "leaders" with one hand on their hips and the other arm swinging through the air as if they were trying to get an airplane to turn to the left before it ran off the runway. I stormed out of there, made my way back to the warehouse to get my plane ticket and get the hell out of there. I felt like I had just been exposed to a badly run "Young Nazi Youth Camp."

What was wrong with this organization? Why couldn't they see the needs of the people should come first? It didn't make any sense to me. There was something wrong with this picture. The chanting, the Gohonzon and the dream of peace were real, but the vehicle had too many flat tires. All I wanted was to find a way for people to be able to chant and pray to this Gohonzon and become happy. What could I do?

One thing was for sure—I wasn't leaving for L.A. that night. All the tickets were locked in a safe, and the warehouse was empty except for a couple of people lying on their cots and one guy sleeping in a chair securing the safe from anyone like me. I spent most of that night sitting and staring at the water and chanting quietly and thinking to myself, "What can I do?"

The next day we departed for the mainland. But first, there was chanting and doing *Gongyo* as a group. Benches had been set up facing the ocean end of the Waterfront Hilton and a Gohonzon was enshrined. The leader was chanting much too fast for me, and when it came to pronouncing the words of *Gongyo*, it sounded like the leader was trying to imitate a machine gun. It really pissed me off. I wanted to at least be able to come close to doing it correctly. Instead, I threw the *Gongyo* book under the bench in front of me, put my hands together and let the bullets rip out of me.

The book slid out in front of Mr. Kikumura. He picked it up, turned, looked at me and handed it back. I don't know what to tell you but that may have been one of the best *Gongyos* I've ever done because in the middle of the chanting, I had an unexpected answer to a prayer I didn't realize I had made. It was a realization I will never forget. Suddenly, it became clear that the only way to a true peace was for me to change myself.

The anger, the frustration and all that I was complaining about would never change until I changed. All that was happening around me was mirroring exactly what I was feeling in my heart. All I saw outside was a reflection of what was inside. The outside wasn't pretty. If the organization is going to change and develop, I had to change and develop. Easier said than done. I needed to become a good friend to myself. I also realized I needed to find a good friend in SGI-USA. Instead of expecting changes outside of myself, I needed to find out how to make those changes happen inside. I later found out this process of inner change was referred to as "The Human Revolution."

Just as we were finishing the morning prayers, someone who was standing at the side freight door called out to the leader that a rainbow had appeared. It wasn't raining. The leader went over to the door and some of the other leaders, including Mr. Kikumura. What the hell? I went as well.

There was a rainbow. That was nice but I wasn't that impressed until the leader came back to the front and said something to the effect that the Universe was showing us that our gathering was a great cause towards "The World's Peace." He suggested we all sing "Somewhere Over The Rainbow." We joined hands and swayed back and forth singing. Not exactly my cup of tea, but whatever. In the middle of the song the leader was again signaled to come to the door. Now a bunch of us went over. A second rainbow appeared. Both rainbows were over the top of the Waterfront Hilton. Now you had my attention. That was amazing. Now I really wanted to understand this Buddhism.

Flying home was exciting. Lynn and I sat together and both of us were blown away by the whole experience of the Hawaiian Convention. On the plane they showed a film called the "Young Americans," a story about a group of singers and their appearances on stage as well as backstage and all that happens in between. One person stood out in the film. He was one of the singers, but there was something about him that caught my attention. About a week after coming back to Los Angeles, Lynn and I were driving in her car to a discussion meeting when I spotted someone waiting to cross the street at the light. I said to Lynn, "Roll down your window."

I called out to the man and asked him if he was interested in going to a discussion meeting about Nichiren Buddhism. He came over to the car, looked in and said, "Yes."

It was the same young man we had seen in the movie on the plane. His name was Ken. He was crossing the street on his way to jump off a building to commit suicide. He decided to chant. That evening he received the Gohonzon and went on to become a successful actor and singer. He had a difficult time getting over his wish to die, but he made it. Seeing and listening to other people's experiences is a reward in and of itself. It added to my own belief and faith.

Was all the running into Lynn when all I was looking for was a hug from a stranger the workings of chanting? Was the whole adventure in Hawaii where we were questioning whether there was such a thing as a Buddhist wedding or being invited to witness such a wedding the workings of chanting? And then the statement from her: "He's changed so much I could almost marry him again."

Was this the direction my, or should I say, our lives should take? Let me sum it up quickly. Although never fully divorced, we got married "again" on September 28, 1968. Yes, it was a Buddhist ceremony. Yes, that's when the real Human Revolution began.

From that point on, the real struggles began to appear. The money from commercials ran its course. There are too many details to share at this point, but from one minute to the next it was one challenge after another. The problems Lynn and I had during our first marriage came back to show their ugly face. The difference was that we could sit down and chant for the solution or answer and something would always happen to lead us in a direction of growth. At the same time, it seemed that it was more difficult to overcome the problems because the solutions always had to come from inside before they revealed results on the outside. The more I chanted and practiced this philosophy and tried to put it into action in my daily life, the more I realized I needed to find things to read and to talk to someone who had a grasp on what was going on. The only person I felt I wanted to talk to was Mr. Kikumura.

That first meeting in Hawaii stuck with me. What stuck was the impression I got from this man. He was a real human being who knew who he was. I trusted him to give me a straight answer to any question I was to ask him. His character and integrity were clear to me.

One evening, either I called or met up with Guy McCloskey and asked if he could arrange a meeting with Mr. Kikumura. That was a day to celebrate for the rest of my life.

That first guidance session I had with Mr. Kikumura started me on a path of practice and study of Nichiren Daishonin's Buddhism that forever will be the beginning of a life I never could have imagined. He never for a moment acted or spoke as if he had all the answers. He always presented himself as a guide to help me find the answers in the teachings of Nichiren. And just as important, he always referred to the writings and guidance of a man named Daisaku Ikeda.

At this moment I can't recall the words of the conversation, but what I do remember is that I felt a complete trust in him. When I joined what was later to be known as SGI-USA and started to practice, I had many doubts about the leadership and the organization in general. What was their real purpose? The majority of the leadership was Japanese. What was going on in the back of their minds? Was this an underground movement to rule and conquer the United States in retaliation for the bombings during the war? Where did the money come from? I wanted to know what went on behind closed doors. I wanted to know everything. Most of all, I wanted to think that there truly was a way for human beings to be happy. For me to take this religion seriously, I needed to see there were no contradictions to my needs and the wishes of all people. I firmly believed for a religion to be true, it had to remove the sufferings from the hearts, minds and lives of the people.

From the moment my mother opened the trunk of her car, pulled out the suitcase and told me that I had to go with those strangers, I knew this wasn't the way life was supposed to be. I didn't know how it should be, but I knew that wasn't it.

On June 26, 2009, I started my 42nd year of the practice and study of Nichiren Buddhism and of being a member of SGI-USA. I never intended to chant for more than a day or maybe two if I didn't see some conspicuous result. I certainly had no intentions of becoming religious. It's almost as if I'd been turned inside out. Appreciation and gratitude don't come easily to a lot of people. When you're as boneheaded as I am, it's a sure bet that I would have turned out to be one of those people who couldn't care less about others. But here I am, constantly wondering what I can do to help others. If I was to look back to see what was my greatest fortune when I started chanting, it would be that I formed good habits. These good habits came to be because the pioneers like Mr. Kikumura taught me the basics of faith, practice and study. That's it.

When I had that first meeting with Mr. Kikumura, I came away with a lot more on my mind than when I got there. He first, and foremost, told me that faith in Buddhism means actual proof in your daily life. He suggested that I set goals for myself and to chant to accomplish them.

He also made it clear that Buddhism was based on the law of cause and effect. The sooner I took full responsibility for my life, the sooner I would see results leading me toward what I wanted and needed to become completely happy. He repeatedly said it would be a waste of time blaming someone else for my problems.

In the beginning, one of the biggest problems I had was listening to the leaders talk about this man who was the central figure of the SGI. President Daisaku Ikeda. He was the president of the international organization, and when people spoke of him, it seemed to me as if they looked to him as one would look to the Almighty. It made me really nervous.

"Who is this man?"

From as far back as I can remember, I've been on guard against letting anyone get close to me. It would be a major event if someone could break through the lock I had put on my heart. I just couldn't allow anyone to burn me again. Too many scars were left from my mother and even my father. When I married Lynn, I kept that lock closed. Now, there was the encouragement to let the wisdom and compassion of this man called President Ikeda, or Sensei, guide me so I could experience this total absolute joy of enlightenment through faith in this Buddhism.

What was most interesting though was the fact that when I chanted and applied his guidance to whatever the situation or problem was, I got results. Mr. Kikumura, in whom I had gained complete trust, always pointed me toward President Ikeda as his teacher and the person to follow. And in everything I read, President Ikeda always pointed toward his teacher, Josei Toda. All these people kept directing me to the teachings of Nichiren Daishonin. Even the writings of Nichiren declared that the law, *Nam-Myoho-Renge-Kyo*, was supreme. One of the writings of Nichiren went so far as to state, "Never seek this Gohonzon outside yourself." [4]

It seemed that the entirety of the teachings of Buddhism always ended up trying to make it clear that everything depended on me. Those teachings always made the point that I had to be the change that I wanted to see. It all came down to my prayer, action and determination. Another important point was how I could use all the personal dreams I had toward a true world peace. How could I use my life to create the greatest value for others as well as for myself? It was made clear that it was through chanting for both others and myself, helping others by giving them the key to changing their fate or destiny and by developing my inner self. This inner change is the process called Human Revolution. It doesn't happen overnight, but let me tell you, it does happen. There is a letter Nichiren wrote to a disciple over 700 years ago called "Winter Always Turns to Spring." [5]

When I asked Mr. Kikumura about this letter, he gave an answer that has carried me through a multitude of circumstances. He said, "Sometimes your life will seem like it's in the most severe winter ever. At other times, Rick, it will seem like it's the greatest of springtime. When you're in that terrible winter, you can either stand there and freeze to death or you could learn how to ski."

I can't tell you how many times those words helped me get through some very difficult times. There is tremendous wisdom in those words and when applied, it's like going

---

[4] *The Writings of Nichiren Daishonin*, ed., trans., The Gosho Translation Committee, (Tokyo: Soka Gakkai, 1999), p. 832.
[5] *Writings*, p. 535

through those times with a friend.

For the next couple of years, it seemed as if my life was changing a little every day. Each day I was learning more and more about how Buddhism could be applied to my daily life. The learning came quicker than the applying. One of the most difficult parts of my human revolution was opening up my heart. There were times when it seemed that I was banging against a brick wall, but when I made a breakthrough, it seemed like I was in paradise.

Lynn wanted to have a child. I was totally against it. It made no sense to me to bring a child into a world that appeared to me to be destined for decay and death. I did have a little bit of the dream of a world of peace, but I couldn't imagine it occurring in this lifetime. Why should I want to allow this hard world to happen to another human being? There was the one thought: what if this Buddhism was all it said it was and through awakening people throughout the world to this teaching, we could change the direction from a living hell to a world where peace and security existed in the hearts of all mankind? The results of my personal practice indicated it could happen, but I wasn't convinced the SGI could get enough people on board to make the ideal a reality.

Looking back after all these years, I find it remarkable that I made it this far. When I began practicing, it was as if I was in kindergarten again, but this time it was the school of learning the facts of life. I know I was reading about what was called the four sufferings of life; the sufferings of birth, the sufferings of maturity, the sufferings of illness and the sufferings of death, but I didn't see clearly that the organization in the United States was going through the sufferings of birth. The leadership was very young in faith and experience and as to be expected here in this country, we approached our practice with a consumer's mind and a "give-me" attitude.

"Chant for anything you want."

It's not unreasonable to expect that in this country with its corporate approach to human happiness, the organization would appeal to the greed in the human heart as a means to stimulate propagation. Unfortunately, the immaturity of some of the leadership and the desire for recognition and fame and fortune became the driving force of their own life rather than the happiness of the people. It was a very real example of the sufferings of birth. Self-centeredness, arrogance, conceit are very real conditions of the human heart and as years passed by it became clear that the central figure of the NSA organization had to go.

Once he was removed, the name of the organization was changed to SGI-USA, and the new central figure was chosen based on his determination and commitment to protect the purity of the teaching of Nichiren Buddhism, and to brighten the light focused on the sanctity of each and every living being. The guidance and direction of President Ikeda, which had been interrupted by the previous leader more for his own ambition and reputation rather than the welfare of the members, was now presented thoroughly and completely for the sake of the people. The oneness of mentor and disciple, the oneness of person and law and faith equals daily life, became the overriding spirit of propagation and the growth of the quality of faith for those who chose to volunteer to help others find the Buddha in their own hearts. Perhaps my greatest fortune is to never give up in my determination to do whatever I can to solidify the foundation of the SGI for generations to come.

After practicing for about one year, an opportunity came my way to go to Japan to meet the members there and participate in a study and training course. Many times when I don't get what I chant for, I do get what I need. This was one of those times.

20

A BABY

...Born Again

As I write this part of the story, today is June 15, 2009. Yesterday was my daughter's 35th birthday. Let me tell you how that happened.

In the summer of 1969, Lynn and I went to Japan with a large group of members from SGI-USA. Coming up with the money could be a book in itself, but we made it happen with a lot of chanting and determination. One of the most wonderful characteristics of the organization is the continuous encouragement to challenge yourself through prayer and action. This trip was just such a challenge. I knew that I wanted to learn all I could about Nichiren Buddhism, but I wasn't sure just how involved with the SGI I wanted to get. Everything told me to continue going forward except the little voice in the back of my head that wanted me to go out and play the games that would put me back on the path of my old bad habits. Those games were always going downhill. By this time in my life I wanted to make that voice shut up.

There were some things about that trip that took my mind back to the whole Waterfront Hilton experience. It was that the organization wanted everyone to dress the same. On the Hawaiian trip we all wore blue and white Aloha shirts with white pants and the ladies matching muumuus. For this trip to Japan everyone was dressed in white pants or skirts and a white and blue seersucker jacket, a white shirt or blouse and of course a blue tie. Even the cardboard suitcases matched, blue for the men and red for the women. Again it was get in line and wait. I made it this time without the flipping of the finger and without having to look for vegetarian food. I was back to meat and potatoes.

After Hawaii, I began to participate in SGI activities pretty consistently. I found that I truly wanted to introduce people to Buddhism and I wanted to study the teaching. I wanted to win over my negativity and become able to get in control of my life without having to resort to anger to get my way. Prayer was becoming my primary tool. The more I was able to direct my chanting and prayer to taking responsibility from within my heart for what was happening in my environment, the more the result became a desire to awaken in both myself and others the potential for good. If I wanted a conclusion of value or good, I would have to come from that position in my heart. I can't tell you how wonderful the realization was that I didn't have to resort to anguish. This didn't happen overnight, but just the hint that it was beginning to happen was like opening the door on a cage.

Mr. Kikumura once explained it this way.

"It's the skunk-skunk principle. If every time you turn around skunks are coming your way, you can bet your last dollar they're attracted to the skunk in you, Cowboy. Get rid of your stink and the skunks will go somewhere else."

Great guidance. Thank you.

Thirteen hours on a plane can wear you out. By the time we got to Japan I was pooped. All I wanted to do was sleep. Forget it. We got into the airport terminal and were met by so many Japanese members it made me feel like I was at the World Series and they just won. They were everywhere. Waving flags, singing songs, clapping their hands and screaming at the top of their lungs. I was shocked. I've never seen so many happy people in my whole life. They were so glad to see us. It must have been exhilarating for the Japanese members to see Americans who practice Buddhism. From their point of view, to see that *Nam-Myoho-Renge-Kyo* had spread so far from their home must have set their hearts on fire. And for us to see so many people in Japan who embraced this teaching, could world peace truly be on its way? This greeting of love and warmth and excitement certainly gave me reason to think so.

President Daisaku Ikeda sent a short message of welcome as we were escorted to buses that would take us to Olympic Village where we would be staying for a couple of days while we did all kinds of activities. I never imagined that there could be this much consideration for others in the entire world. From one minute to the next we were treated like royalty. As the buses made their way to the village, members were lining the streets with flags and banners, jumping up and down, smiling and waving. It was incredible. We arrived, got our assignments for sleeping. Fresh fruit was waiting for us and more messages from President Ikeda. Everything was happening as smooth as silk. The care and the smiles could melt rocks. There was no room for complaint. It seemed that this was the way the whole world needed to be, happy and caring.

For the entire trip, every minute, there was something to do. The schedule was full of opportunities to chant, to study, to participate in question and answer sessions or eat. Probably one of the most important activities was to meet the Japanese members up close. Dialogue was difficult if you didn't have a translator, but the communication from the heart was more valuable than understanding the words. The Olympic Village had been constructed to house the participants in the 1964 Olympics in Tokyo. I had two primary objectives that I wanted to accomplish during this trip. First was to see President Ikeda in person and listen to him talk about Buddhism. Second was to chant to the Dai-Gohonzon that was inscribed in wood by Nichiren Daishonin in 1279. It was located at the head temple at the foot of Mt. Fuji.

At that time our organization supported the priesthood both in spirit and financially. Since that time, the 67th High Priest Nikken Abe excommunicated the entire international membership. There was tremendous jealousy on the part of the priest Nikken toward Daisaku Ikeda who was receiving international recognition for his compassion, wisdom and action to establish peace throughout the world. That priest's envy and incessant desire for control over the laity removed any compassion or wisdom he may have once had. The actions and words of Nikken revealed his true nature by demonstrating his anger, stupidity and folly. When confronted with the un-priestly behavior of his and other priests, the total lack of appreciation and gratitude they demonstrated toward the generous support they received from the laity, they responded with the excommunication. I don't think it would be too wise to follow a man with such a display of stupidity.

Since that time, the SGI has by grown leaps and bounds and no longer has to give attention to the temple, nor does it have to concern itself with their personal doctrine. Our greatest concern is for the members of the temple and the effect of having been influenced by the misleading interpretations of Nichiren teachings. The SGI has all the teachings of Nichiren Daishonin. There are no secrets being kept away from the eyes of the laity by the priests. The priesthood has gone so far as to try to alter the intent of the Daishonin's teaching and to accuse the SGI of conferring counterfeit Gohonzons on the members. They also imply that because of our refusal to obey the dictates of the High Priest, we were destined to end up in the "hell of incessant suffering." What they can't alter is the actual proof of prayers being answered, the written words of Nichiren himself, and the growth, happiness and faith of the members of the SGI.

Back to 1969.

We had gone to the temple to chant to the Dai-Gohonzon. First, a picture-taking ceremony was scheduled on the steps of the Grand Lecture Hall with President Ikeda. That would be the only time I would see him on that trip. The SGI membership in Japan was about one in every ten people at that time. President Ikeda's schedule was and is incredible. We were fortunate to be able to have him come to take that picture with us. His responsibilities were enormous.

He came out in a suit, we had our picture taken, and he quickly took off his jacket and began to speak. His voice, though not loud, was powerful, clear and warm. I had no idea what he said but I knew he meant what he said. President Ikeda then asked if we wanted watermelon.

"Yes."

He went to a table that was set up and began to cut up the melons. They were delicious. The thing I noticed about these few moments with him was his complete confidence and total attention to what he was doing. This offering of watermelon wasn't a ceremony or just a ritual to him. He was sharing a part of his life with each of us. Each action and movement had a harmony and rhythm that sent a message to me that this man was totally united with all around him. He seemed to envelope everything and everyone in his life. I don't think I can make it any clearer than that. He personified all that I knew about Buddhism at that time. That was the beginning of a relationship in this life that I believe I had been seeking forever.

He had other picture-taking ceremonies with members from other countries. People from all over the world were coming to this summer training course. He gave as much of his time and attention to as many as he could. I had to know more about him. Who was this man and what did he mean to my life? That became my prayer.

Now it was time to go see the Dai-Gohonzon and to chant for world peace. All I remember was that we were all squeezed like sardines in a can. The building where the Dai-Gohonzon was enshrined was small and everyone had to first stand as close to each other as possible and then sit down on our feet. I don't know how we did it. It was so uncomfortable that it was very difficult for me to have much sincerity in my prayer, but I did my best. We weren't allotted much time, as there were not only people from other countries, but there were hundreds, if not thousands, of members from Japan who were anxious to chant as well.

Lynn and I had gone in at the same time, but we were not side-by-side when we chanted nor were we together during the picture-taking with President Ikeda. During most of this trip we were running separately but in the same movement. After seeing the Dai-Gohonzon everyone was invited to have some free time for a little shopping.

There was a town just outside the temple grounds that had a lot of souvenir shops as well as Mom and Pop stores for the local citizens. There were also a few places where we could buy accessories for our altars. We could buy incense, scarves, postcards, books, and pictures—just about anything we wanted or needed. We could also buy prayer beads. The beads came in all sizes and shapes, colors and different materials. There were sandalwood beads that were wonderful to have in my hands, as they gave off a fragrance I would expect to faintly smell walking through a forest. There were beads of stone, other woods and even plastic.

Lynn and I were now in this wonderful little shop that catered to members looking for something to take home for their altars. I was looking around and a pair of tiny baby beads caught my eye. I was compelled to buy them along with a tiny scarf to wrap them in. It was almost involuntary except that I knew what I was doing. I just didn't know why. A warm glow began to rise in my heart like the sun peeking over the top of a mountain at dawn. Something dramatic had changed in my heart. I wanted to have a baby. Lynn wanted children and had been chanting for me to want them as well.

This was the beginning of a world I had never experienced before, the world of a parent. I had to find a way to learn to be the best parent I could. Who could teach me?

Where could I learn the art of raising a child without letting the way I felt about my experience with my parents negatively affect a child? Could I use the example of parenting that I had from my mother and father to help me by not doing as they did? All these questions and thoughts were racing through my mind when I looked over to see Lynn looking at me. She saw me select the beads and scarf. We looked at each other in silence but our hearts spoke to each other through our eyes. These were the feelings and thoughts being sowed in my heart and mind.

I'd been a Buddhist for a little over a year at that time. In many ways, I felt like I wasn't in control of my life anymore. Not that I had been doing such a great job before, but at the very least I had held on to a little pride knowing that I was never looking outside of myself for help, guidance or direction. I had lived a solitary, angry existence growing up as I did. Even during those three years with Lynn before we found this practice, I lived alone in my heart. Putting a religious system of thought as a center of focus, especially one as foreign to the western way, and more importantly to my way of thinking, caused me to approach every day with both eyes wide open. Before taking up this practice, when I looked forward in my life, I found that I was always alone. And now, baby beads. What more did I need to know about which direction my life was leading me?

Set a goal, have a little fun under the sheets, have a baby. Read a few books, find a house big enough for three, make sure the room is painted with a unisex design, check the nutrition balance in the diet, be sure to take the doctor's prenatal advice, cross your fingers and pray. I'm sure I must be forgetting a few things but really, what more can you do? Well, now that I think of it, perhaps looking into the financial costs would have been a good idea, but I didn't have to worry too much about that because in no time at all, I was going to make a big step forward in my acting career. I was sure of that. I was always sure of that. I'd just be satisfied working in construction for the time being until that big move. No need for me to have a real job, I was an actor with no doubts. Too bad I wasn't a smart actor with some sense.

Another good idea would have been to put a little more concentration on our relationship. Most of the time I put a lot of emphasis on my relationship with Buddhism, thinking that it would naturally flow over to a better daily life. I had the impression that when someone said that faith equals daily life, everything depended on my development of faith, and it would automatically be mirrored in my everyday existence without my having to pray and concentrate on the problems in the marriage.

The reality is that we were struggling. I was working in both construction and film. When an acting interview or a job came along, I didn't think twice about walking away from construction. One day on "Mod Squad" was worth a million dollars of joy working in my art. Three shots on "Quincy" as a hit man, a coroner and a doctor in another could keep a smile in my heart for weeks. The "Incredible Hulk" and a lot of others I can't remember at the moment kept my spirits up but didn't do much for the budget or Lynn's mind toward peace and security.

From the time we returned from Japan, we tried to have a baby. As time went by and nothing was happening, it put added pressure on the relationship. The fact was we couldn't conceive.

The baby beads and scarf sat near the altar. After a couple of years of trying, we went for medical advice and an evaluation. The conclusion was that although there was no discernible medical reason for not conceiving, it could be that physically we were not compatible. At this point we decided to get guidance and see if there was a solution to the problem from the viewpoint of Buddhism. The conclusion was that we needed to approach the goal from inside. The point was made that although it appeared that the lack of being able to get pregnant was physical, it was inseparable from the spiritual.

We followed that guidance, changed our strategy in prayer and within a fairly short time we were able to conceive. That internal journey produced results that were very conspicuous. Lynn was pregnant, happier than I had ever seen her and we were united in heart and mind as never before. We started reading the baby books, looking for the house, just being excited about the prospects for the future when hell appeared. We miscarried in the fourth month.

There is no way I can imagine the discomfort, disappointment and depression Lynn must have felt during that time. We got her into the hospital for the care she needed, and I took care of the unborn. Removing the remains of that child from our bed was the most difficult thing I had ever done. That image will forever be etched in my life.

All through that time, many other experiences helped

with the development of understanding and belief in Nichiren Buddhism—a new house that would be perfect for a baby, a lot more work in both commercials and film, including a co-starring role in an independent film shot in Florida. I also did a number of print jobs for magazines and generally felt good about the direction my career was going. I didn't make the big bucks but I felt that would come naturally. The one or two day jobs on "Cannon" or a small role in "Crazy Mama" kept my spirits up, but those roles were very unsatisfying.

At the same time that I was hoping to get the roles that would let me truly reveal the freedom I felt artistically in my heart, I had a very distinctive desire to never lose my privacy. I was definitely at cross purposes with myself.

The most significant personal development was that I was given the opportunity to escort and provide security for President Ikeda when he came to the United States. Even today, as I look back, it amazes me how that occurred. There were three of us who were in the closest proximity to him during his movement. I was the third. I don't know how faith is evaluated, but it can't be revealed in numbers. It must be something that shines from within one's heart.

From the beginning of my practice, I developed a seeking mind. I wanted to know the truth of life. I clearly remember the day my mother opened the trunk of her car, pulled a suitcase out and told me to get in the car with the strangers. From that day, from that moment, I believe my life began a journey of destiny that would take me to the place in my heart and mind where I now live. The experiences I am having and have been having—chanting to the Gohonzon, my involvement with the SGI-USA, studying the teachings of Nichiren and hearing the words and reading the works of Daisaku Ikeda, caused me to want to break out of the walls I had built around myself and establish the caring for others that was inspired by this exposure to Buddhism. Sharing my experience with the members and the people I know and meet, is the happiest life I could ever imagine. Little did I know just how long it would take for me to truly make the internal changes I would have to make to feel this way.

Being given that chance to watch President Ikeda as he moved through his daily life had to be an answer to a prayer from the deepest recesses of my life. The skepticism and even the fear of involvement with religion in general, more specifically, with an organization of religion, had diminished quite a bit, but there was this one part concerning the mentor-disciple, teacher-student, relationship that was a big hurdle for me to get over in order to experience the essentials of faith, practice and study.

Trust was something another person would have to earn from me before I could freely give my heart the freedom needed to unite with the heart of another. At that point Mr. Kikumura was the closest person to my heart of trust in the world of Buddhism. Trust would have to be the basis of my decision to follow the guidance or direction that was presented in order discuss my problems, the continuing changing circumstances of my life and to try an alternate way of thinking and responding when facing an obstacle or an unfulfilled dream.

"Don't follow your leader," Mr. Kikumura said. "Support the position. If I was to tell you to follow your leader and one day you came to my house, found me standing up in my bed doing something I shouldn't be doing, you'd think you were supposed to go home and do it yourself."

That was as clear as a bell to me. The leaders also need to do their own human revolution. No one was exempt from having to do the human revolution, the inner transformation, a spiritual awakening. A primary responsibility of a leader is self-development, particularly if they feel a sense of caring for the welfare of others. It's pretty hard to encourage someone to challenge him or herself if you're not doing it yourself. But when you do accept that responsibility to cause a change for the good in someone or something outside your own personal life, an expansion begins to take place in your own heart and it shows up in others as well. And it's a mind blower when you actually live it and see it and watch it unfold in front of your very eyes. And then you realize the reward of faith. You believe. And then from that level of faith you go for more. More good, more beauty, more value.

This dialogue with Mr. Kikumura has stayed with me all my life.

"They may still be struggling with some of their own bad habits, and if I told you to follow them, it could cause you to have a very misguided understanding of Buddhism."

Then he said, "Read what President Ikeda has to say. Find out what kind of person he is and see what he does. See what he has to say about leaders and leadership."

Although he never had children of his own, I felt as if I had a real dad for the first time. By example, he showed me something I will never forget and will always try to emulate. He never failed to let me know he had a teacher, and he never failed to point me in the direction of the teachings of Nichiren, the Gohonzon and President Ikeda. He never pointed to himself. Wouldn't it be a different world if we had more "Dads" like him?

Mr. Kikumura was 82 on August 13, 2009. Whether it's pride or ego I don't know, but one of my great treasures is that I was also born on August 13th. If that's the skunk-skunk principle,. I buy it. It was with Mr. Kikumura's recommendation that I was given this most important assignment to aid President Ikeda in his travels while in the United States. I gave my word that I would do whatever it took to allow him to complete the purpose for the visit.

"Thank you, Sir."

The selfish part of being able to accept this opportunity was that I would be able to create more good fortune for my family.

After the miscarriage, my doubts were pretty strong concerning the chances of ever having a child, but Lynn and I decided we wanted to see Mr. Kikumura for guidance about continuing our expectations to have a baby when he interrupted our questions with, "Do you want to have a baby, Rick?"

"Yes, Sir."

He continued, "If you think in any way it's your wife's fault that you can't have a child, you are not using Buddhism to overcome the problem. Your mind is attached to an inferior way of thinking."

Then he turned to Lynn and said, "And Lynn, if you think it's the cowboy's problem, the cause for not being able to have a baby, you are not looking in the right direction. The problem and the solution always are within your own life. Buddhism is a teaching of inner transformation."

He spoke very clearly and left no doubt that we could change this around. I felt it in my heart that the problem was mine and the solution was my spiritual determination.

Then very gently he said, "Go home and have a baby."

It was one of those moments when you just kind of space out for a moment. Mr. Kikumura had turned away to speak to someone for a second. Then looked back at us and said, "What are you waiting for? Go home and have a baby."

It took about 30 minutes to drive home. Five minutes later Kelli Richards was conceived. That first 30 minutes was foreplay on the freeway.

By January, 1974, we were in our fifth month of pregnancy. I felt completely confident that we were going to go full-term and have the most wonderful baby the world has ever seen. Monica Kaneko Kelli Richards. That girl broke open my heart and released a love I had never known or even suspected could exist. There isn't a cell in her body I would change even if I could. They may write poems and songs and fill greeting cards with all kinds of words and images about love, but nothing has ever come close to expressing the gratitude I feel with the entirety of my life for having the opportunity to spend some of this lifetime with her.

Fourteen months later, our son was born. Andrew Shinichi Richards. Another kind of love came out of me. And as thrilled as I was to have this boy in my life, it appeared, early on that a great part of his mission was to get me to deal with the fundamental flaws in my personality and character. And fortunately for me, he's still doing it. He keeps trying to train me to get on board with today. His giving me this computer and challenging me like he did is exactly what I'm trying to say. From the beginning I had to stand back sometimes and just watch him in action. Very smart, very creative in his approach to whatever caught his fancy and always a learner regardless of what he was trying to accomplish. He had all the markings of a winner.

I've heard many members of the SGI refer to children born to a Buddhist family as "Fortune Babies." Of course with my mind of greed I hoped that it meant that my personal fortune would automatically increase. But Nooo. It really meant that they had a mission to keep the parents in the mindset to continuously polish the tarnished mirror within their own lives. Again, the word gratitude isn't nearly clear enough to explain the feeling in my heart for the appearance of these remarkable people in my life. The fortune is mine.

From 1972 until 1981, I was able to accompany President Ikeda whenever he traveled to the United States to encourage the membership and to solidify the development of our organization. It became clear to me that the purpose of the SGI was to be a two-way system of communication. A true world peace must first happen in the heart and lives of the people.

"A great human revolution in just a single individual will help achieve a change in the destiny of a nation and, further, will enable a change in the destiny of all humankind."

These words of President Ikeda express his personal conviction, the heart and spirit of the SGI and the purpose behind the teachings and efforts of Nichiren Daishonin.

It was May of 1972 when I was first able to participate

in one of President Ikeda's trips to the States. I remember going to the Los Angeles Airport to greet him and, along with others, escort him to Malibu where he would be staying at a Training Center during his time in L.A. Because I was involved with the security part of his movement, I was able to watch him from a vantage point that would give me the best view of his actions and behavior. Even though I had determined to do whatever it took to make his trip successful, I was still very leery and suspicious of the intent of the entire movement. The only thing I couldn't explain was that as I continued to chant, I continued to see positive results. How could this Gohonzon be so great and be the center of the system of thought of Buddhism if the organization had ulterior motives without them being exposed? Having this opportunity would give me the best advantage for catching them in contradictions. If I caught the organization at cross-purposes with the intent of Buddhism, as I understood it at that time, I would have dropped them like a hot potato. I've been on guard for one thing or another most of my life so now was going to be a good chance to use it to find out what the top leaders of this organization were doing when no one was looking.

It might have been a day or two after getting settled at the Malibu Training Center that about 10 of us got to sit on the lawn in a circle with President Ikeda and ask him any questions that were on our minds.

When it came to my turn, I amazed myself by saying, "I want your trust."

I shocked myself with the statement. It came from my heart, not my mind.

"You already have it or you wouldn't be here."

He looked at me and all I can tell you now is that I wanted this man for my teacher. I asked if he would name my children. He said yes, but he would wait for a while and think about it. Not knowing we were going to experience the loss of our first pregnancy, he wrote the names Kaneko and Shinichi on two pieces of paper, and they were given to me. Kaneko is the name of his wife and Shinichi is his name in the novelized history of the Soka Gakkai. Lynn still has those pieces of paper.

Monica Kaneko Kelli Richards. Andrew Shinichi Richards. I love the sound of their names. It was shortly after this that one of the interpreters came up to me and said something to the effect, "Don't spend too much time telling your children who they should be. Spend that time finding out who they are."

He also said something to the effect that with whatever time I did have to spend with them that I should make it the most important time of their lives.

Apparently, President Ikeda sent that message to me, and I have done my best to practice that throughout their lives. And let me tell you they are two amazing people, and they are my great friends. You just can't have too many "great" friends. Looking back now, I can only wish I had done a better job implementing that guidance.

21

THE GAMBLER

...Born Again

I felt that the best way to express my gratitude and appreciation to Buddhism for being able to share this life with my children was to involve myself even more thoroughly in the activities of NSA, the organization's name before it became SGI, and accept more and more responsibility as it was offered. I thought my wife understood and agreed with this direction I was taking, but I misunderstood her.

Being able to have the children after so many obstacles were overcome gave my faith a great boost, and that boost was not only for my own life as a husband and father. It became clearer that the path to world peace started in the homes and hearts of people. Waiting for someone else to step up and take responsibility wasn't the answer. I had to want to step up and exert more effort. The organization had to grow and develop a foundation of faith and activity that would spread throughout our nation and the entire globe. How else was I going to provide peace and security for my children on the most fundamental level?

I started spending more and more time at night encouraging members and less time at home with my wife and children. They were always on my mind. Everything I did, I did with the faith and determination that soon I would have a great turnabout in my life and be able to provide both the time and material fortune that I envisioned. The more deeply I got involved with the members and listened to their doubts and problems, the more determined I was to do everything I could to help them with their faith and practice. I saw that one of the essentials was study. Without knowledge of the teachings from Nichiren himself, it would be easy to approach Buddhism expecting that something or someone outside of me was going to solve all my problems.

If I was going to help others, I had to raise my life condition so that when I spoke to members and tried to give them hope, it would be based on my own experience. It's easy to quote what someone else said, but when it comes to motivating another human being, it's best to do it based on one's own actual proof. As far as my wife was concerned, I'm afraid I didn't do a very good job of showing her the actual proof she wanted to see for her own life.

It was during this time when the children were coming into our life that I was offered that opportunity to provide security for President Ikeda when he came to the United States. That meant that I would spend at least a month or more involved in his movement. It also meant that I wasn't going to be around very much, and that also meant I wasn't working. Traveling as an aide to President Ikeda even took priority, in my mind, over an acting job. I just couldn't see anything being more valuable than spending this time with him, doing my best to see that he was protected and able to complete his purpose in solidifying the foundation of our organization and clearing up doubts in the minds of the membership. I considered these activities to be the primary purpose of my life on this earth.

I was still at the stage of developing my faith that required the approach of a detective. At that time in my life, with all that I was experiencing and hoped to experience, everything seemed to hinge on my relationship with President Ikeda. It wasn't the same type of gamble as it was in the first stages of practice. But at this level of actively pursuing the solutions to my personal and family problems, and believing that the answer to the problems of humanity—physically and spiritually—could be found in practicing the principles of Buddhism, I needed to rid myself of all doubt.

It's not too difficult for me to understand how I became such a skeptic. I was suspicious of everyone. The time I spent with President Ikeda gave me a great opportunity to evaluate this Buddhism on the words and behavior of the world leader of this movement. Having faith in my own experience wasn't enough to convince me that this was the superior religion, philosophy or system of thought in the world. I also thought it extremely important to be able to trust the leadership with all my heart. I wanted to know what was going on in the back of his mind.

I think I was born with the heart of a gambler. As a kid I was always taking chances with my life whether it was getting caught doing something I knew was illegal or hitching rides with strangers. Physically, I had the nature of a daredevil. When I needed something, I usually found a way to get it. I might have made a pretty good magician because of the skills I developed while slipping foods or other things and stuffing them into my pockets, up my sleeves or under my clothes without ever getting caught. Wait, that's not true. I did get caught once stealing a half pint of bourbon. It fell to the floor and broke. I had a hole in the pocket of a jacket I had stolen and claimed as my own. But when it came to booze, food and cigarettes, I was pretty slick if I do say so myself.

Probably my biggest gamble was when I decided to practice this Buddhism. Over the years I had chances to get involved with a number of different religions or religious organizations but passed them up quickly. Any time it became apparent that I had to fake believing in what I couldn't believe, I was out of there.

If nothing happened within a very short time of my first experience of chanting, if there was nothing going on pretty soon, it made no sense to me to continue. What the hell is the use of going to work if you don't get paid? It made even less sense to chant and pray if your prayers don't get answered. Horse sense I had, wisdom…not.

The teachings of Buddhism come from a human being, not an invisible entity that I could neither see nor hear nor become. Nor could I ever be able to emulate something that was considered to be a "creating" life force that determines my destiny. One of the most attractive principles of Buddhism for me was that I was entirely responsible for my destiny or fate. That meant that I was totally in charge of my life. It gave me the freedom to change those things I didn't like about myself. It also removed my being able to put the blame on anyone else for whatever circumstances I found myself in. That's a hell of a lot easier said than done.

The good part about the realization that I was in charge of and responsible for the entirety of my life was the awareness that I had this new way, this new opportunity, for my life ahead of me. The hard part was that I could no longer hold my mother and father or a god responsible for my being born to the people who conceived me. That is not an easy pill to swallow. On the other hand, when I did awaken to the fact that I arrived in this life with my own set of baggage, that it wasn't handed to me by someone else, it caused me to stop to think about what I was doing and saying on a daily basis. Was I thinking and acting based on my resentment and anger toward my parents or anyone or anything else, or was I now taking action and giving consideration today toward my future incorporating the practice and teachings of Buddhism? It was all up to me. It gave me a sense of freedom that I had never experienced before. It also made me aware that I didn't have the wisdom to see clearly what action to take, let alone having the correct prayer in my mind and heart.

Nichiren Daishonin writes "one should become the master of one's mind rather than let one's mind master oneself."[6]

All I could think of when I read that was "How the hell do I do that?"

It was very important for me to be able to completely trust President Ikeda as my teacher. I had to remove all limitations from my mind and heart toward him. Completing that transition to a oneness of Mentor-Disciple relationship was the primary intent I had in my life as I spent time in his company when he traveled here to the United States. I also studied everything I could get my hands on. President

---

[6] *The Writings of Nichiren Daishonin*, ed., trans., The Gosho Translation Committee, (Tokyo: Soka Gakkai, 1999), p. 390.

Ikeda was constantly writing about Buddhism. The teachings of Nichiren, translated into English, and the words of President Ikeda became my greatest friends. I never felt as if I was alone in my pursuit of this thing called the Human Revolution. I realized that becoming the master of my mind didn't mean surrendering my mind, but to elevate it to the level of the Buddha's mind, or to put it another way, to become one with the mind and heart of the mentor. This is a never ending journey, not a destination.

There are all kinds of friends. To have a friend who occupies a permanent place in your heart and mind and whose constant wish is for you to be victorious in every aspect of your life is to have the ultimate friend. This is my great fortune.

Unfortunately, for both Lynn and the children, a dark spot in their heart was forming, and I was the cause. I did truly believe that I was doing everything I could to ensure we would have a great future. Slowly but surely, Lynn and I were growing farther apart. Both of us had great communication problems. It was very difficult for her to open up to me, and I didn't take the time or have the wisdom to listen to her heart and hear what her words didn't say. It never was a tight, close relationship in the first place but as time went on, we just got farther and farther apart.

There is no value in saying one was more responsible than the other. The one common thread was and is the children. Even when we got to the end of the line in the marriage, we didn't put it out there for the children to see. As a matter of fact, I didn't realize we were at the end of the marriage until the day she said, "I want to end it."

Adding to Lynn's disappointment was this karma or

attraction I've had with horses all my life. Between the trips I made aiding President Ikeda, the off and on again jobs in construction or the one or two days on a television show or commercial, I met some of the most beautiful horses I could ever imagine. This all happened during the time we were trying to have a baby and had the miscarriage.

We had been given a dog we named Jesse James. She looked like a miniature Rin Tin Tin. I took her for a walk in Griffith Park near the stables. Walking along, feeling like a million dollars with horses all around, I spotted a horse unlike anything I had ever seen before. It was an Andalusian stallion named Califa. I was stopped in my tracks. You could have shot me and I wouldn't have fallen over. I couldn't take my eyes of that magnificent animal. The rider and owner was a prayer being answered. I had chanted to meet a film director that I could have a good friendship with and that would also lead to work, and here he was sitting on a horse that had more presence than ten movie stars.

You'd think that by this time I would have learned my lesson. When I chanted for the television, as I first got involved with this Buddhism, I had forgotten to chant for a TV that worked and was a color set. When I chanted for the director, I forgot to mention in my prayer, "…and one that was working." Budd Boetticher had directed something like 58 motion pictures in his career but was having a very difficult time getting more work. Let's just say he also had a very strong presence. For a lot of people in the industry, his reputation as a hard drinker with an ego that resembled a combination of John Wayne, John Ford and John Huston, meant they would have their hands full if they got involved

273

in one of his projects. When he hit some hard times, the industry used it as an excuse to keep hands off.

Standing there mesmerized by the beauty and the action of this wonderful horse as Budd put him through his routine, I must have looked like someone in a trance.

Budd brought Califa over to me to say, "Hello," and that was the beginning of another great adventure in my life. We spoke for a while and he invited me back to his barn to see his other horses.

"Follow me."

I did and I knew I had found heaven again.

One of the first thoughts that occurred to me upon meeting Budd Boetticher was to be a listener because he gave the impression that he had just about all the answers to any questions you might ask. Best to be quiet and let him take the lead in conversation. Another great lesson I learned as a kid—speak only when spoken to.

For the next four or five years, I did everything I could to spend as much time with those horses as I could. I ended up riding those incredible animals and doing and learning as much as possible. Getting to know him and his beautiful wife, Mary, became a wonderful association and friendship. Unfortunately, I lost track of them when my basic activity in life became survival after Lynn and I separated.

During that time spent with Budd and his horses, he had to call in a trainer to help Califa overcome some bad habits he had picked up. Califa had previously been owned by Gaston Santos of Tampico, Mexico. Gaston was widely known as a rejoneador, a bullfighter who fights the bulls totally from horseback. Califa was a veteran of quite a few fights and was highly skilled. Budd received this animal from Gaston, brought him to the United States and gave exhibitions demonstrating the skill and relationship that must be established between horse and rider. It must have been a very difficult transition for Califa, especially after spending six months in quarantine. Before being allowed to cross into the United States, he was quarantined as a precaution to determine whether he had a blood infection called piroplasmosis. He was cleared and came here under the ownership of Budd Boetticher.

Califa had to adjust to the riding skill of Budd as well, and that's the reason trainer Glenn Randall had to be called in. Randall, as I mentioned earlier, was the same man I had met in Cincinnati, Ohio, when I had my adventure with Trigger. It took a while, but the memory eventually came back to him.

"Oh yeah," he said.

"First thing I remember was that I thought you were a smart-ass kid."

The time with the horses, the willingness to quit a job at the drop of a hat, the trips with President Ikeda and probably a million other things all added up to my not being a good person to partner with for the rest of your life. Looking back over that time in my life, I have no trouble understanding why this might end up as a non-permanent relationship. But I never lost hope that the time would come when it would be good for all of us as a family. But that hope could easily diminish as time goes by.

I wasn't doing my best to make the light of hope burn brighter. I was having a hard time wanting to come home at night when I knew Lynn was still awake. There were way too many times when I would come home, find the lights were still on, and rather than go in, I would go to a bar and have a stiff drink or two waiting until I was sure she was asleep. Whatever had been the attraction between us was long gone. Even though I still wanted to take care of her as best as I could, it was becoming more difficult just to be there. For the sake of the children and the desire to validate my faith in Buddhism, I would have never taken steps toward a divorce even though in many ways the marriage was more on paper than in my heart. At the same time, I was shocked. I think it was on a Wednesday morning just as she was about to leave for work. We were in the kitchen, the children were getting ready for school, and she said, "I'm dying inside."

There was a pause on my part and I probably said something like, "Let's talk about it tonight."

The rest of the day is a blur except for the churning of thoughts as they raced through my mind. Anything and everything one could think about after "I'm dying inside" became a maze of words and emotions and different scenarios. That day seemed to take a year to pass. I know I must have picked up the kids from school, but I don't remember it. My brain was like a crossword puzzle with every answer being incorrect.

Dinner must have been a very quiet event. I know that I was scheduled to go to a discussion meeting in Oxnard that evening, but I called and gave some excuse and apology in order to stay home. We waited for the right time when the children would be in bed. It would be unfair for me to try and quote Lynn's words at this point, but things were made very clear. She wanted to end it. For her the marriage was over.

Interestingly, she had become friends with someone who was also born on August 13, the same day as me. He wanted to break into show business as a stunt driver or maybe it was that he wanted to be a cop, and he was Chinese. It immediately made me think that the odds were pretty good that she was going to jump from one pot into another pot.

I imagine someone will say that I'm beating around a dead bush, but Lynn became someone who could take care of herself. It's true that I didn't do a very good job of taking care of her, but at the same time she went from being a frightened little girl who got out of an abusive family relationship to become a woman who was able to get her feet under her and think for herself. This girl who couldn't boil water became a mother who had two amazing children. And these two children are both standing up in society with outstanding principles and have the hearts and willpower to surmount any obstacles they encounter. I truly believe it's a strong reflection of Lynn being able to take care of herself. It's better than depending on someone else to do it for you. I hope, at the very least, my prayers have contributed to her life, even a little.

That first night of the decision that she wanted to end it didn't take long to draw up plans. There weren't many details to work out. Didn't need a Ouija board. I knew instinctively this was something she had to do for her life, and to fight it wouldn't be the answer.

When we first met at Corriganville in January, 1963, as I have mentioned before, I felt as if I had met someone I couldn't turn my back on. She needed a friend, and I decided to be that person at least during the time I spent at Corrig-anville working the stunt shows. It was shortly after we had posed for the cover of the RV magazine that I asked if she wanted to go to a movie. She felt she had to tell me her story.

I have to give her a lot of credit for overcoming a swamp of negative experiences and moving on to a level that enabled her to stand on her own two feet. She had given birth to two great children and developed the courage to shed herself of someone like me who just never got to the place where I could take care of her as she had hoped.

On that Wednesday when she said she was dying inside, I said to her, "Give me till Saturday and I'll get out of here."

I wanted nothing from the house, no money, no furni-ture, nothing except some clothes and the old 1967 Mercury. What the hell am I going to tell the children? If I remember correctly, I waited a day or two and came up with a story. I told the kids I was going to Florida to make a movie. It was a lie, but my emotional state was getting pretty shaky. This was hitting me a lot harder than I could have imagined. By this time the children, Kelli and Andy, as he was called then, were 9 or so years old. I don't know for certain. During all this divorcing and separating, the number of the years, the dates, the days of the week, all became a maze of confusion. The clarity came with the realization that I wasn't going to be able to kiss the children good night. I wasn't going to have a home to come to. I was back on the street again, but this time it was going to be a lot lonelier.

If anyone has gotten this far reading this story of mine, you have to know by now that I'm not a master of words. I've met people who tell a story or share an experience with the clarity of a painting. When they speak or write, you can see the picture, and experience the lifeblood of the characters. Daisaku Ikeda is just such a person. I can only wish to relate what was going on in my heart and mind when I left the house on that awful Saturday morning. I had to keep a good face to say "so long" to the kids.

"I'll see you when I get back."

All the while in my heart I was scared to death that I might never see my children again. I was beginning to get a sense that I was going to face some very hard facts of life. My mother may have been right all along.

"You'll never amount to anything. You're just like your father."

And he was already dead.

I was a total failure and no one could have convinced me otherwise. I needed time to think things out. I called Mr. Kikumura and let him know I wasn't going to be available for a while. I don't remember what reasoning I gave. I just needed to think. This was one of the darkest times in my life. My behavior wasn't anything to be proud of either.

I remember that I went to a Copper Penny Restaurant near the studios and just sat there staring at the newspaper when a woman I knew, Budd Boetticher's daughter, came up behind me and bit me on the neck. I had never been unfaithful to Lynn. Under any other circumstances I'd be in pig heaven, but the timing just didn't suit the occasion.

That night I ended up in a bar across the street from one of the studios and went home with a cocktail waitress that I shared a mutual chemical attraction with. Looking back, I think that was an act of stupidity designed to have the purpose of revenge. Leaving her place, after way too much to drink, I totaled the Mercury by running into the rear end of a tow truck. I didn't even scratch the truck but I did save myself some money. He hooked me up, towed me off to a side street where we removed the plates, registration, and ID number. Saved $25 on the towing fee.

After a month or two, Lynn and I talked, and we decided to try and see if perhaps we could work out some of the problems. It was time to get down to the details. It was time for me to make some adjustments.

We never did see eye-to-eye as to the importance of the need to develop the organization to become not just capable of taking care of the members that were practicing at that time, but to raise capable leadership for the future. I felt a great responsibility toward the future of not just the organization but also the entire world. As I saw it, the population of our country, and the world in general, was conducting itself with little or no regard for the continuing existence of the human race on this planet. I felt compelled to do everything I could to ensure the peace and security of not just myself and my family, but also all living beings.

The picture of the possibility that a world of peace could be created through the propagation of Nichiren Buddhism and the practice and study activities of SGI was becoming clearer in my mind. It was also becoming a little clear that the actions and attitude I had toward my daily life left a lot to be desired. I can't say I had a well thought out plan but I can say with all honesty that I wanted to consider the possibility of Lynn and me giving it another chance.

It was apparent that I needed to do my best to clean out

the darkness of my family. It is of little value to tell someone else to clean up his or her back yard when my own is filled with crap.

I remained in the same leadership position as before but altered my activities from as much as seven days a week to two or sometimes three days. Lynn seemed satisfied with that. I started spending more and more time at home with her and the kids. I remember that we got a pool table that the kids loved. Lynn always wanted to play the piano. We got a piano and even hired a teacher to come to the house. Kelli amazed everyone by walking up to the piano and making herself at home with it. She even began to compose music on her own. It was as if she was picking up something that was familiar to her. I remembered that my grandmother, Nana, had been a concert pianist when she was very young.

And I got a job. I promised I would keep the job and not quit for any reason unless there was a lot of money attached to something new. That job was as hard physically as any other work I had ever done. I was paid $75 a day cash for construction work but after a little over six months, I hurt my back so bad I couldn't even walk for a couple of days. I worked my ass off. That job came to a halt when the owner made some huge mistakes in measurement, design and construction of a building we were putting up in Downey for Enterprise Rent-A-Car. Within three days he packed up his home and moved to somewhere in Washington State. He had always planned on the move but made the quick exit rather than take responsibility for the repair and costs to rectify his errors. Telling me that when he did move on to his dream home in Washington, he was going to leave his accounts to me, and I would pay him a small percentage to use his contractor's license. The problem was that with his running out, all he left me was his lousy reputation.

At home, I painted the entire inside of the house to give us a feeling of a fresh start. That didn't work. I moved the rooms around so Lynn and I had a more private part of the house for us. That didn't work. We spent time watching television with the whole family. That didn't do much to bring us closer either. Once again I was chanting like I was going to get blood out of a rock, but it seemed that we were slipping farther apart. And I was keeping in touch with my leaders by phone, but inside I was yearning to be out with the members. Then after about a year something strange happened. I got an audition for a film and got the part. The strange thing was that it was just about one year to the day from the time I lied to the children about going to Florida that I got this film, and we were going to shoot it in Florida. The lie turned into the truth. It just took a year for the flip to occur.

Another unexpected event had happened a month or two after I came back to the house. There is something like a current of electricity inside of someone who is an artist by blood. Acting is as much an art as painting or dancing or performing music in any form. The greatest art is the art of living a truly value-creating life.

The frustration of not being involved in the art of acting got me to the point that one night, as I was chanting, my only prayer was for something to come out of me that would allow me to ease this anxiety and experience some creative satisfaction.

A photographer friend called me the next day asking me

to give him a hand moving his studio to a new, bigger location. We met up and after a long day's work and a drink or two, he handed me a block of clay he used to prop up still-life pieces for his photographs.

"Here, take this home and give it to your kids."

That evening I took the clay home, expecting that the kids would have it mashed into the carpet before I could count to ten. Instead they said, "No Daddy, you make something."

Okay. I went to the kitchen, got a dinner knife and a spoon, a plate to put it on and we sat in front of the fireplace as I began to play. I'm not going to evaluate my talent, but I sculpted a bust. I just seemed to know what I was doing. It was as if a treasure burst out that had been locked up inside of me. I haven't stopped sculpting since. Every opportunity, I was sculpting. My concern was that Lynn might have been thinking, "Here he goes, off on some artsy-fartsy trip again."

The film in Florida was called "Cease Fire." It was a small-budget story concerning a Viet Nam soldier having to deal with all the problems adjusting to civilian life as he began to go through the post traumatic stress disorder associated with his combat during the war. It was great to work and get away for a while, but it didn't pay much. It became another reason for the hopelessness to grow even thicker in our marriage. At some point I remember sitting on the steps going down into an office area in our house and pushing Lynn for an answer. Did she want to continue this relationship or not?

"I want to end it," was her reply.

Now comes the hard part. I had to tell the children. As I write this, right at this moment, I recall those minutes telling

Kelli and Andy that their mother and father were going to get divorced. My heart is still there.

I was a mess. I think it's safe to say that I was sobbing as I tried to talk to them. They were crying with me. It must have been just as difficult for them as it was for me. Lynn was distant. I felt no sense of loss from her. I don't remember if it was one day later or when it was that I left. All I took was clothes and $30. Where I went that night or what I did is not in the recall ability of my mind.

The one thing I clearly remember from the day I left was a phone call I made to Lynn that night, asking how the children were. She told me that for quite a while she didn't see or hear them and found that they were down in that office area sitting alone. She asked how they were. Kelli said something like, "Daddy's hibernating like a bear."

Lynn said that later on Andy came into the kitchen and asked, "Whose idea was this?"

Lynn said that she and I had discussed our problems and agreed this was the best thing to do.

Andy again asked, "But whose idea was it?"

Again Lynn said we had discussed it, when Andy came back with, "I want to know who had the light bulb go off in their head first?"

That's my boy.

Time to move on to the next stage of my life. Maybe the next chapter should be called "Starting Over."

22

STARTING OVER
Again and Again and . . .

It took quite a while for me to awaken to it, but life is a constant new beginning. That's all well in theory. The hard part is knowing it and living it on a daily basis. It's so wonderful to have teachers and friends who become reminders of these important principles of life—how the human and cosmic forces within the universe can be so powerful when the two are not two but together are one.

This was clearly a time to start over. For all practical purposes the marriage was over. At that time I couldn't say that I felt a great loss in the relationship with Lynn. For quite a few years before the splatter from the fan hit the wall, it was apparent that there wasn't that much attraction between us. And along the way, I lost any determination to make it any better. Even though I prayed and chanted for the relationship to grow, the truth has to be that the prayer wasn't coming from my heart. I did want it to work out, but it was for the sake of others, for the sake of the children, not for me. It's fair to say that I was a hypocrite.

I have always had a very solitary nature. I like being alone.

I sought out the company of people because I needed something like food or shelter or some temporary love. Altogether there have been four separate times when I lived on the street. Perhaps the saddest part is that I didn't mind it that much. In some ways I was very comfortable with that life style. Though it was as if living in a dark tunnel, there was a certain sense of victory by not having to share space or property with others. There I was again, homeless, without love, without a horse to talk to. But not for long.

During the time after the separation, before we called it off for good, I was able to buy a yellow 1969 Mustang. I moved into that car. That was my "'horse" for a while. For the next year or more, the things and people and places are again a maze in my mind. Much of the darkness of my life came to the surface, and as a consequence I don't remember the order of things as they happened. Adding to the trash that was coming out of my life, I aided it with drink. When you want to escape your reality, or should I say when you want to avoid your reality, a cheap bottle of anything helps. Help is the wrong word.

Most everything I did during this time added to my debt to the universe. Maybe the only good thing was that I never failed to chant for the members and pray for my children, though even that was difficult. Whenever I would deeply focus on them, I would cry. It took almost a year before I could see beyond the moment without having to look through the distorted vision that my tears created. But I never missed or skipped my practice.

My children were, are, always have been, and always will be inseparable from my heart. The day after my father died, my grandmother died. From that moment on, for the rest of my life, I will pray for them and their peace and security. It was probably one of the most significant experiences I had in my development of faith during those early years of my practice when I prayed for them. I prayed with the intent that my chanting would reach their eternal lives and comfort them.

My grandmother, my Nana, was 84 years old when she passed. A year before that, she had visited Lynn and me at our home—that must have been in 1972—and had noticed the altar with the Gohonzon enshrined in it. We had candles and a small cup of water and a couple pieces of fruit on a table under it as well. There was even an offering of evergreen. Nana, with her very gentle manner asked, "What is that?"

Not wanting to scare the hell out of this woman who had professed a faith in her God all her life, I replied, "It's an oriental object of art."

"What's the fruit for Dick?"

I've mentioned how much I hated the name Dick, but this is Nana. She kept at it.

"What's the water for Dick? Why the bush?"

Finally it was time to tell her.

"Nana, Lynn and I are Buddhists. We chant *Nam-Myoho-Renge-Kyo* to the scroll and it's making us happy."

There was a long pause and some very serious thought on her part.

"I've believed in God all my life, but it hasn't made me happy."

The next week Nana came to our house to an introduction meeting, joined the SGI and received her own Gohonzon. Lynn and I enshrined it in her apartment.

With my grandmother and father dying one day apart, I had only one thought in mind as I prayed for them. I prayed for them to be at peace. Is it just a coincidence that up until this time Lynn and I couldn't have a baby, but soon after the deaths of my father and grandmother we were able to have a daughter and son just 14 months apart? I don't think so.

When I left the house for the last time, I had a credit card. Not necessarily a good omen for someone in the state of depression I was headed for. I rented an apartment. The building was pretty run down from neglect but had a charm that was hard not to like. It was cheap, with a large living room and a kitchen with an oven that worked. No microwave. Frozen dinners were the menu of the day every day. The oven was also very important because I had found a new kind of clay that I could sculpt and then bake in that oven. When the clay cooled it would become hard. I could add to it, cut it or sand it until I got just what I wanted. Sometimes I would stay up all night, playing with my clay until I couldn't see straight. It was great but I knew it couldn't last. I knew very well I wasn't going to be able to keep going in this direction without running into a wall. But in the mean time, I was really enjoying the creative process.

The "Ozzie and Harriet" family—Ozzie and Harriet Nelson—had owned the apartment. I think it had 18 units and would be used for out-of-town guests as well as a location for party scenes in a couple of the shows when Ricky Nelson first began his singing career. It had a kidney shaped pool with a two-story rock waterfall at one end. The water didn't pump and run down the falls, but that didn't mean it couldn't.

The manager and his wife seemed like very nice people.

The morning after I moved in, I picked up a paper and sat by the pool like I was the happiest man of leisure when the manager's wife walked by on her way to her car. She stopped for a second and said, "Hello."

She asked if I liked my apartment, and then said something like, "If you happen to be around, keep your eyes open for the ducks. There are 26 of them. They'll pull up in a little yellow bus any time now, park in the back and come onto the property to do their chores."

I didn't pause for even a second.

"Okay, thank you."

She continued, "Each has their assigned responsibilities. Some do the laundry; others paint or take care of the landscaping. The newest duck is a carpenter. If you see any of them sitting around or not working, please let me know. I may have to scold them."

She said good-bye, walked off and went on her way to work. Do you have any idea what it's like to meet your mind's twin for the first time? It's one of the most precious events in my life.

The next morning I made sure I was sitting in the same spot as she left for work.

"Good morning. By the way I did see the ducks, and I honestly can't say I saw them doing anything they shouldn't have, but they sure were here. Look at the pool."

She went to the pool's edge and saw the evidence. At the bottom of the pool, sitting on the drain was one white egg. Slowly she turned to me, "Thank you. Perhaps we had better wait until we catch them in the act. Maybe we can get a photo for proof that they have not been doing their job."

The following morning same set up, only this time the white egg was sitting up on the edge of the pool at the foot of the waterfall. And down at the bottom sitting on the drain was one black egg.

I apologized. "Sorry, but I don't have a camera."

She was about 23 or 24 years old and had a mind or creative imagination that had to occupy a very important place in her heart. A couple days later she must have taken a day off from her work as a nurse or technician at the children's hospital. We got to know each other very well and the link of our minds discovered a path of its own.

Although she and her husband were still living together, she told me they were separated and would be going their separate ways in the near future. That gave us a license to meet by the pool in the middle of the night to create a world that until now was unknown.

Day by day or night after night, a new life began to reveal itself. The water began to flow from the top of the falls. The white egg, now wearing a sombrero and slanted eyes, made its way to the top as the black egg followed, ending one tier below, off to the side, with clay horns protruding out of his head.

At the bottom of the fall was a lagoon. If you look closely you could see tiny miniature empty beer cans sitting on a lava rock where the ducks would take a break and quench a thirst. The water, with the aid of food coloring, became a "Blue Lagoon." I looked everywhere but never did discover where Brooke Shields was hiding.

Slowly, one day at a time, with the help of rubber cement, artificial grass and a hobby shop, you could find a herd of horses, a family of pigs and a pasture of cattle as they moved into this world. Crossing the bridge at the bottom of the Blue Lagoon was a mother duck and her family of ducklings making their way with great caution to the other side. A herd of sheep could be seen climbing a path to green grass. The shepherd was sitting on a rock with his back to us, but if you moved a little to the right or left, you could tell he had one special sheep that was his favorite. The pretty little thing had her head in his lap. The shepherd had a dazed smile on his face. Not all sheep are the same.

There was the dancing horse, the cow with the bedroom eyes and of course the nudist colony that was doing its best to not be seen, except you could easily catch a glance of them through the cyclone fencing. Finally, I did get a camera, and I must say the pictures reveal a gathering of images created in the minds of twins who met and came together to foster a community of people who enjoyed the life they led but may have limited themselves by becoming a civilization that kept its back to the object of worship. Can you imagine such a thing?

One day in a conversation with the manager's wife, she told me that once she had a good chance for becoming a part of the United States 1984 Olympic swimming team, but she had been in an accident that caused a severe injury to one of her feet and kept her out of the trials. That woman sure could swim.

My apartment was on the second floor in the corner. One Saturday afternoon I came out on the balcony and looked down over the pool. Several people were sunbathing and she was swimming. With no disrespect intended, I'll just say that her body made me think that she could have skipped like a pontoon across the pool and whipped anyone to the other end. In a lap pool I doubt anyone could have caught up to her. The problem with the apartment pool was that it was small and kidney shaped. The wonderful thing was that she was doing her best to make the most out of what she had. She would circle the edge of the bean-shaped pool and go around and around until she felt like she had enough. Watching her go made me envision Flipper trying to find a way out of a trap.

It was interesting to watch as the residents of the apartment house became aware that something was going on around the waterfall. Almost daily they would come to the falls and check to see what was new. None of us could figure out how it happened. Perhaps it was…oh, never mind. It would only be a guess on my part.

Time to move on, dictated by the fact that other than having a great experience at Ozzie and Harriet's, I was digging deeper into my dark side. I needed to start over. I needed to make my way back onto the path that Buddhism had revealed to me.

I moved back into my car. I was able to comfortably pack everything I owned into that '69 Yellow Mustang. I was broke and didn't even have money for another meal. This time living on the street, or I should say in my car, was quite different than when I was a kid. No stealing or perhaps I should say no more permanent borrowing of stuff.

Thoughts were coming out of my mind that I might be on the last stage of living. I had to face the fact that I had failed in every aspect of my life. In a very short time I went from having a family to only having memories of having a family. I had never failed to kiss my children goodnight regardless of when I got home from trying to help others practice and study Buddhism. If I didn't go immediately into my daughter's room to kiss her goodnight, she would be out in the kitchen looking up at me with those beautiful eyes, holding on to me while I finished making a sandwich. Soon as I was done, she would have a bite and I'd carry her back to her bed, kiss her goodnight as I quietly sang "Hello, Kelli" to the tune of "Hello, Dolly."

My son Andy on the other hand was a different story. I could drop a rock on the house and this guy wouldn't budge. Except for one night after I had kissed him, I took my sandwich to the living room and turned on the "Tonight Show." He came out, sat down on the couch, leaned against me and apologized for having been such a bad father. Could he be the reincarnation of my father? You figure it out.

The weights of my failures were getting heavier by the day. I wasn't able to fulfill my responsibilities as a member in the SGI and that was just as bad as failing to be the anchor of my family. I failed the members, but most of all I failed to live up to President Ikeda's expectations. It seemed to me that there was little purpose left in my life. Truthfully, there were several times during this period when I didn't expect to see the light of the next day. I had no purpose or sense of mission. The only glimpse of hope was during my daily prayers and reading the words of Nichiren. Or when I recalled something President Ikeda had said. Sometimes it was just a short flash of hope, but ultimately it was enough.

I got into the habit of parking at night in a lot near the

Burbank Studios so when the drivers for the transportation department would come to work, the noise would wake me up. I'd chant and do my morning recital of prayers then go to a 24-hour health club and clean up.

The first time I tried to walk in the health club they stopped me and asked for my membership card. I didn't have one. I acted as if I got mad at myself and promised I would bring it tomorrow. The next time I went to that club I had them believing I left it, with my money, in another pair of jeans. It ends up that I seemed to have joined three different clubs by the time I was finished needing them. Squeaky clean and refreshed, I would go to some main commercial area like Victory or Ventura boulevards and knock on doors.

I would go door-to-door and ask for work. If there were no jobs available, I'd ask if there was anything I could do to make $20. And if that were the case, I'd initiate a conversation about Nichiren Buddhism and the SGI. It never failed that by the end of the day I ended up with enough money for a meal and a little something to drink.

Then one day I just needed to take a break and hang out with some horses, so I went to the L.A. Equestrian Center to walk around, say hello to the animals and smell the aroma. I felt like I was at home again. It was only a temporary joy, but I needed it at the time.

Then I got a great idea. Why not move into the Center and set up a stall for myself? Find a stall in the farthest barn that would probably be the last one to be used during an event and move in. The one I picked was near the restrooms by an outdoor exercise area for the horses. All I had to do was wait a couple of days and move in on a Thursday when the center and the participants in the next show, a "Bill Pickett Rodeo," were getting set up. Perfect timing I thought. There would be so much activity taking place no one would notice me as I put six bales of straw in my stall and arranged them so I would be comfortable and at the same time concealed from anyone sticking their heads into my new home while I slept. The men's restroom had a couple of showers that the workers used to clean themselves up after a hard day's work before they went home. What more does a lonely homeless cowboy need? Well…there is one thing.

One thing about horses that's very important is exercise. During my stay in the stall, the center used to sponsor indoor polo matches. The Los Angeles home team and the visiting teams would house their horses in the Polo Barn. Polo ponies are incredible athletes and need to be kept at their peak for a very fast, strenuous sport. Each player will have somewhere around six ponies to be available at any given time during a tournament. Just like any other great athlete, they need care and management. Most of the time, the care and exercise was in the hands of the "Pony Girls." They would ride one pony while leading three or four more, sometimes two or three times a day, to keep them limber and stretched out. Then they would bring them back, wash them down and give them what they needed in preparation for either a workout or a match in the indoor rink. The diet of each pony is individually monitored. The responsibility of the Pony Girls is crucial to the performance of the animal.

When one of the Pony Girls that I had said hello to a few times found out that I was living in a stall, she insisted on seeing it for herself. If I was to take in a deep breath right now, I could almost float back to that barn. Getting up close and personal with a woman who's been riding bareback on a polo pony for the last two hours becomes a wonderful memory of the senses. The missing ingredient is love.

For the next month or maybe two, I tried to get my feet under me and to stimulate my faith in myself with my practice and study. After a while of just spinning my wheels, I really knuckled down in the prayer department and chanted as if it was life or death. One morning I woke up with the compelling feeling like I had just risen out of the mud and was getting a fresh breath of air for the first time in quite a while. That day I decided to go over the hill and get a cup of coffee.

top: Gene Autry and Rick at Cincinnati Gardens around 1953.
bottom left: Young Rick with his 'Nana' at a party, 1943.
bottom right: Rick's parents, Jean and Ferdinand, at their wedding, 1940.

top: Rick, 17 years old, when he first met his dad.
bottom left: Rick as an actor in Hollywood, 1965.
bottom right: In the Army, 1961.

top left: *Working on a commercial, 1965.*
top right: *Stunt man for a western show in Corriganville, CA, 1964.*
bottom: *Photoshoot for LIFE magazine as the Honda man, June 18, 1965.*

You meet the nicest people on a Honda. Besides being a ball to ride, prices start about $215.* Upkeep is hardly a concern. And insurance refreshingly modest. The 4-stroke, OHV engine is a brilliant blend of craftsmanship and engineering. In a word—dependable. Going on from there, Honda has the largest parts and service network in the country. And speaking of scope, there are 15 models to choose from. Any one will add something to your life. HONDA

Rick riding in front with Guy McClosky following behind him, at a SGI-USA event.

Rick with Daisaku Ikeda as part of the SGI security team.

top: At Corriganville with Lynn, his first wife, where they met.
bottom: Rick and his two young children, Kelli and Andrew.

Rick (far right) travelling in Hawaii with Daisaku Ikeda.

Rick with his mother and children.

left: Kelli and Rick.
right: Andrew and Rick.

Rick with Lady Joanne, and friends at Hermione Baddley's home inset: Hermione Baddley, 1986.

top: Eva's parents, siblings and grandfather.
bottom left: Dancing at their wedding reception in their backyard.
bottom right: Rick and Eva's wedding ceremony, 1990.

Rick and Eva at a club in 1992.

Rick and Eva at a party in 2000.

Mr. Kikumura whom Rick loved as a dad.

Rick with Eva's dad, Jose Muñoz.

Rick and his children in 2008.

23

THE FOG

on Carmar Drive . . .

There used to be a coffee shop on Sunset Blvd called Ben Frank's. When I was in that part of town for an interview, I would almost always end up stopping there. If people were collectibles, that was a good place to find them. It became one of those places I centered on whenever I needed a cup of coffee and a place to think and read the paper or do some people peeking.

Around 1970 someone sat down at the counter next to me with a drawing pad, sketching out some changes he was going to make to a garage. He said, "Hello."

I asked if he was in construction. He told me that the house belonged to a British actress by the name of Hermione Baddeley. He was disappointed that I didn't know of her but introduced himself as John Rebel, and he was her general contractor. I felt very uncomfortable around this guy. Just a little too friendly, a little too loaded and I was certain that he was interested in finding out what my favorite sexual positions might be. I'm sure he must have said something about his relationship with the film industry, but by this time I wasn't about to give him the time of day, let alone talk about any of my interests. I went back to the paper and pretty much froze him out by responding with a slight turn away and a more intense reading of the news.

About five years later, again having a cup of coffee at the same place, I turned to see who had just sat down at the counter next to me, and there he was again. He didn't remember me, and I pretended that I didn't recognize him. The truth is that every time I came into that place, I always had a flash of hope in the back of my mind that I would not run into him again.

Of course he started a conversation and I, as coldly as I could, returned the hello. That started an information bulletin telling me that his biggest problem was that he was the personal manager to one of the greatest character actresses in the world by the name of Hermione Baddeley. And to top off his problems, he lied and claimed he was also her son. I counted to nine under my breath and asked a question. Lesson learned. If you are trying to discontinue a conversation, never, never try to end it with a question. I was planning on a refill of my coffee but seeing that he was going to order something to eat, I decided to get the hell out of there. Another good reason was his breath. The smell of booze was bad enough, but he also had the lingering odor of someone who had just eaten his three-week-old dead dog.

The next time I saw him was at least eight or ten years later. It was over for Lynn and me. She had moved to San Jose with the kids and had gotten remarried. She had also quit chanting and become a Christian. I was still practicing and studying the best that I could while living in a stall at the Equestrian Center when I had that rush of thought to go over the hill and have a cup of coffee

Why I thought I could afford a cup of coffee and the gas to get there is another mystery to me, but then I've already removed the concept of coincidence from my mind. The reason became clear when someone came up behind me wearing boots that didn't fit. It sounded like an old war-horse was walking on a brick road. I turned and saw a man with long matted hair and a string of beads with a red cross fixed in the middle of his forehead. He was wearing a pair of camouflage pajamas and engineer boots with taps on the heels. And of course he sat next to me. It was John Rebel again, drunk out of his mind. The dead dog was still on his breath and his eyes looked like the bull's-eye on a dart-board. I immediately turned away from looking at him but could feel him looking at me.

With a tongue that had to be as thick as five gallons of mud he said, verrry slooowly, "Excuse me, but don't I know you?"

This wasn't in my plans. As a matter of fact, I was flat out of any plans that didn't pertain to survival. There wasn't much I could do but respond with a lie.

"No, I don't think so."

That didn't work. He nailed it to almost the exact time we last met. How he did that in his condition I'll never know, but he did. Now I had a plan. Get the hell out of there as soon as possible. I had just been served my coffee and I was determined to finish it. It might be my last meal for the day and I needed the energy. He kept talking. What the hell! I wasn't going to shut him up so I tried to be as cordial as possible, which wasn't easy.

Looking at John Rebel while he talked was very difficult. He was wearing a set of false teeth. I knew this because as he talked, the upper plate would sometimes fall. And between his tongue as thick as mud and his upper teeth floating around, I had to look away. This man was scrambled. He had the appearance of a bad cartoon, and at the same time I felt the suffering he was going through. I became more aware that although my circumstances of living in my car and keeping my eyes open for an opportunity to find a base to attach myself to wasn't the best way to live, I was in much better shape than this man. I decided I had to tell him about Buddhism and how much it affected my life.

In my jacket pocket I had one piece of my sculpture. It was a three-inch tall bust of a character that came out of my imagination. Not many people knew of this talent, but I decided to tell him the story of how I had chanted one night out of artistic frustration to find something that would give me some sort of a creative avenue to get me through the times between acting gigs. The opinion of those who saw the pieces I had done was definitely positive, and everyone thought I had a gold mine with this talent. I decided to tell John about how the chanting brought about this discovery. I pulled out the piece from my pocket. He took one look and he lit up like a Xmas tree. It was almost as if the drunk left and was replaced by a jewelry inspector. I didn't even get a chance to mention Buddhism before he had a million questions.

"Where did you get that? Who made it? Are there any more? How much are they worth? Do you sell them?"

His excitement got the attention of those close by and I suggested we go to my car to show him 14 other pieces I had in my trunk. It was time to get out of there and be on my way.

It's funny how someone can sober up when they really want to. I opened the trunk, showed him the other characters, and it became clear to me that he smelled money.

"You've got to show these to Hermione Baddeley."

"OK."

"Follow me to the house."

First thing on my mind was, What the hell am I doing following this guy? The second thought was, What have I got to lose? Just be careful.

I was right from the start about being careful. This man drove like a runaway wagon in a 30's John Wayne western. He was driving Hermione's 1976 Cadillac Sedan de Ville as fast as he could, but that thing was floating all over the place. Here I was following him up Laurel Canyon to Mulholland Drive and over to Carmar Drive to Hermione's home.

We got out of our cars and he said, "She's going to be mad at me for bringing you up. Don't worry. It'll be all right."

I was thinking, Great, another first impression based on anger. Just what I had hoped for.

We went in and I sat at the dining room table as John went to get Hermione Baddeley. Someone was raising his or her voice in the back of the house. After five minutes John came out. Don't forget, everything he said was filtered through a bucket of mud behind teeth that he might choke on at any minute. Slooowly,

"Sheee'll bee riiight ooout."

Meanwhile, three dogs came running out from the back straight at me with tails wagging so hard I was thinking something was going to be broken and it would be my fault.

Finally, she came out and that face left a striking first impression. I recognized her immediately. I wasn't a habitual viewer of "Maude," but she was unforgettable and very good in her character. She was Mrs. Naugatuck, the housekeeper. who drank Gin from a teacup and told everyone she was a cousin to the Queen of England. Hermione came in and sat at the table as John slowly tried his best to conduct a formal introduction. It was clear from the start seeing the interaction between them that there wasn't a lot of love. The look on her face during the introduction told a story without words. I don't think I'd be too far off the mark to say that she had a "crispness" about her. With a stiff-legged crispness in her walk, she could easily have played James Cagney's mother in "Yankee Doodle Dandy."

Hermione must have been close to her 80's at that point, but she had the wooden-legged walk of Mr. Cagney when he danced as George M. Cohan. She was shorter than Mickey Rooney, and the sharpness of her speech was like that of a British prosecuting attorney who never needed to take a breath. I know it can't be so, but Hermione didn't appear to have any lips. When she spoke, the words coming out of her mouth were sharp enough that you could have the impression she cut them out of a magazine with a razor blade. Soon the formalities were out of the way.

"Let me see what John's so excited about."

I opened up the box, pulled out the characters one-at-a-time and gave her a brief storyline with their names. It was going well. I was showing her a character named Monk.

Monk has been a car thief most of his life but recently ran into a priest, and he decided to change his ways. He followed his namesake and joined a monastery. He couldn't stand it there so he stole the robe they gave him and a box of Bibles. Now he was on his way to Jamaica to see if he could make some money.

I could see she was caught up in their appearance and laughed at the stories. About half way through, someone came from the back of the house and stood there looking at us. Now there was a character like no other. It was the Honorable Lady Joan Austin-Mutton-Smith. Her presence sparked up the room. This isn't going to be easy, but I have got to try to describe her to you so you at least have an idea of what I saw.

Lady Joan, or her preference, Joan, was close to 5'11" in heels. She stood tall, but with the posture of a reversed letter "S." She was as thin as a telephone pole, and her feet were pigeon toed in shoes with a strap around her heels. She wore a red two-piece polyester pantsuit and a man's belt pulled tightly around her waist. A printed scarf adorned her neck like an ascot, with another matching scarf wrapped around her head. Her hair was fire engine red and peeked out from under the wrap. On anyone else, at any other time, in any other place, she would have seemed so far out of place someone would have thought she was a missing person that no one was looking for.

Her face was a renaissance master's dream. Long and thin, her chin jutted out toward the horizon with her head tilted back to help her keep her balance. Lady Joan carried her shoulders back, but the longer she stood there, they slowly folded forward, and then she would throw them back to adjust her posture so she was standing as erect as possible.

Within a minute, the shoulders had moved forward again and she would straighten up again. And when she smiled or laughed, you heard the voice of love. When we were introduced halfway through my presentation, I felt as if I was in the company of royalty. It may have been that she no longer had a castle to call her own, but you knew she deserved one. There was honesty in her presence that made me feel secure. I immediately wanted to get to know her. She offered to make Hermione and me a Gin and Tonic, not forgetting to make one for herself as well. Lady Joan mixed a hearty drink.

I continued with the presentation. When I finished, Hermione was the first to comment that she thought they were "wonderful," and she wanted to introduce me to a good friend who was an entrepreneur. His name was the Baron John Mendes D'Costa. She thought that he could help with some ideas toward marketing these characters.

And she said, "If these figures, these people, were ever to appear on television or film, perhaps one of the ladies would have an English accent."

"Of course," I said. "Of course."

John Rebel was more than a little disappointed that he wasn't included in the marketing conversation, so he chimed in with the idea that he would like to produce a movie with the characters in an adventure. There was a noticeable silence and that "look" from Hermione. Then John fought back while holding on to the wall.

"Oh yeah…but I found him."

Lady Joan said nothing for a second then announced, "I like them but why did you have to make them so ugly? If only they were pretty like angels."

I didn't know what to say. Lady Joan proposed we all have a second drink.

Slowly from under his breath and through the mud John said, "How come no one asks me if I want a drink?"

Hermione quickly announced to all, "John, you are a drink."

Lady Joan, Hermione, and I moved to the bar area in the kitchen while John went to his room and came back with a half-gallon bottle of vodka that he drank without a glass. It was about 3 in the afternoon and this was the norm for life on Carmar Drive.

Joan knew how to pour so as to not feel cheated on the gin. After almost two hours and at least three drinks, it became time to go. I was thanking everyone for his or her time when out of the corner of my eye I saw that Lady Joan was falling backwards. I was able to move quickly enough to catch her head and keep it from slamming into the marble floor. She had fallen asleep while standing, in the middle of saying our "Good-Byes." It was obvious she was in pain. I think Lady Joan was in shock, and she said her leg hurt "something god-awful." Hermione was angry with her and blamed it on the "Narcolepsy Devil."

John went to his room to get his Fireman's Rescue Manual so he could pick her up, sling her over his shoulder and carry her to her room. I told Hermione to call 911 and have an ambulance come to the residence. John came back with his book but couldn't find the right page. I convinced him to just go get a blanket and a pillow. We would keep her covered until the ambulance came.

Hermione asked me, "Please follow Joan to the hospital

and see that she is taken good care of."

While waiting, she started telling me of the long relationship she and Joan had and that they were the best of friends "even though Joan is a bit of an eccentric." Joan was lying there on the marble floor with a blanket pulled up under her chin, listening as Hermione told stories of their 50-year friendship. Joan was Hermione's biggest fan and they met at a racetrack when Lady Joan's family had a red roan horse competing in a steeplechase event in England. All I could think was that this was one of the most unusual collections of people I'd ever heard of, let alone met. Of course, then I went back to my Buddhist roots thinking, How do I fit in here? Maybe it's the skunk-skunk principle again.

Following the paramedics as they put Joan into the ambulance, Hermione saw my car parked in front of the house and noticed that it was packed to the roof with everything I own. I volunteered that I was moving. I just didn't tell her that it's been a long time moving. She suggested that I take her car and follow Joan, stay with her as long as needed and report back to her. John was standing around looking like a lost puppy, thinking nobody cared about him.

It turned out that Lady Joan had a fractured right femur and would have to stay in the hospital until the doctors felt she was healing well enough to be cared for at home. There was also the danger of pneumonia setting in as it does with elderly people when they break a hip or anything that keeps them bedridden.

I stayed at the hospital until she was settled in and was falling asleep. It might seem backwards to say it, but I'm glad for that time as I got to know a remarkable woman in unusual circumstances. She was Hermione's greatest fan and the best friend anyone could want. As she started to doze off, I leaned over and gave her a kiss on the forehead. Back at the house I reported everything, said good-bye and headed for the door.

"Young man, would you mind telling me where you are planning to live?"

Before I could say anything in response she asked, "Would you like to live here in the room off to the back?"

I think my life just took another unexpected sharp turn, this time for the better. It was getting dark as she suggested we sit down for a little talk. It was a question and answer period with the outcome that she showed me the room off to the side and back of the house and pointed to the lounge bed that I could sleep on that night. I gave her a thumbnail sketch of events in my life, like a totally unexpected divorce, the heartbreak of not seeing my children and a career that was not only not picking up steam but seemed to be running out of gas. In addition to letting me stay at her home, she offered to pay me $50 a week if I would drive her to interviews or social occasions and maybe some shopping. That was just what the doctor ordered.

"Yes, Ma'am."

John was nowhere to be found. Hermione told me that he would sometimes stay up for days on end, drink himself into a stupor and then sleep for three days in a row. After the ambulance left with Lady Joan, he went to his room and crashed.

She said, "That's a relief. Maybe there will be some peace and quiet for a day or two."

It wasn't said but both of us knew that this was going to cause a pause with John. I was thinking that it might cause him to have a fit at the very least, and I had better be on my toes. She ordered pizza; we had a couple of gin and tonics and sat out by the pool until it became time to sleep. What a day this had been.

The following morning I was up at the first crack of light and walked out by the pool to discover that her property sat at the edge of a 250-foot drop down to a park where you could take your dog off the leash and let it run. The drop started less than six feet from the edge of the pool, which ran parallel to the house and stopped six feet from my room. The room was about 14' by 14' with a brick fireplace and ceiling-to-floor-windows on the pool and park sides. The only thing missing was a bathroom, which was in the house. What? Me complain? Nooo way. From the pool, looking at the house, the entire poolside was glass. What a view!

After Hermione got up, I began to walk around inside the house and get to know its layout, but I also found out how the place operated. Lady Joan did the cooking, John did nothing but drink and get in the way of peace and comfort and Hermione spent a lot of time in her bedroom keeping away from John, who she just seemed to tolerate. I wondered if maybe he had seen a skeleton in Hermione's closet. It didn't make sense that this woman who was very sharp-witted and liked to be in control would put up with the manners, behavior and appearance of a man like John Rebel.

Lady Joan had a few things that played against Hermione's way of life as well. Just to name a few, Joan never had to brush her own hair as a child or adult. Between hair dressing appointments her hair became matted and she covered it with a scarf. Even after a shower she didn't know to comb it out. Her family apparently always had people to literally do everything for them. Her mother thought her feet were too big so she had a "specialist" who would come to the castle or mansion daily and bind her feet in such a way that they stopped growing in a normal manner. They took on a size and shape that caused her to constantly fall out of the shoes her mother insisted she wear. At almost 80 years of age, she was still wearing the same two pairs of shoes her mother bought for her when she was 18. Every six months she had new soles and heels put on one pair while she wore the other.

Lady Joan also didn't know how to use the telephone. She would talk into it if it was handed to her, but she had never called out herself. Someone had to do that for her when she needed it. She had a difficult time counting and folding her money. And though she never learned to cook when she was younger, she developed a liking for it in her later years. The only difficulty was that if it couldn't be roasted, baked, or fried in a one-quart saucepan, it didn't get cooked. Her specialty was hard or soft boiled eggs, though she apparently had a tough time remembering when she put the eggs in the boiling water. But she and Hermione were the best of friends. That was enough. They ate out or ordered in a lot. They had to.

The next couple of days were spent getting settled in my place and becoming comfortable with Hermione and she with me. I drove her to the hospital to visit Joan, took her to get her hair done and got to listen to her tell stories about her life and career. Walt Disney brought her to Hollywood in the early 1960's to star in a series of five films he wanted to make where the lead was an older British woman. The negotiations fell through so he put her in a couple other films, including "Mary Poppins." I was later told that it was around that time that John Rebel was introduced to Hermione for the purpose of escorting her to celebrity occasions. He'd been around ever since.

More than a year had passed since leaving my home and living in my car. It had taken its toll on my body and to some degree my mind. There were several times when I thought I had come to the end of my lifespan, and I expected to die having failed to be a positive addition to anyone's life, let alone the world in general. Now, being able to have a roof over my head and being shown a little appreciation for my talent and actually being needed was like a new springtime appearing from within my heart. I felt this was a fresh start. For the next couple of days I regrouped physically and spiritually. With Hermione's approval, I was able to enshrine my Gohonzon and focus on it. It also became the subject of conversations with Hermione and Joan when she came home. John Rebel did not want to talk about Buddhism.

About two days later John Rebel woke up and decided to join humanity again. He was as sober as he could get and seemed like a different person. He was very polite and even gracious in asking how everyone was and asking where Joan was. Hermione started to tell him that she was in the hospital when he started to remember. She informed him that I was now living in the back room. He took time to pause, think, and remark, "You mean my study, my office?"

Hermione responded, "You've never studied there and

what could you possibly need an office for? Most of the time you can't write your name let alone have a business you would need an office for."

Not a happy time for John. He turned, went back to his room, came out with his half empty gallon of Smirnoff, pulled it up to his mouth and having forgotten he had left his teeth in the room, tried to gulp a slug of the booze and ended up with most of it running down his shirt and into his pajama bottoms. He returned to his room and came back with a plan.

"We need to reach an understanding now."

Before he could say anymore, Hermione spoke.

"The only understanding we need to have is that this is my home. I pay for everything and you, Mr. Rebel, had better be on your best behavior or you will use up your welcome. Do you understand that this is the understanding you need to reach right now?"

John said nothing, picked up the bottle by the handle and went out to sit by the pool. Hermione looked to me and quietly said, "Make yourself at home."

The exchange between Hermione and John set the stage for the rest of the story. It was very difficult to get a clear picture of the relationship between them. She obviously took care of him, but it also seemed that she was very guarded when he was around. I decided to leave well enough alone and just go about my business of getting healthy in body and mind. My children were constantly on my mind, and I was strengthening my determination to change my life around so that they would have no worries about their father, and I would be able to provide them with a home away from their home in San Jose.

In the meantime, I was grateful for everything that was happening. I was also aware that I needed to watch my back. John Rebel was probably less than pleased that I was around. And I was sure that he wasn't happy with the possibility that Hermione might be a little more secure in her own home.

For the next couple of weeks, I could feel my inner-self becoming stronger physically and my determination and dreams were again coming out of hiding. With the passing of time, I started to find the rhythm of life was such that I was better off not getting involved in the internal workings in the main house. At one point when sent on an errand, I was able to buy some clay and began developing a series of new characters that I called "Just Some of My Friends." It was wonderful for my inner creative peace as well as something to keep my mind and hands occupied.

Playing with my clay was almost meditative. With my hands and one side of my brain I was creating something new, while on the other side I was going over my history and having some very distinctive memories of the many things I should have done, should have said, and the changes I should have shown for my family. It also became very clear that I was not the kind of person that my wife needed in her life. Getting rid of me was probably the best thing she had ever done for herself. With me not around she was released from a lot of the burdens of having to give consideration to the fact that I was around. Now she could move her life forward.

Hermione would come out to the room and sit with me and watch me work the clay as well as tell me bits and pieces about her life in film and on stage. The most interesting conversations were the little bits she would disclose about her relationship with John and the life inside the house. Apparently there was a short period of time when she and John did get to know and like each other, but that didn't last long after finding out what was really driving his desires. It was his greed, his anger and his stupidity. It became clear to her that he was after all she possessed, and he was going to get it.

She also began to ask me to help her with some of her paper work and banking. I found that she had very little support from anyone and was very nervous about her property and even her mind. She was scared of John and believed he would be very happy if something would happen that would give him the opportunity to be in charge of her life.

Lady Joan came home after about a month in the hospital and could get around without the aid of a cane or walker. Clearly Hermione was happy to have her there, but at the same time they began their little cat and mouse routine that I only had a glimpse of before the fall. Hermione was the cat and Lady Joan was the mouse that always appeared just as the cat wanted to take a nap. The odd part was that the cat never really gave chase. John was the rat, the real pain, and if he took a bite, the cat could lose. It became clear as time went on that I was the unexpected obstacle in his life.

John tried to woo me with promises of success because I was "such a great artist." I was also "so handsome" that he dared not "make advances sexually" because he knew I was straight, but if I ever just wanted to let him have some fun with me, he would be delighted. He also wanted me to know that without his teeth, he could give me "an experience that I would never forget." I picked up a leather-working tool I had, showed it to him and described what the effect would be if ever in the middle of the night, I were disturbed from my sleep and had to use it. I quietly told him I wouldn't hesitate, for even a split second, to cut a man's throat, ear to ear. I used my powers of recall to reveal the silent rage I had in me. He got the message. He also reported to Hermione that she might think again about having me live there because now he's afraid of what I might do. Hermione asked me about the incident later. I told her what went on and she took a long look at me and said, "Good boy."

Lady Joan began to open up to me as well. She loved to do the food shopping for the house. I really enjoyed going to the store with her. She was a delight to be around. She was one in a million or probably 10 million, a true original, a study in motion of a human enjoying all the moments of life. She was like a child seeing its first circus. In many ways Joan was much more entertaining than the "Greatest Show on Earth." Sometimes when she would see something that wasn't pleasant, she would turn away and remark, "We need to erase unhappiness from life."

At times she would talk about John.

"He's such a good boy, but he's lost control of his mind. It's the drinking, you know, that has a hold of him. What do you think we should do?"

Answering her own question, she went on, "We've tried to get him to seek help, and it just makes matters worse. He gets angry and starts screaming and running around like an animal. It's better not to do anything. Perhaps we should just ignore him, except he has such an influence over poor Hermione, the dear. He really is a good boy."

I had been there about two months or maybe more when one night as I was working with my clay, Joan came out to my room and knocked on the sliding glass door.

"Please come in, Rick. Please hurry."

She was moving as fast as she could toward the house. As I passed her I could hear a god-awful yelling that sounded like a hyena barking. As I entered the house I had to open a sliding glass door into the dining room. The screaming stopped. I got to the living room to see Hermione sitting in a chair in the corner with John Rebel walking in a circle in front of her.

Dead silence until I asked, "Hermione, are you all right?"

She answered, "Yes."

John was flushed, drunk and doing his best to remove the anger from his face.

"We're just having a little family dispute, just like all families do," as he lowered himself to the floor and took one of her feet in his hand.

"She's my queen. I'm her jester. My queen is unhappy and I want to tell her that I will always be with her, to protect her, to guard her against enemies of our kingdom. Can you understand that, Rick? Can you?"

If he thought he was going to get me into a conversation, he had another "think" coming.

Lady Joan was standing at the edge of the living room when I suggested, "Lady Joan, would you please take Hermione to her room, and I'll be there in a minute. John and I want to talk."

I waited until they left and were in Hermione's room and was about to speak to John when he said, "I don't want to talk right now, I'll talk to you tomorrow."

I felt that would probably be better. It would give everyone a chance to rest, and I would be able to see how Hermione was doing. John took his bottle and went to his room.
I could hear that he had turned on his TV, and I went to
Hermione's just as Joan was coming out.

"She's tired, her door is locked and she said she would see
you in the morning."

Tomorrow was important. I had to know just what was
going on in this house. From my room I could see into the
dining room-kitchen portion of the house, and I didn't see
any movement. John stayed in his room. I was beginning to
feel signs of stress across my back. It's always been hard for
me to hold back when I see something needs to be done.
Self-control was a challenge.

The next morning I woke up in the dark. It started off with
the most beautiful sight I had seen in an awfully long time. A
thick fog of at least six shades of gray swirled gently in a wind
that pushed it in horizontal circles and lifted it before causing
it to dive down to the dog park below my window. It was a
dancing mist; it mesmerized me. It was like I had awakened in
the middle of an early Robert Mitchum movie.

Again, the great artist of nature took away all feelings of
separation from happiness and caused hope and beauty and a
desire to be at peace with the universe to rise from my heart.
The chill in the air, the fresh beginning of another day, played
with my imagination, wanting to take me into another realm
of oneness with nature. That was interrupted with the sound
of the opening of a sliding glass door.

Lady Joan wanted to offer me a cup of tea or "coffee if

you prefer." I went in to help.

She wanted to be sure that I was OK. We were whispering so as to not wake up the "blurry one," and to our surprise Hermione came out to join us. We all went outside, at my request, to stand on the edge of the hill and become a part of the "Fog on Carmar Drive." When we came in and sat at the dining room table, Hermione informed me that she had to go to her lawyer's for a business appointment at 10 a.m., and then she wanted to drive to the valley to look for shoes at a specialty store. She was always on the lookout for shoes for Joan. Never did find any that Joan would accept. It was another of their cat and mouse games. I decided to wait till then to bring up the subject of John and his behavior toward her the night before.

As Hermione and I were about to go to the car, John Rebel came out of his room in those ridiculous camouflage pajamas asking where we were going. Hermione didn't interrupt her brisk walk to the car, as John slurred, "Oh darling, let me take you wherever you need to go. You know how much I want to look after you and see that your interests are the priority."

This guy had about as much charm as a dead fish. We got down to the Hollywood side of the canyon and I asked, "What was going on last night? Do you want me to get rid of John for you?"

She took a beat and said, "Mind you own business. John has been in my life for twenty years, and there is nothing that can be done."

I thought for a minute, "Hermione, I'm not talking about violence. I am saying to you that I will see to it that John will no longer be a threat to you or Lady Joan."

"Let it alone Rick. It's not your concern."

Again, I kept quiet and by that time we were at her lawyer's. I saw her to the office and waited for about an hour while she took care of business.

She wanted to stop at a couple of stores and the subject of John didn't come up again. Other than telling me where we were going, not a word was spoken. On the way back to the house I said, "Hermione, I can't sit around and watch this. If you won't let me do something about it, then I had better leave."

She looked at me for a long minute and said, "Then perhaps that is what you should do."

I slept there that night, got my things into my car and the next morning we said our good-byes. During my stay I had gotten a pager and before leaving I made sure both Lady Joan and Hermione knew they could always reach me if they needed or wanted something. Between the three of us, the good-byes were not happy. The fourth person probably was laughing all the way to the bathroom. One week later Hermione paged me. I called.

"Rick, would you be a good boy and stop by when you have time?"

Actually, I was relieved not to be staying there because the stress was building and it wasn't healthy for me. The other point was that I was staying with a lady friend, and we shared a couple things in common. Talking wasn't one of them. So when Hermione called, even though I knew I was not going to be 100 percent welcomed, I had developed enough respect and concern that I wanted to respond.

The look on Lady Joan's face told it all the second I arrived at the house. Within five minutes, Lady Joan and I were in quiet conversation with Hermione in her room. I was asked if I would be able to move back in. John must have been sleeping off another bout with the devil of darkness in his room. I got everything out of the car and back into the room by the time John awoke, got up and saw that I was there.

"You're the worst mistake I ever made."

He stood there at the opened sliding door with the eyes of a mad dog.

"You're right, John, because I'm the witness."

At that point I started moving around the room as if I were doing a dance from "West Side Story," snapping my fingers. "I'm the witness. I'm the witness."

John just stood there. He was lost. I think I succeeded in making him think I was crazy. He knew I wasn't going away. He went back in the house, got his ever-present vodka and I heard him call out, "Hermione! Hermione!"

That slow muddy speech now also had the sound of a lost child. He was going after me with the only weapon he had. He started to beg. He was going to cry and show fear of abandonment.

About five minutes later Hermione with great cheer and that "Cagney" walk came out to my room with Lady Joan trailing as quickly as she could with news that made them both very happy—John D'Costa was expected in two days. Hermione delivered the news and Lady Joan delivered a verbal essay on just what a wonderful man the Baron John Mendes D'Costa was.

"Oh, Rick, you'll love him."

John Rebel didn't love him. He came out dragging his feet, listening to Joan sing the praises while he slowly sank lower and lower into his lonely hell. I should have felt a little more compassion, but all I could see was him plotting his next move. If he didn't do something quickly, he knew he was about to lose every opportunity he thought he had to gain control of Hermione and her fortune. His was the face of Evil.

24

THE FOG
on Camar Drive . . .
Part II

The news of the Baron John Mendes D'Costa's arrival time was as if a light was being shined on the house. The entire atmosphere inside was changed—both in the hearts of Hermione and Lady Joan and in me. It even caused a change in John Rebel. He suddenly became kind, considerate, warm, and he welcomed any suggestions about how he could better support the arrival. He wanted to buy a suit, to get his hair cut, to slow down his drinking and in general join the household as a member. That significant change in his demeanor lasted about two hours. Later that day, as he slipped deeper into his private hell, he announced he was going out of town.

Hermione asked me to make myself available to take John to the airport. I don't know how he was able to pay for the trip, but I suspect he got it from Hermione. She was probably more than happy to get him out of the house. She told me that it was difficult for her to invite friends to her home because whenever someone did come, John would always force himself on them so he could be the center of attention. Many of her friends refused to visit, knowing he was

332

there. What could it be in her past that he held over her head as a threat? With the welcomed news of his departure, I felt it best to just let sleeping dogs lie. No conflict today.

With John hovering over me, I made the calls for his flight and was very surprised to find that he would be going to New York for two days and then on to Europe. He said he was going to London to take care of some "very significant personal business" and would make arrangements from there. He was really trying to give me the impression that it was time for him to "get back to the work he was destined to do." And of course I was a big part of his plans. He would let me know what our "future in show business would be" as soon as he returned. If this man had a dream, it would have to have been a nightmare.

The following morning I drove him to the airport. What little conversation we had revolved around the great fortune he had being a member of Hermione's family. I said nothing until I dropped him off at the International Terminal.

"If you don't make it back, John, don't worry. Hermione and Lady Joan will be fine."

At that point I drove off hearing John yell, "What the fuck does that mean? Wait, I'll be back."

The next day was exhausting. The girls wanted their hair done. Both wanted this or that. Both were like little kids.

Being out in public with Hermione and Joan always ended up being an adventure. I really had to think on my feet. Listening to and accompanying these two "wonder women" never failed to get the attention of all the eyes and ears of those who spotted them. Watching them walk down the street could be called a chase scene.

Pigeon-toed Lady Joan trying to keep up with "Cagney" Baddeley always led to Hermione getting so far ahead. You could lose that tiny springboard of a lady in a crowd of three. When she would realize she couldn't find Joan, she would come clipping back as she scolded Lady Joan for being so slow.

Once Lady Joan responded with, "Well, Hermione dear, you know my feet hurt and my shoes don't fit very well. Why don't you try walking backwards? That way we can always keep in touch."

They had a great time with their differences.

"Where shall we go to dinner when John comes? Let's have a party with all our friends. Too bad you don't cook, Rick. We'll have to find someone to clean the house and all the windows."

It became a circus overnight. The dogs had to have baths so a trip to the vet was arranged. I don't know how it all came together, but the ringmaster was Hermione. It was as if new people appeared from within the bodies of both Hermione and Lady Joan. As hectic as it was, it was wonderful to see the joy coming out from under the gloom when Rebel was there.

During all of this running around like a chicken with its head cut off, Hermione made my day when she said, "I hope that when the time comes, you'll be able to have your children come up here for a swim. I'd like to meet them."

That raised my spirits and energy to an almost forgotten level. What a wonderful image to carry around in my mind. It had been too long since I had last held them, kissed them goodnight and heard them laugh or even yell at each other. Magic appears in my world when I'm with them. During all this time since the separation, whenever they came in my mind, I cried. The depths of the hell I felt in my heart was at times so unbearable that I truly thought it would break and I would die. Never before had I so much as even imagined the pain of not being able to be with them. Middle-aged crazies, male menopause, old age and probably my second childhood all happened at once. I thought I was going nuts. The only hope came with the chanting, the prayers of my faith in Buddhism and the faces of my children in my daydreams. And now I had a renewed vision of seeing them again, and maybe soon.

The benefit of being here at Hermione's home was becoming a little clearer day-by-day. In many ways I was very much out of touch with the reality of most people and their daily life. Even when married I continued to hold on to the survival mode of living that I was branded with in my heart and mind as a kid. I blew the chance to grow up when I was with Lynn. I think I was afraid of taking responsibility for my life, my family and directing it toward being the best husband, the best father and the best provider I could be. I was still expecting that something was going to happen that would make me change. This time at Hermione's began a period of realization that I wanted in the bottom of my heart but still didn't know what action to take. What was wrong with me? Was I to be a born loser all my life?

The fact that I was able to be able to have this roof over my head, to study and practice my faith comfortably and eat well for the first time in quite a while, gave me hope that I was perhaps on a curve toward getting more positive control over my life. And now I have a visit with my kids to look forward to.

When the Baron John Mendes D'Costa walked through the door, the first impression was that this man had a lot of fortune. The second thought was that I wondered where he got it. He had the appearance of royalty and simultaneously he could have been the head of an organization or mob. Legal, illegal, inherited or gotten from actions that could have been described on a wanted poster were just some of the thoughts that went through my mind. He had a million-dollar smile and a smirk that went with it. He was as tan as a dark camel with teeth that shined under dark eyes that gave the impression he had just woke up or he was just dead tired. The most telling part about him was seen in the way the ladies just loved him. He was bringing a breath of fresh air into their lives. That was good enough for me. As they hugged and kissed I watched from a distance. After a few moments of greeting, I was introduced, received a firm handshake and I quietly slipped out to my room.

It was probably two hours later when Mr. D'Costa knocked on my glass door and asked to come in. It didn't take long to find that we were comfortable with each other and to realize our common determination was for the welfare of Hermione and Lady Joan. It was refreshing for me to have another voice and opinion about the circumstances in which I found myself. Our immediate agreement was that John Rebel had to go. I related my experience so far and the fact that I had confronted Hermione about my getting him out of the house and then my leaving unless I was able to take care of Mr. Rebel. With Hermione's call for me to come back and now John D'Costa's arrival, I hadn't been able to implement any action but was happy to have this chance to discuss it with a friend of the ladies like himself. With the sudden "vacation" Rebel decided to take, it all seemed to be going in the right direction.

The stories that the Baron began to tell me were all I needed to hear to know that my instincts weren't too far off track. Apparently a number of years ago, Hermione had agreed to return to England to appear in a play, and on the advice of John Rebel she signed power of attorney to him just in case situations would occur that needed immediate attention. While she was performing on stage, her friend John Rebel sold a house she owned in the canyons for $800,000. Although Mr. D'Costa didn't have all the details, it seems Rebel was working with a lawyer and was able to not only sell that property but purchased another house for less than half that amount. Many months later when Hermione returned to California, it was explained to her that there was evidence from a geological survey revealing that her property was in immediate danger from a hillside sliding from under her home.

Hermione Baddeley was one of the most respected character actresses of stage and screen. One day she showed me one of her most treasured possessions. It was a handwritten note that was handed to her backstage after a performance.

The note read, "Dear Miss Baddeley, you must change your name to Goodeley."

Signed, George Bernard Shaw.

She had told me that she started acting on stage at the age of six. The list of her credits would choke a horse. She started her career in the 1920's and didn't stop until her death. I took her on several appointments for work as late as June 1986. By then she must have been almost 80 years old, but the moment she thought she was going to work, she got as excited like a little puppy hoping someone was going to give her a treat. She did it all. She was nominated for an Oscar as Best Actress in 1959 for "Room at the Top," and she won a Golden Globe as Best Supporting Actress in 1976 for her performance as Mrs. Naugatuck in "Maude." The show was produced by Norman Lear, and Hermione was featured in 45 episodes. They loved her on the talk show circuit— "The Merv Griffin Show," "Dinah." She did everything from "Little House on the Prairie" to "Charlie's Angels" to "Magnum P.I." And there I was watching her near the end of her years being controlled by a man in the disguise of a friend.

After about an hour talking about Lady Joan, Hermione Baddeley and their history with Mr. Rebel, as John D'Costa knew it, I was invited to go out to dinner with them and to relax and enjoy myself as well. It was a good beginning to the next month or so when Hermione and Lady Joan started receiving invitations to parties, dinners and friends would call and come visiting. John found himself an apartment at the bottom of the canyon near Sunset, got himself a car and a beautiful girlfriend named Wendy. The Baron John Mendes D'Costa was a ladies man with all the charm and charisma of a Cary Grant. He wasn't tall but his appearance always caused people to take the time for a good look. John was Italian, raised in England, and he dressed like a cover of "GQ." He also had the ability to make you feel like you were the most important person in his life.

One evening John suggested that he and I go out for a

night on the town. I met him at his new apartment dressed in my best Levi's and the only sport coat I had. He came to the door dressed entirely in black with two exceptions. His tie was pure white, and pinned to his fly was a three-inch long diamond studded question mark. "Attention"… "Attention." You couldn't miss him if you tried, and that was exactly what he wanted.

"I wouldn't want anyone to think I was judgmental."

That's all he said and off we went.

About three weeks after John's arrival, he called me at Hermione's. He had asked her if it would be all right for him to ask me to do some things for him. To make it simple, I'll just say that John had a friend who was caught up in a bad habit of freebasing cocaine. He had all the "eight balls" he needed but was too stoned to go out and get a new lighter.

"Would you mind going to the local home center and getting a butane torch and a couple of Bics?"

I said I would do it and privately let John know I didn't like the idea of contributing to someone's downfall. He understood and asked me if I would help him help his friend get off it. I was glad to do just that, but John thought that right now wasn't the best time to start the intervention and that I should go ahead and get the torch and lighter. I did come back to find the man going through a really bad time. For a minute or two I again thought it might be best to call for professional help, but with John's assurances, we sat with the man.

At the friend's repeated request, John and I tried it ourselves. From the moment it began to have its effect on me, I knew this was something I would never do again. I know people who swear that all their drug experiences helped them expand their minds, but in my experience I couldn't find that expansion. It was more like shattering a mirror and scrambling it in my brain. John worried me when he kept saying he felt like "King Kong." I was afraid he liked it, especially when he pointed out to me that every hair on his body was standing up like a porcupine in heat.

I kept in touch with Hermione and Lady Joan by phone as John and I sat with his friend for about four days as he withdrew from behind the "8-Ball" and was able to somehow get his feet under him. Both of us felt assured that this trip to the dark side was over for him. Shortly after that, John had to leave town on business, and I had to brace for the return of John Rebel. He had called the house and informed the ladies he was coming back in a week and was bringing a friend with him.

And come back he did, still with that muddied mouth, but this time dressed like he had been somewhere important with his new friend. I can't remember his name so I'm going to call him Pepe. Poor Pepe had become dependent on John Rebel to protect him and guide him in his first trip outside of his native country, Portugal. He was very frail, very feminine and very young. It was also clear that the kid had some kind of emotional or mental problems. Hermione, Joan and I were uneasy with the young man being there, but John had assured Hermione that he was going to stay for just two weeks, and then he was going to put him on a plane and send him back home. She agreed and that was that. She also didn't have a problem with the news that they would be sleeping together. It's what we didn't know that became the start of another adventure on Carmar Drive. It was late when they arrived and close to the time for everyone to turn in for the night.

The fog came in that night thicker than ever. It was the most beautiful sight I had seen in quite a while. It was as if 20 shades of a palette of gray oils were spreading in slow motion throughout the canyon. The wind was the painter. I awoke and went to the side of the pool, wanting to fuse with this mystical magic of Mother Nature. At that moment, I cried with a wish that my children could experience this with me.

The rest of the day was uneventful other than taking Hermione's dogs to the veterinarian for a checkup and a bath. Those dogs were a strange group. One, by the name of Rusty was a deep red longhaired, uncoordinated mix and may have been one of the most simple-minded animals I ever met. Time and again I watched when a ball was thrown for him to fetch, and it didn't matter where he caught up with it, on the way back he would fall or slip into the pool. He just never seemed to notice it was there, and the surprised look on his face as he went in the water was worth a million. On the way in, he would look for someone to make sure he wasn't alone.

Peaches had Lady Joan by the heart from the moment she laid eyes on her. Peaches carried herself like a queen at her coronation. And she always seemed to be walking in slow motion. If you threw a ball for her to retrieve, she would just look up at you as if to say, "Are you serious? I never chase anything. It always comes to me."

The third dog ruled. I can't remember her name, but if the others stepped out of line by not giving her the number one spot in the pecking order, she would walk right up to their face and in a very low growl straighten them out, walk to the door to enter the house and sit there. The other dogs weren't allowed in until she was ready to let them in.

On the way back to the house from a little shopping spree, Hermione said John Rebel had asked her if I would drive Pepe and him down to the Strip for a little sightseeing and a drink or two. I couldn't say no, but I sure didn't like the idea. It was around eight that night before they were ready to go and had already had quite a bit to drink. While driving down Sunset, Pepe spoke up. And after two attempts, I understood him to be asking me if John was the brother of Larry Hagman who played J. R. Ewing on the "Dallas" TV series. They were both sitting in the back seat of the Cadillac and in the rearview mirror I could see John putting his hand over his mouth, knowing he was busted, and hoping I was going to back him up.

"No, Pepe, I don't think so."

Pepe looked at John and then back to me.

"He's not J. R. Ewing's brother?"

I knew I was spilling a can of peas John wasn't ready to clean up, but it was too late now.

Pepe said, "You lie to me. Why?"

John tried his best but through the mud in his mouth and the fact that Pepe just couldn't drink, it became clear that I needed to get them both back to the house before all hell broke loose.

The change from this sweet little boy from Portugal, who thought he was in love with J. R. Ewing's brother, into an angry, scared unbalanced kid, was shocking. We had arrived at the club John had wanted to go to when this all came down and Pepe wanted out of the car. John said they would get a cab home and for me to go back.

I have no idea when or how they got back to the house. The next day they didn't show themselves until later in the afternoon. The ladies had eaten around 4 p.m. and weren't interested in anything but their gin and tonic from then on. I had made a sandwich, had a healthy gin and tonic of my own and was in my room for the night, content to play with my clay. Apparently, John and Pepe had straightened everything out and were going about their business. Pepe had offered and was excited to cook dinner for the two of them. Cooking was one thing he did well, and it was to be a celebration of a new beginning for them, at least as far as Pepe was concerned. A fresh start for John always was accompanied with his trusty half gallon of Vodka.

In my world, with my chanting, the clay, and being separate from the house, it was a nice quiet evening until I heard the crashing of glass coming from Hermione's room and heard something land in the pool. I ran outside, then inside and almost got run over as John Rebel was struggling to get outside through the dining room as Pepe staggered after him carrying an iron skillet raised above his head, going straight for John. As Pepe went past, I managed to grab the skillet from his hand, but it didn't deter him from targeting John who had fallen down, probably from fear and exhaustion, and was lying on his back next to the pool curled up in a fetal position like a puppy who was surrendering.

The second that Pepe got to him, he started kicking and screaming something in Portuguese. While all this mess was going on, Hermione and Lady Joan followed the action, yelling and screaming like a flock of chickens. Hermione had grabbed the iron skillet and was headed for Pepe to whack one of them to stop all this commotion. I had to hug and stop Lady Joan from entering the fight. Hermione swung and missed with the skillet as it slipped out of her hand and into the pool. I wasn't too interested in stopping the kicking. It soon wore itself out, leaving John with a lot of bruises and Pepe with a sore foot.

I got the girls into Hermione's room and saw that the loud crash of glass was from Hermione's television having been thrown through the sliding glass door into the pool by Pepe in his anger. He was seeking to punish John for refusing to eat the dinner he had prepared as a celebration of their newly formed determination to make their relationship into something wonderful. I think you would have to say that it was getting off to a rocky start. It was a bumpy ride so far.

John and Pepe went into their room; I sat with Joan and Hermione and made the point that the police had to be called. At first Hermione balked at the idea but realized that for the sake of insurance, it had to be reported. I went to the kitchen, called 911, reported the domestic disturbance and added that it probably wasn't over, and it would be wise to send a patrol car to the house. The kitchen looked like someone had set off a little bomb. Food was everywhere, dishes were broken and the floor was as slick as ice from the grease used to cook the dinner. I decided to wait before cleaning up so the police would have a clear picture of the disturbance.

Everyone remained in his or her rooms and all was quiet when I answered the door. The police first wanted to hear my account as I saw it, and then asked for Hermione to come out to the living room. Both she and Lady Joan did their best to tell the story. It was difficult for the officers to get a good picture as the girls kept interrupting each other, but finally as one officer continued the questioning, I took the other to Hermione's room, then out by the pool, pointing out the television lying on the bottom. Back in the living room Hermione was saying that she would not press charges. After a good effort by the police, they had to say that there was nothing they could do under the circumstances. I suggested they at least meet and talk to John Rebel.

They agreed and I had him come out of his room to the foyer. He, of course, had on his good face and showed no emotion, but the mud in his voice gave him away. After a very strict warning, the officers said they were leaving, and I walked them to their car.

I asked them, "Please don't leave. Something is going to happen here tonight, and I believe someone could end up dead. Please come back in and at least speak to the young man who was involved with John."

They followed my advice and we went back in.

John was trying to explain something to Hermione when I came back in with the LAPD officers. He came out of the living room and was asking what they wanted when a very sharp sound came from down the hallway. It was Pepe trying to break an empty bottle of Schweppes Tonic on the bedroom doorframe while holding a large hunting knife John had given him as a gift. The boy was clearly out of his mind. John started screaming like a wild chimp with one officer telling him to be quiet while the other went toward Pepe to disarm him. The kid tried to get by the officer. The knife was taken from his hand, and he was thrown to the floor and handcuffed.

All this was taking place with John screaming and running around in circles calling out, "Don't hurt him. Leave him alone."

After the officer repeatedly told John to be quiet and sit down, he hit him in the chest with his baton. He was quieted instantly except for his gasping for breath.

Witnessing all this convinced Hermione she had to press charges. She refused to press the charges against John. Just Pepe. John was told to go to his room. Pepe sat on the floor while the officers filled out the complaint. They put the kid in the car and assured Hermione the boy would spend the night in jail and appear in court in the morning. He would also receive a restraining order to keep him from coming on her property again.

They might have known John Rebel from some other occasion because as they left one of the officers said, "It's not my place to say this, but you may want to consider whether you want to continue your relationship with Mr. Rebel. He could be your worst enemy."

Pepe spent 10 days in jail. John hardly came out of his room. The house was as quiet as a library until the day when Pepe was released and Hermione asked me to drive John to pick up Pepe and take them to a hotel. Again, John got money from somewhere and was getting the boy ready to go home to Portugal.

John Mendes D'Costa came back in town during this time but was only staying for a couple of days before going on to Australia for business. This man was so bright that when

I was around him I felt like I was getting a tan. He loved to laugh and most importantly he was good medicine for the girls. He took them out for dinner and brought their spirits up with the promise that when he came back, he would take them out again for a night of theater. He also convinced Hermione and Joan that it was time for them to let me take care of John Rebel and see that he moves out of the house.

The day before Pepe was released, with Hermione's consent, I called her travel agent, booked a flight for two days later to John Rebel's hometown in Arkansas. His flight was to leave around 9 in the morning. The night before, on the way back to the house after taking Pepe to the airport, I informed Mr. Rebel he needed to pack a bag because he was leaving in the morning. By the time we got back to Carmar Drive, he was as quiet as a mouse. The moment we got in the door he went directly to Hermione's room to find that both she and Lady Joan were locked in and he was locked out. He looked at me with spit in his eye.

"We'll see about this in the morning."

I never knew where he got his Smirnoff from, but I never saw him without it. That night he sat at the dining room table and must have drunk half the bottle. I sat in the chair and never took my eyes off him. He couldn't take that for very long, so he went to his room. I stayed in a position where I could keep my eye on his door.

I waited till one hour before we had to leave for the airport the next morning before I went to his room and unlocked the door with a key Hermione had given me. I stood by the side of his bed and gave him a hard slap across his face. He must have thought he had been shot dead in bed but woke like lightning had struck him.

"John, you have 30 minutes to get your shit together before we leave."

I went into the hallway, closed his door and waited for about five minutes to at least give him a chance to get moving before I went back in the room. The poor fool hadn't gotten out of bed yet.

I took the knuckle of my middle finger of my right hand and struck him just below his left eye with enough force that I was sure he got the message that time was up. I again went back into the hallway, left the door open and watched as he packed a bag, got dressed, put on his shoes, and we headed for the car. We were out of there. The plane ticket was in my hand and I kept it there until we got to the airport, parked, got to the terminal and I handed it to the attendant. I stood there watching him going down the tunnel to the plane.

The only words that were spoken came from him as he started to board, "I loved her once, you know."

How sad, too bad.

Back at the house the ladies had been sitting on pins and needles waiting for the news. Once it sank in that he was gone, there was dead silence until Lady Joan spoke.

"I think the puppies are going to miss him."

Hermione asked if there was any ice cream. Joan suggested a gin and tonic, and that was the beginning of the next chapter in life on Carmar Drive. The fog had lifted in the hearts of everyone.

When John Rebel was there you couldn't get a rat to come into the house, but from the moment he left, the ladies' friends appeared and the invitations for dinners came out of nowhere. Where were these "wonderful friends" when she needed them. Real friends are extremely hard to come by.

Mr. D'Costa came back in town with beautiful Wendy. If John weren't around I'd have done my best to get all of her attention. My children came down to Los Angeles. I picked them up in Hermione's Cadillac, and they came to the house for a day of swimming and hugging. The greatest treasures in life are the ones buried in the deepest eternal recesses of the heart.

My children are more treasured than all the jewels in the universe. True fortune can't be counted. That one day of swimming together with them caused an internal journey to restart in my heart. I knew I had to change my life from the inside out to not only relieve them of worry about their father but to show them the power of my faith. My determination soared upward from that day. A fresh start, a new beginning for the sake of others. I determined I would start each day with that in my mind and heart. I also knew that I wasn't going to just up and leave the ladies without someone around to be there for them when needed. At the same time, I knew I had to create a new life for myself.

Another fog came in over the canyon, but with it dancing in the air, there was an almost musical background with it. You could say it was a fog like so many others before. But with the change in the hearts of that house, the fog, though gray, seemed to have a glow of joy attached. Amazing how a change of the heart is reflected as a change in the environment. The sun coming up seemed to absorb the fog and draw out the joy from within the ladies. I was in my room when I heard Hermione's shoes coming my way, walking with that crispness that was only hers. I looked up and there she was. All of her nearly five-foot frame stood in my doorway in her bathing suit.

"Could you be our lifeguard? Do you swim well enough to save Joan and me if we go under?"

I looked out at the pool and there was Lady Joan sitting in a lounge chair next to a table. She had set it up with ice, gin and tonic. It was almost noon.

"Not too soon I hope?" said The Honorable Lady Joan Austin-Mutton-Smith.

"Not for me," said I.

This was another day for the books. Hermione swimming like a frog, Lady Joan sitting in her chair like the Queen herself and me playing the butler, lifeguard and "hey, boy" all at one time. The day went great until Joan tried to get out of her chair but couldn't quite manage it. The gin had played its part in combination with the sun to make her a little out of balance. It was time to get her back to her room. Hermione was out of the pool, sitting with a drink while I escorted Joan back to her room where she lay down for a little snooze.

I went back outside to find Hermione bending over touching her toes with her back to me. I had to give her a lot of credit for being so limber, but it seemed that no matter where I moved to, she kept moving in my vicinity, turning her back to me, bending over to touch her toes again. It wasn't exactly the most intriguing picture I had ever seen or imagined, but I did recognize that I was being flashed. She probably wanted a little poke for fun and to feel a little tingle, but it was an itch I just couldn't get up to scratching. The protective forces of the universe protected me that very moment. The phone rang. John and Wendy wanted to come up for a swim.

The next month or more was a time for everyone to reclaim their comfort and begin to settle down to relaxing, having friends over for an evening of conversation and in some ways becoming reacquainted with each other. John and Wendy were good friends to the ladies and went out of their way to give them the love and attention they deserved after so much of their time had been spent looking over their shoulders wondering what kind of trouble John Rebel was going to cause. I took this time to elevate my faith and practice of Buddhism and to sculpt and think. I also was able to take Hermione to a Buddhist discussion meeting at an SGI community center.

Hermione was genuinely interested in the Buddhist view of life and death. When we arrived at the center, a number of people who I had known for quite a few years came up and I think it surprised her that I knew so many people there. There were also those who remembered Hermione from so many of the shows she had done on television. A lot of them were young and she seemed flattered they were aware of her work and showed a true respect and appreciation for her.

During the meeting when it became time for anyone to ask questions, Hermione quickly raised her hand, got to her feet and asked the person leading the meeting, "If I were to chant, could I chant to come back in the next life as a pussy cat?"

The audience roared, not just at the question but the way she asked it. She pulled out all the many years of theatre in her life, dug down into her bag of dialects and tickled the funny bone of everyone in the room. The member's response gave her a great amount of pleasure. This woman loved to be wanted and needed to make people laugh. She laughed along with them. It must have been quite a while since she had had a good laugh herself.

Compared to all the time I had been living on the hill, the events of the next four to six weeks were boring but pleasantly relaxing. I really was enjoying the evenings with the ladies. Listening to the stories from Hermione and Lady Joan over a couple stiff gin and tonics was fascinating. Then when they would turn in, I would go sit by the pool and watch the night pull up its blanket and the world would slowly go to sleep. At times, that blanket would be the fog that has never left my mind of dreams. By midnight on most nights, I was ready to put away the clay or lay down with a book. The last thing I would do was to look out my window toward the house to be sure all the lights were out. One night they weren't.

Perhaps Hermione had fallen asleep with the light on so I decided to walk inside to check everything out. Going down the hallway I noticed her bedroom door was open so I quietly looked inside to see Lady Joan sitting in a chair by the side of the bed. Hermione was tossing and turning, but seemed to be asleep. Joan told me that she did this sometimes when she had a little too much to drink. She had taken a sleeping pill and Joan thought Hermione was restless because she had piles, hemorrhoids.

"Would you be a good boy and carry Hermione to the potty so she could have a go? Please, dear, Rick."

She was as light as a feather and I was able to get her

seated. Her eyes were closed but she took care of business. She put out her arms. I picked her up, carried her and put her in the bed. After a minute Lady Joan said, "Thank you. Why don't you go to bed and get some rest!"

I went back to my room but couldn't go immediately to sleep. I saw that the light was out and was getting ready to turn in for the night when I looked out the window and saw that the light was on again. For a moment I thought I would let it be, but a second thought made me go check on the ladies again.

25

THE FOG

on Camar Drive . . .
Part III

This time as I entered the room, Lady Joan was sitting on the bed, Hermione was still wrestling around with her eyes closed and Joan again asked if I would carry Hermione to the bathroom. I picked her up and was headed to the bathroom when all of a sudden she stiffened up like a board and her arm shot straight up in the air. I immediately put her back in the bed and called 911. Joan kept herself collected. I was very proud of her. The look on her face showed all the love, concern and respect she had for this woman who was so much more than just her very best friend.

In no time at all the paramedics were there, administering to Hermione with great care. Their first suspicion was that she had had a diabetic seizure or perhaps a stroke. Without hesitation, they got her in the ambulance as I called John D'Costa and asked if he could come to the house and sit with Joan until I got back. I followed the ambulance to Cedars Sinai and stayed until she went through emergency. The doctors that I spoke to were pretty confident it was a stroke but didn't want to reach a permanent conclusion until they were able to do more tests. I got back to the house a couple of hours later to find John and Lady Joan waiting. I reported all I knew and that we would have to wait until tomorrow to know the details.

We did make a decision that we were not going to notify any media of Hermione's condition with the single purpose of keeping the news away from John Rebel. The last thing we needed right now was to have him doing his act of grief for the press. He would milk this for all it was worth. The other concern John D'Costa and I had was the condition of Joan's mind. During all this time I had spent surrounded by so many British, I saw at least one consistency; for the most part they don't like to reveal troubles or concerns publicly. It had taken quite a bit of time and effort to get Hermione to reveal just how much she was afraid of what John Rebel might do if she went against his wishes. It might have been the "stiff upper lip" syndrome.

John, Joan and I went to the hospital the following afternoon to visit Hermione and speak to her doctors. In the room everyone was silent until I spoke.

"Hermione, Joan and John D'Costa are here to see you and to let you know we love you and are praying for you to recover and be well."

Just then her nurse and a doctor came into the room. The doctor asked us to step into the hallway to report that, so far, the tests revealed she had a major stroke. He wanted to wait another 24 hours before coming to a definite conclusion as to the severity, but it appeared that the brain stem was affected and the results would produce extreme limitations with little or no control over her vocal and bodily functions.

The doctor left and we all agreed not to discuss our conversation with him in front of Hermione, but we did need to notify her two children in England. Back in the room, we talked to her in general about the dogs and that she needn't worry about the house or anything. It was very unnatural to see this woman remain still. If she ever wanted a nickname, Sparkplug would have fit perfectly until today.

Lady Joan was the one we were most worried about. Outwardly, she revealed little emotion, but in her eyes, the pain and worry were very clear. It was very difficult knowing the depth of the suffering in her heart, and there was little that we could do. Joan showed her affection with her eyes. Hugs seemed to be uncomfortable to her. I wondered how much physical touching she received from her family as a child. I suspect little or perhaps none. I could certainly relate to that. That afternoon, when John had gone back down the hill to his place, Joan and I sat by the pool saying very little. I reached out and took her hand in mine. It took a second or two, then she relaxed and we held hands for a while. I think it was good for both of us. She already had a permanent warm place in my heart.

Later that afternoon back at the house, John D'Costa called and spoke to Hermione's children and reported that their response was not to keep her alive through artificial means. They suggested pulling the plug. We didn't relay that to anyone because we held on to the hope that there might be some improvement in her condition soon and it would be better to give her more time.

Lady Joan wanted to invite some people who she thought were Hermione's better friends for a party and tell them what had happened. It seemed too much like a surprise party with a bad ending, but that was Joan's wish. John and I agreed that it would be better to break the news that way rather than on the phone and let the story get out of hand and into the ears of the tabloids and the eyes of John Rebel. Asking everyone to keep it a secret, the party was set for the next weekend. Having John D'Costa around was a great benefit. He took charge of the legal and administrative side of the situation while I took the responsibility for the physical end as far as the dogs and the property were concerned. We were both keeping a close eye on Joan.

Everyone arrived within a half hour of each other at the announced secret surprise party. Joan put on her happy face, greeting everyone with champagne. Cheese and crackers and maybe some vegetables with dip were as far as we went for something to munch on. I could see by the look on their faces the guests were expecting more but quickly understood as John made the announcement regarding Hermione's health. By this time there was no uncertainty about her future.

John announced to all, "She would at best be bedridden for the rest of her years and although she was remaining alive without a respiratory support system, there was little, if anything, to be expected as far as her ability to ever speak clearly or communicate with anything other than a squeeze of her hand. At this moment she couldn't even do that."

As John spoke I watched the expressions on the faces of these friends and to tell the truth, I didn't see a lot of change beyond the disappointment in the food. Someone suggested a toast to her but that took some time before it happened as most everyone had an empty glass already and wanted more champagne first. Those who still had some champagne left in their glass quickly finished it off and stood waiting for another pour. The toast was pleasant and over quickly as everyone began milling around and talking to Joan and John. We wanted to make sure that we kept this out of the press to keep John Rebel out of the way at least until we knew the state of affairs regarding her estate and the conditions of her will. On that point everyone seemed to agree immediately.

There were a couple of the guests who expressed that they had at sometime or other given a couple items to Hermione as gifts and wondered if they might just let John and Joan know that they would be happy to take them back if at all possible. When I heard this, the hair on my neck went straight up in the air. Greed with a voice that needed to be addressed. John handled it with all the diplomacy he could muster. One of the guests was a lawyer who had handled some affairs for Hermione in the past. He had a title of some sort that gave the impression that he was a member of a royal European family. The "holier than thou" look on his face as he entered the house gave me the impression that his opinion of himself was that he was the Savior. His driver and "man around the house" lover was very uncomfortable as he followed at the correct distance behind his master. He took the wrap off his man and stood off to the side watching everyone.

The master carried his tall self around the room using his nose like a Geiger counter, sniffing all the news he could snort. Everyone changes the nature of a room when they walk into it, but it's a little unusual to immediately get the sense that a fish has just arrived. I never did like fish.

Lady Joan and John D'Costa were making the rounds with everyone trying to get the scoop on everyone else's business. Some people live to find out the secrets of others. The whispers for the day were, "What about John Rebel? Why did she put up with him? What did he know? What's going to happen when he finds out?"

I had to get away from this for a minute and went outside by the pool. In no time at all, the royal lawyer sent out his lover to tell me how relieved they were to know that I was staying here and taking good care of Hermione's interests. There may not be too many things I'm good at, but one is that I can smell bullshit from a mile away. The last thing a person should do is to try to bullshit a bullshitter. This guy was following orders to make me think I was invaluable. I had enough of this crap and went back inside. Lady Joan caught my eye, and we went into the kitchen so she could tell me a story.

I listened and knew immediately that while as I was being praised by his lover, the royal pain in the ass lawyer was removing an article from the house to his Rolls. He told Lady Joan that he had given Hermione a crystal statue of Jesus to keep for him while he was in Europe some years ago and that because she liked it so much he never even thought of taking it back. But now would be a good time to return it to his home. I didn't think so.

When I had first seen this wonderful piece, I asked Hermione about it, and she told me how and where she had purchased it, long before she ever came to live in America. She revered it almost as an object of devotion. I saw it as an extraordinary piece of art. It stood about eight or nine inches tall with great detail, and being crystal, its reflected light gave it a presence that was mesmerizing. The art is wonderful.

I love an adventure. Now I was on a hunt for Jesus. I slipped out the back of the house, went around to the front to the Rolls Royce and found it to be locked as expected. Peering in through the back window on the passenger side, I saw just a small piece of the statue sticking out from under the footrest in the backseat behind the driver's side. That was too easy. Just as I was going back into the house through the front door, the lawyer and his companion were saying good-byes and extending their sympathy to Lady Joan. I walked them to the car, opened the passenger door for the lawyer, walked the driver to his side, waited for him to close his door and quickly opened the rear door by the statue. I reached in, picked up the piece and announced that it would be going back in the house or up your ass.

I closed the door, walked around to the lawyer's side and said, "You're going to take this back, give it to Lady Joan and tell her that you changed your mind."

He started to tell his lover to do it but I said, "No. You." When John D'Costa found out what went down, it gave him a great delight.

Over the next few weeks I did a complete inventory of the property and house. There was little or no change in Hermione's condition, and it was clear there wasn't going to be. Although John and I talked about the possibility of having her children talk to the doctors about keeping her alive or to stop giving her anything to sustain her life, Lady Joan let it be known that there would be no effort made to limit her stay on this earth.

There were very few days when Hermione didn't have a visit from one or all of us. I went almost every day and would chant by her bedside. I may be mistaken but I do believe she appreciated and was comforted by my chanting. I reported everything to her. Talked about the dogs and Lady Joan. Hermione didn't like Joan being referred to as Lady Joan. She had corrected me a number of times about that but never explained why. I figured it was either the sound of it or perhaps there was a silent wish that she had a title of some sort. In the fifth week after her stroke I decided I was going to have a serious talk with her.

"Hermione, hi, it's Rick."

I could almost hear her saying, "I know it's you, silly."

"I want to read something to you. I hope you understand my heart, even if you don't understand, what I'm going to read. This is from a letter Nichiren wrote to one of his followers back in 1255."

The letter I read is entitled "On Attaining Buddhahood in This Lifetime." It's an extraordinary piece that had been a mainstay in my life for all of my experiences with this Buddhism, and I felt compelled to share it with her, especially because she revealed a genuine interest in Buddhism's way of viewing the true nature of birth and death. It is a clear verbal picture of the true nature of life and it's activities, as well as a wonderful explanation of *Nam-Myoho-Renge-Kyo*.

After I finished reading, I held her hand and reported again that all her property was secure. The dogs were healthy and happy even though they missed her. John D'Costa was taking care of anything to do with money or paperwork and although Joan was sad and was constantly thinking of her, she was doing well.

"Hermione, I know you must be feeling trapped inside this body of yours, and I would imagine your only wish is to be free. If you want to pass now, I promise you that everything will be taken care of, and I promise that for the rest of my life you will be in my prayers each and every day, morning and evening. It's OK if you want to go on. Every time I see a kitty cat I'll be thinking of you."

I sat there and chanted for a few minutes before giving her a kiss on the forehead and leaving the hospital. Approximately two hours later, we got a call at the house that Hermione had passed.

A day or two went by with little being said or done. Lady Joan had held on to the hope that she would laugh and talk with her old friend again. Outwardly, she didn't reveal a great deal of her disappointment but a little of her heart went with Hermione when she left. The first couple of days were spent keeping an eye on Joan until the three of us sat and discussed plans for the future. The children were called in London and it was agreed that Hermione's properties from inside the house would be crated, stored and shipped. The house would be sold, with the monies put into the estate, and arrangements for Joan to go back to England would be made. We also had to decide on the best way to announce Hermione's death to the press. That couldn't be avoided. Neither could the expectation of hearing from John Rebel.

The house was sold almost immediately with a very short escrow. The new owner wanted to take possession as quickly as possible. The crating, shipping and a total inventory were completed. With the permission of the children, the lawyer revealed that her will provided that the dogs and Hermione's Cadillac would go to John Rebel.

The news of Hermione's death was broadcast on all the network news programs. In no time at all, John Rebel was on the phone. First, his muddied lingering sobs and a confession as to his undying love for her took up a lot of time before his announcement that he would be leaving for Los Angeles as soon as possible to attend his beloved's funeral. John D'Costa was on the phone listening to all this when he cleared the air with a question to Rebel.

"Can you afford a round trip ticket to London, John?"

D'Costa looked at me with a smile that would kill a cat.

"It hasn't been decided where or when Hermione will be buried nor even if there will be a memorial here. Why don't you let us have your phone number, and as soon as we know anything we'll call."

John D'Costa was slick. This gave us a little more time to get things settled before having to deal with Mr. Rebel. John got the number and informed him that Hermione had requested that he received the dogs. They needed to be shipped as soon as possible so John elected to be there waiting until the dogs arrive. We got the address in Arkansas and told Mr. Rebel we would call when it was time to send them to him.

"Did she leave any money for me? I'll have to feed the dogs you know."

With that, Mr. D'Costa hung up on him.

Very shortly after that, the dogs were flown, at his expense, to his home and they arrived safe and sound. I do know that although he never lifted a hand to take care of them before, he did like to play with them when it suited him.

It was probably three weeks later that John Rebel flew into town to pick up his 1976 Cadillac Sedan de Ville and a couple of boxes he had stashed in the garage. All this time I had a bug in my stomach about turning this car over to him. The dogs, OK. But the car? I just didn't like the idea at all. I personally didn't think he should have a thing coming to him, but there was little I could do or say about it. Well, almost nothing. In the back of my heart I knew it wasn't the best cause to make, but I did have one idea that kept digging its way into my dreams. So…what the hell? Just do it.

He wanted to come up to the house but we said no. He could come up the next morning at 10 a.m., pick up the car and leave. About a half hour before he came up, knowing that I wasn't being the best person I could be, I poured a quart of milk under the driver's seat without telling either John or Joan what a bad boy I was. A cab dropped him off. We said hello and good-bye in almost the same breath, gave him the keys to the car and stood in the driveway to see him off. That bad taste was gone. If anyone contributed to Hermione's stress and even her stroke, it was John Rebel. Two days later we got a call from him. He was going through the Arizona Desert and by noon he could no longer tolerate the smell, and he started to get sick. He couldn't understand what had gone wrong but he had to abandon the car at a junk yard and was making his way to the bus station to continue on his way home. Too bad, so sad, but I was glad.

The last night I spent in the house on Carmar Drive was like going to the theatre and someone comes out and begins to reprise the story just before the curtain comes down. As the last Fog on Carmar Drive I would ever see began to roll in, it was as if a prayer was being answered.

"A man going through the middle-age crazies, homeless, comes across an invitation to move into the home of an elderly British actress who basked in the fame of international recognition. No longer sought after for those wonderful juicy character parts she was so delightful in, she has little applause to respond to and perhaps even fewer good friends to call out to. The charm of a devil had brought her to the edge of her humanity and she could only hold on to her sanity by paying this devil his dues."

The estate gave me $2,000 to help me relocate, and the next morning was to be my last. John D'Costa was going to escort Lady Joan back to England, and I would be very much in the same boat as when I met Hermione the first time except I had a very healthy determination toward the future.

With that instinct to look for horses, I ended up renting a studio apartment next to the Los Angeles Equestrian Center.

Love the smell of that horseshit.

26

HORSES
in the Neigh...borhood

When the breeze was blowing in the right direction and the windows were open, the aroma was like perfume to this want-to-be cowboy. Anytime anyone ever referred to me as a cowboy I had to tell them, "I've known way too many real cowboys to ever call myself one, but I think I have a cowboy's heart."

With the Equestrian Center out the window, a Mexican restaurant and bar down the street, a bowling alley with five pinball machines 100 yards away, and even an ice rink, I was as happy as I could be under the circumstances. Attached to my apartment building was a stable for people who were staying there and wanted to board their horses. At night I would walk along the rows of stalls and talk to them. The apartment also had a good-sized pool and just about the first thing I did was call the kids in San Jose, tell them about the place and give them my phone number. Yep, I had my own phone, first one in a long time.

My place was studio-size and that was enough. There was a little kitchenette with an oven that worked and a bar with three stools that separated it from the rest of my new palace. When the kids did come, I would use that oven and make them one of their favorite foods from Dad. We called it Sheep Dip Pie.

I enshrined my Gohonzon and chanted with great joy in my heart. Another fresh start and it was like getting an infusion of faith. I didn't have a car yet but I called a couple of members of the SGI in the area and began going to meetings nearby. I think the next thing I did was bring out my clay and tools. I was ready for the next stage of my life.

The $2,000 that Hermione's estate gave me didn't last very long. The apartment was $600 a month. Having to give them first and last month's rent, get a phone, buy a shirt and a pair of jeans and put some food in the refrigerator took me down to the end of the money. I made sure I had enough to entertain the kids but that was about it.

Kelli was the first to visit and stay with me in the apartment. She had come down to L.A. with her mother. As I remember it, Lynn's parents weren't doing too well. Their health was deteriorating, and Lynn and the children wanted to see them more often. Up to this time I never had much respect for them, but they were my children's grandparents, and I am happy to say that toward the end of their lives they had turned a big corner. They had found relief and guidance in their religion. The relationship between them and Lynn had changed and they were much closer. That was a good thing for both Lynn and the children.

At one point while either visiting or maybe it was after Lynn had moved back to L.A., I had asked and found out that Hoytt, Lynn's dad, had said it was all right if I visited him and his wife, Marie. I had gotten on their list of the un-wanted. Hoytt was very sick and had been unable to take care of himself for quite awhile. Lynn was tending to him when I arrived that day. The rest of the family were sitting around the living room with what I felt was the distinct feeling they were waiting for him to die. If I had worked on it I probably would have felt closer to everyone, but at that time in my life it just wasn't a part of my determination.

I found that Lynn was in the bedroom trying to insert a pain medication for her Dad. Had he been able, he would have never wanted his daughter to do this or see him so helpless. She came out to ask for help, but no one moved. I wanted to help and went into the room with her. She needed someone to hold her father in a certain position that would allow her to help him get more relief from his discomfort. I had my hands on his back and hip to keep him steady when Lynn placed her hand on mine. I don't know if she was aware of it or thought it was her Dad's hip, but for me it was a magic moment. It removed a lot of the distance that had grown between us, and I was able to feel a closure to my re-lationship with her parents. For Lynn, being able to provide that love to her father must have been very difficult but also very rewarding.

Hoytt was a good man and I'm to this day very grateful for what I was able to learn from him. Anytime I work on a project around the house, I call upon many of the things he showed me.

When Kelli came to visit me I think she was about 12 or maybe 13 years old. She immediately made friends with other children in the building and, I think, had a good time. I loved having this time with her.

Kelli has always played a very important role in my life. She seems to be a guardian angel for me. Many times it has been her words or actions that have protected me from making a fool of or hurting myself. One time in particular stands out.

Before the divorce, Lynn, Kelli, Andy and I, were having dinner one night when I received a phone call from a stunt coordinator to go over a couple of details in reference to a job I was being offered. The kids were about 7 or 8 at this time.

The job entailed driving a car along a wooded rural road during the eruption of a volcano. The film had already been shot and they felt they needed to embellish the action. At 60 miles an hour, the gas tank was to explode and cause the car to flip over on its roof, slide down the road, come to a stop against a tree and explode again.

The car was going to be equipped with a cannon located in the trunk area that would be set off by the driver, me, with a switch that would shoot a pole into the ground causing the car to vault over onto its roof. At the same time, a second switch would lock the front brakes, giving the car an even better opportunity to complete its action. I would be setting off this action as I drove. After this part of the stunt was completed, they'd cut to a different angle, we would see the car explode, and that would be that. I was happy to get the job. And we certainly could use the money.

I thanked the coordinator for the opportunity, told him I would do my best, and hung up after setting the time we would meet the next day to get familiar with the car. I went back to my meal and took a look toward Kelli. Her face was beet red, and she was mad as hell.

"You're going to do what? You're going to blow up a car and kill yourself."

Dead silence. I looked at Lynn and Andy. Not a peep; not a word.

Then she said, "Have you been practicing?"

I knew I was in serious trouble with this little girl. She turned to her mother and with the same red-hot words, "And you're going to let him do it aren't you?"

I think I probably tried to say something like, "It's going to be all right. I'll be safe."

But that would have fallen on deaf ears. There was nothing I could have said that would have cooled her off. The rest of dinner was in silence. Looking at Andy was like looking at a kid who figured his big sister was in a lot of trouble, and he was going to welcome the chance to see her get straightened out. Lynn was as wide-eyed as me.

The silence wasn't broken until a little later when Lynn and I were in the kitchen washing dishes and cleaning up. I whispered to her, "What the hell was that?"

At this point I knew that I had to make a decision. If I were to go ahead and take this job and ignore my daughter's heart and mind, I would leave a dark spot in our relationship. Lynn and I talked about it and she agreed. I made a call and turned down the job as Kelli listened. This experience with my incredible daughter is one of the highlights of my life. The hug and exchange of love between us after the phone call is also right up there.

After the visits with Kelli and later Andy, I was broke. I had to do something, so I began chanting for some kind of opportunity to appear that would enable me to stay there. Otherwise it was back in the street again.

Having my children visit me for a week or so highlighted my life. Both Kelli and Drew are, without a doubt, the greatest treasures in my life. Many times when the light at the end of the tunnel was as dim as it could get, just seeing them in my mind would give me a boost of hope in my heart and a reason to never give up. The baggage, or karma, of my life sometimes appeared to be defeating me and taking me into a deeper hell, but when I thought of the kids or looked at their pictures, it lifted my spirits and caused me to want to keep fighting. They are my good fortune.

Another source of encouragement appeared one afternoon as I was walking down the hall toward the elevator. I spotted a woman walking ahead of me with her little dog. I was immediately fascinated by the movement of her hips that were being embraced by a pair of perfectly fitted white cotton jeans. Everyone has a way of walking that is unique to them, but this was the first time I had ever watched someone walk with such enjoyment and pleasure coming from hips that seemed to be doing a dance. They were happy hips. As I watched her, I wondered if perhaps she was double jointed. I hoped so and I think I must have had a look on my face that revealed what was going on in my mind as she stopped at the elevator and turned to see who was coming up from behind her.

Of course the first words out of my mouth were, "Nice dog; does she do any tricks?"

I mentioned I was going down to the stables to say hello to the horses. She had not been there before and one thing led to another, and I invited her and the dog to go for a walk with me. It would be fun for all of us. That night, the lady and I went to dinner at a Mexican restaurant and while eating a burrito, I found out she wasn't seeing anyone at the time. Later on, I did find out she really was double-jointed.

I think it was the next afternoon, and I had just come back from walking around the equestrian center. As I closed the door to my place, someone knocked. Standing there was a tall man with a head of cheap bleached blond hair, wearing engineer boots, jeans and wearing a leather jacket with a chain attached from his belt to his wallet. I had seen him in the building another time.

He asked if he could "use your phone for a second?" to call his wife and see if she was coming back to her apartment soon. He and his wife were separated. She lived down the hall with their daughter. He had to go to work soon and needed to talk to her. The daughter took ice skating lessons across the street at the Pickwick Gardens rink. He had picked her up and was bringing her back, but the mother wasn't home. He made the call, all the while looking at 10 pieces of my sculpture that were sitting in a small suitcase Lady Joan had given me.

Listening to his voice as he talked to his wife, I sensed he was a good man. As soon as he hung up he said, "Thank you," then immediately asked, "What are these?"

I loved it when someone showed some interest or curiosity about my characters. I explained to him how I happened to be given some clay one day and this is the result so far. I took out a couple of the pieces and told him one of their stories.

"This is Whistler. Everywhere he goes he whistles. The other day he went to the funeral of a friend and started whistling the theme song from 'The High and the Mighty.' Someone threw their hand over his mouth, and he blew out his right ear. He still whistles but he keeps turning to the left."

He insisted on hearing all the stories and looking at all the pieces. After I finished he asked, "Do you sell them?"

I ran a thumbnail sketch by him of what my life had been like for the last few years. I finished by telling him that I wanted to take the case of characters downtown to the L.A. Mart. But at this point in my life I had to concentrate on making enough money to pay my back rent, get a car and then begin trying to find out what the reaction would be by showing "Just Some of My Friends" to buyers. If the responses were positive, I would then look into a way to manufacture them and get them out to the public.

"Here."

He gave me the keys to his old Cadillac. I think it was the same year as Hermione's.

"Let me tell you something. I've been looking for a way to get out of the business I'm in for about a year. Let's just say I deal in illegal substances and leave it at that. I like your stuff. Take the car and go out to the Mart and see what they say. If it's good, let's talk more. Okay? I'm really serious about wanting to change my life. I've got a kid and a wife I want to take care of them, but the way I'm going, I probably don't have much of a chance of it happening. My wife just can't live with me anymore unless I stop this dealing. So take some time and let me know. Here's my number."

We talked for a little while and he left. The man had six

vehicles. He would change cars every day thinking it would make him less conspicuous. I was going to say something about changing his hair from an obvious bleached blond to something that might not draw as much attention, but on second thought I decided not to.

When he left, I just stood there stunned for a moment and immediately went to the Gohonzon and chanted with my head spinning like a top. This was like a chunk of fortune just landed in my lap. I had to give myself a good talking to about not getting too excited and just play the hand that was being dealt.

The next morning I was up before the chickens. I got my case of characters as presentable as possible. Chanted with great excitement and appreciation, rehearsed the short stories I had for each piece, locked the door and headed for the Cadillac.

The tank was full and I headed straight to the L.A. Mart. My good fortune continued as I realized I couldn't pay for the parking but found that it was free. Now to get in the building and take the "Friends" around to see what happens.

As I approached the entrance, I noticed that everyone who was coming out had a cloth badge stuck to his or her shirt or jacket. I stopped one man and asked what the badge was for. He explained that everyone who entered the building had to show his or her business license to get in and was given the badge as a pass. It wasn't open to the public, just wholesale distributors or manufacturers. Nuts. Now what was I going to do? Using my thinker for a minute or two, I came up with a plan.

I waited for the next man who was leaving to come out and I approached him with,

"I'll give you 12 cents for your badge."

I did have the 12 cents, by the way, but that was all. He gave me the badge and shook off the 12 cents.

I stuck the badge, upside down, on my jacket and walked straight up to the security officer on the door with all the confidence I needed. He looked at me and smiled before noticing, "Your badge is on upside down sir."

Perfect.

"It's Okay officer. I put it on this way so I can read it once in a while and remember who I'm supposed to be."

He looked at me for a split second like I was off my rocker before asking, "What do you want?"

I gave him my best monkey business grin and whispered, "I want to get around you to find out what the people think of my sculptures."

On his desk, I opened the case and showed him one character named Willard. I told him, "Willard wants to be a movie star but refuses to do anything unless Charles Bronson has already turned it down."

He laughed, paused, "Elevators are over there, ninth floor."

That day I presented my case of Friends to about 20 managers of these offices and display rooms for wholesale representatives. Out of the 20, 19 said, "How soon can you get these to me?"

Now what was I going to do?

As soon as I got back to my place, I called my new friend. A little later he came over and we talked. He wanted in. He would pay my back rent, supply the car and finance the research to see what had to be done to get these characters out. He truly liked the idea that he would get out of the dealing business, and he also liked that I was not interested in getting loaded on his stuff. I still liked a good stiff drink or two at night, but the drugs were not anything I wanted to be a part of. When he found out that I was a Buddhist, that added to his trust in me.

At one time or another I had tried just about anything you could smoke, snort, shoot up or drop. The one conclusion I reached after each experience was that I didn't want to do it again. From the time of my introduction to Buddhism, I became aware that all the artificial highs that drugs were supposed to supply, in reality became blinders to the true transformation available on a permanent basis by going on an internal journey to experience my own natural self. And then to top it off, turning on someone else to this celebration of his or her higher self seemed to multiply the entire meaning of my own purpose for living. Too bad I didn't wake up to the drinking problem I had.

For the next month or more I worked day and night trying to put all the pieces of the puzzle together to complete the picture of what had to be done to get this thing up and running.

Where do I start? Make a list. I've got to reproduce these things.

A friend turned me on to someone who could do the job as I wanted it to be done. Packaging. They will have to be shipped safely as a set. Graphics. Assembly.

Then it dawned on me that I was getting in way over my head. I needed to get legal advice in reference to protection, licensing, raising manufacturing money. Give me a pound of clay and put me in a corner, I'll be just fine, thank you. With my background and minimal education, I get nervous putting my hand in my pocket to count my change. I needed help.

When I was living at Hermione Baddeley's home, I met a lawyer friend of hers who specialized in the entertainment field. I remembered his name, looked him up and made an appointment for lunch. I figured if I met him outside his office, the odds were more in my favor that he wouldn't charge me.

We met at a coffee shop near his office in Beverly Hills, and I naturally brought my Friends with me. The hope and plan was that if he fell in love with them and smelled money at the same time, I might get him interested in partnering up with me and we could advance this project together. It worked.

While sitting at our table, I decided to bring out the characters, tell their individual stories and position them so they sat on the table staring at him. It wasn't a part of my plan but as I did this presentation, people at the tables close by started watching and some even came over for a closer look. And they liked them as well. I think it was the response of the patrons' of the restaurant that closed the deal.

We got down to discussing the business of turning this into a corporation with the intention of raising $100,000 by selling stocks for $5,000 to limited "S" partners. My not knowing anything about business was both a blessing on one hand and an obstacle on the other. The obstacle was that I had to trust this man and also trust my own faith that I would be protected from getting ripped off. I felt a little at ease when he volunteered to take care of both the work of incorporating as well as putting up the money to cover the fees. That turned out to happen at just the right time as my dealer friend was running into money troubles of his own and could no longer continue supplying either the car nor money for the rent and research. I felt sorry for the man. He just disappeared after that. I can only hope he is well and happy.

Very soon Rick's Thumb, Incorporated was born. A number of years before all this, while still married and probably even before the birth of my children, I had gone down to the SGI administration building to get personal guidance from Mr. Kikumura. I don't remember what it was I wanted to talk to him about, but I'm sure it was a question about how to use Buddhism to change something in my daily life.

When we were finished Mr. Kikumura said to me, "You know Rick, I've met thousands of people all over this country, and I find that most of them fall into just a few different categories. Like the fingers on a hand, they each have a different purpose or mission. Each one is a little taller or a little shorter than the other. Some are thicker or thinner than the next one, but each has its own character. Rick, you're a damn thumb."

The name I gave to the corporation was to honor Mr. Kikumura.

Things started moving pretty fast. Within just a matter of a couple of weeks we had verbally raised $40,000. We picked up $15,000 and the first big mistake was made. We opened an account, had the checks made, and contacted the L.A. Mart to make the arrangements and pay $1,500 to reserve a space at the Los Angeles Gift Show coming up in a month and a half at the Convention Center. We agreed to go ahead and start producing. I contacted the mold maker, gave him the originals to make the mother mold. Each of the molds, made of metal and latex, cost $250.

I had to have a car so I bought a used Ford Festiva for $1,000 from a neighbor at the Equestrian Inn. I'm not going to make a list of all the expenditures, but let's just say the money was running out pretty fast. As a matter of fact it was running out just about as fast as we were spending it. What a coincidence. Here comes that hindsight again. I think that we should have concentrated on raising all the $40,000 before we went ahead. We really should have waited until we collected the original goal of $100,000.00 before we did anything. My personal mistake is that I didn't have the slightest bit of wisdom when it came to business, let alone how to start one or generate monies. I expected my lawyer, partner, to take the lead on the raising of money and the business part of the business. It may be that my brain was or is made of clay.

The good news is that Just Some of My Friends was a hit. Within 45 minutes of the first day in the show, nine out of the ten sets of the ten characters were sold. From that time on, for the next five days there must have been 500 or maybe more people in the gift business that came by and looked at the one set I kept for display. I kept the originals hidden at my apartment in the case the Honorable Lady Joan Austin Smith had given me. They're still in that case.

All kinds of opportunities appeared during the show. One company wanted to talk about putting pictures of the Friends on T-shirts, calendars and coffee mugs. Each character had its little story printed on cards that were attached by an elastic string around its neck. A Chinese exporter wanted to get together to discuss getting thousands of sets to representatives in Hong Kong and other cities. They said that if they would be Made in America and if I would sign them, it would add to their value and put them in a category beyond just small gift shops. They would become signature art and that they would fly me to China to be introduced as the artist.

Another rep for Denmark, Norway and Sweden wanted exclusive distribution. A producer of animated films wanted meetings to discuss his becoming involved in developing a series. He also talked about doing the merchandising and licensing. They just kept coming. As more and more interest was being revealed, I recognized I was way out of my element.

I'm going to reach the conclusion as quickly as I can. Just about the same time the show ended, we ran out of money and unfortunately, my lawyer friend ran out of interest. I think his expectation was the same as mine. One other guy was going to wait for the other guy to do the other work to make this thing go. Another great lesson in my life: don't wait or expect anyone to do anything. I also think that I may have been protected again. The drinking was burning a bigger hole in my life, and if the success of Just Some of My Friends had shown itself, I may have taken a big dive into my personal hell. Now I'll tell you what I really think.

27

NEVER AGAIN

During the time of the gift show when I had the verbal commitment for $40,000, I got in touch with my seniors in the SGI-USA, and they almost immediately appointed me a district leader. Always in my heart was a yearning to be back in the mainstream of the organization with the purpose of encouraging the members in their faith and practice. During the entire time of the homelessness and living at Hermione Baddeley's, I had been consistent in my practice and study of Nichiren Buddhism and had tried to tell as many people about it as I could. It seems as if I had come full circle.

When the divorce hit, I was a leader of a territory that covered a very large geographical area and I was out almost every night to help people practice. Within one day, I became a general member. And now with the hope falling apart for "Just Some of My Friends" getting on the market, the money running out, and the appointment to the district position happening at just about the same time, I again had to start over. I had the Ford Festiva, and it was to become the roof over my head. I decided not to say anything to the SGI leadership or the members about going backwards and having to move into my car. I was going to do my best to fulfill my responsibilities to the district no matter what.

My own disappointment with my failures, and not knowing what to do next with whatever talents I had, moved to the back of my mind when I decided to renew the dedication of my life to helping others deal with their dreams, their disappointments and their frustrations. At one point in my studies I read something saying in effect, "Lighting the way for another will light the way for you." And in my Mickey Mouse mind I could easily imagine being lost in a tunnel of darkness with a friend, bringing out a flashlight, taking the arm of this friend. I would help the friend leave the darkness in his life behind, and I would at the same time be finding my way out as well.

With this fresh dawning in my life, I had to set some very important goals and targets. I pledged to myself and to my faith that I would change the direction of my life, my heart and my mind. I was sick and tired of being sick and tired. I felt with all my heart that the key to this change of destiny was through the practice and study of Buddhism. I wanted and needed to go deeper into my inner self and find the treasure that Buddhism was leading me toward, and I knew the first step was to do everything I could to help others do the same. The members of this new district were going to become my focal point.

I was also determined to do whatever it took to release any doubts my children may have had toward their father ever becoming happy. I was going to have a home where they could come and feel as if it was theirs as well. Another important determination was that I would never, ever get married again. I just wasn't cut out for that kind of life. And that was for sure.

That first district meeting I went to was, in my mind, an important and very special event. The women's leader was a dear friend named Norma Sanders. We had known each other for a good many years and to be assigned to this district with her was a gift. Being introduced as the new men's division District Leader was a magic moment in my life. It was as if I was an old warhorse who had been lost for five years and had just come back to the barn. Quite a few members I had known over the years were there as well as a lot who were new to Buddhism.

I tried to make this fresh beginning of mine as comfortable for everyone as I could, but I later found out that some of the newer members weren't too happy with this turn of events. They were happy with the way things were with Norma as their central figure and weren't ready for some smart ass man to be up there with her. One of the first things I did after the meeting was to approach each person at the meeting and make a list of all the members' names so I could chant for them. I felt that had to be the best strategy to start this new chapter in my life. If I was going to win their trust, I knew that the first and most important thing I needed to do was pray, chant for them and pray for me to open up my life and find within my heart the compassion and wisdom needed to lead them to study and practice this Buddhism the way Nichiren and President Ikeda taught. Another part of the strategy was to continue to polish myself and make sure I was practicing correctly.

Each day I would keep my mind on two very clear goals: to become the kind of person the members could completely trust and to concentrate my prayer on each of them individually. With the name list sitting to my side, I would keep them in my mind as I chanted for their good health, long life, prosperity as well as for their dedication and prayer to accomplish world peace.

Going down the list of names, I found that I was spending a little more time chanting for one of the women I had met at the first couple of meetings. My first impression was that she was not a happy person. She had a very hard look on her face and little or no life in her eyes. I hoped that my prayer could help her have a breakthrough and that I would see a smile on her face soon.

She and Norma were close, but my presence created a very definite barrier that needed to be dealt with. I later found out that my instinct was correct. The unhappy look on her face was reflecting her feelings toward me. She couldn't stand the sight of me. If I were to say that she thought I was arrogant, self-centered and perhaps too self-assured for her liking, I would be correct. Those qualities of mine might be only a couple of many other opinions she had toward me. I do know that I had a tendency to intimidate people with my intensity, but I didn't know how much until later.

Her name was Evangelina Muñoz. What a beautiful name. The sound of it makes my heart smile. But that wasn't always so. Every time I went over the list of members and would pray for their happiness, I found myself getting stuck on her. After a while, she became more comfortable with me around and even asked me to go with her to visit some of the people she was helping with their practice. I have to think that the reason she asked me to go was because Norma may have been encouraging her to do so.

I remember the first time we went on one of these home visitations. I had the best time being with her. I found her to be a wonderful person who was genuinely concerned with the happiness of the people she communicated with. I also found myself feeling like I had known her for years. I wanted to spend more time with her until that one day when I felt like someone had dropped a rock on my head. It suddenly raced through my mind that I was wondering about a relationship with this girl.

What the hell was I thinking. No...don't think this way. Never again, remember.

I was thinking those ridiculous romantic things I didn't want to think, especially towards a member. I had rules. Don't date members. It becomes too complicated. Most importantly, it can interfere with their faith. In those days, it was an unwritten rule in the SGI that you don't loan money to members, you don't go into business with them and you don't go around having intimate relationships with them for the sake of your own gratification. All these points were for the protection of the members. Today those rules are in writing. And the last thing I wanted to do was to cause someone to stumble in faith because of something I said or did. That was a rule of my heart.

So for the next six months I just crossed out any possibility of allowing me to give even the slightest consideration toward having anything but a nice faith, practice and study relationship with this woman named Evangelina Muñoz.

But it wasn't working. And I was spending way too much time praying and concentrating on not praying and concentrating on her. Besides she wasn't my type. I liked blond, fully endowed women with great nipples, a butt that reminded me of a full moon or two kittens fighting to get out of a gunny sack and sparkling blue eyes that were half closed and said, "Let's go to bed."

Eva's clothes were too big to tell what was going on under there, and her eyes were as black as the ace of spades. She didn't even have a wiggle when she walked. And looking at her, one minute I thought she might be Asian, the next minute she could have been Puerto Rican or any number of nationalities. Of course, when I found out she was pure-blooded Mexican-American and proud of it, I was even more intrigued. There I go again, thinking about her too much. And she was 15 years younger than me.

Stop it.

But then there was a smile on her face that could wrap itself around me and shoo away all the worries of the world. And on top of that, there are the dimples. She has dimples that only a Leonardo da Vinci could create.

There were a number of times during that first six months when things would happen or something would be said that seemed to have an undercurrent of a suggestion that implied a deeper connection between us. Phone calls to discuss members with her would turn into personal communications about things that were happening privately in our lives or minds. On my side of the conversation, I would be thinking from the back of my mind that she was telling me some things that were happening in her heart that concerned me.

Later on she told me of an experience she had while attending a wedding of a friend. As she was sitting there during the ceremony, she suddenly became aware that she could see us getting married. It freaked her out but added to the mystery of our connection. If that had happened to me, I probably would have left town and joined a circus.

Then one night as the activities were closing down, Norma, Eva and I were standing outside an SGI Community Center in North Hollywood when I mentioned that I enjoyed listening to jazz at a local bar called The Residual. By this time I had moved into the Festiva and would find strategic places to park and sleep for the night. I gave myself a couple hours of vacation from reality on Sunday evenings to go to this bar, have a stiff drink and listen to the music.

"Oh, I like jazz, too. Why don't you call me and let me know when you are going, and we can go together."

That was Eva. I wasn't announcing that I liked to listen to jazz because I was hoping someone was going to invite themselves to go along. I remember saying, "I'm not going this Sunday. Maybe the next, I'm not sure."

"That's OK. Call me when you're going to go."

There she goes again.

Where did this come from. I certainly didn't think I was giving any hints about being lonely. But I did say I would call. I was hoping that she wouldn't remember and I was sure that I wasn't going to remind her. This was making me a little uneasy. I looked over at Norma and she had this little shit-eating grin on her face that made me think a dirty little devil had decided to occupy her mind, and she was excited about seeing a rope being put around my neck.

It was time for me to get out of there and find a nest to park my car in for the night. I'm just now remembering as I write this that it was the night when I woke up around 2 a.m. to find the nose of a coyote trying to squeeze through the crack in the passenger window of the Festiva. Lesson: don't sleep in your car at night with an open package of beef jerky next to you. Just in case you didn't know that.

I was telling the truth when I said I wasn't going to be able to go to the bar to listen to the jazz that Sunday. By this time I was sure Eva had forgotten about our conversation until the middle of the next week when she casually said, "Don't forget to call me this Sunday. I'll be home by 4:30. Call me then."

Now I have got to be honest. My biggest problem wasn't that I didn't want to call her. My biggest problem was that if I did and it looked like we were going to meet for this musical event, I wouldn't have enough money to buy her a drink or two. Then what was I going to do. Just about the same time I asked myself that question, I heard a voice from the back of my mind say, "Chant fool, chant."

So I did, and somehow I did have enough money, not much, but enough. I figured I would call her, make arrangements for us to meet around 8 p.m. at the bar, and I would stop at a McDonald's and have a $1.99 buffet salad for dinner before I got there.

It was probably 4:30 on the nose when I called. I asked if she still wanted to meet at the bar and she said yes. She also said something like, "What about dinner. Why don't we meet for dinner first and then go. I know a great soul food restaurant in Sherman Oaks."

My mind was prepared to say, "No, let's just meet at the bar," but my mouth interrupted me with OK. I think it was at this point that it began to dawn on me that I was losing control or that I had two minds.

Again I wondered, What the hell is happening here.

I have a vague memory that the meal was good, but the memory of the food was nothing compared to the wonderful time we were having. There was a lot of laughing and lively talk. The talk seemed to be loud enough that we were drawing a lot of attention from the others who were there for their dinner. We started talking with the other patrons. Everyone in the place was having a party. Even the owner and the chef came out from the back to see what the excitement was and to join in. I think it was about this time that I began to wonder about my rules. This seemed to be too right for it to be wrong. We were introducing the whole place to *Nam-Myoho-Renge-Kyo*. Joy was filling the restaurant.

We finally left and headed for the music in separate cars. At the club, the jazz had started and we were about half way through the first song when I decided to light up a cigarette. I really enjoyed smoking. Aside from the fix from the nicotine, I liked having the cigarette in my hands. If I felt like leading the music, it became a baton; to paint a picture in the air, it was a brush. Along with the toys I made out of matches, I used it to give me something to stare at when I wanted to take time to answer a difficult question like, "Do you have to smoke when you're with me? I really wish you wouldn't."

"She talking to me?"

This day needed to be recorded as the day that the Rick

I knew was now on his way to becoming another Rick—a Rick I wasn't planning on becoming. "Never again" was my motto. I'll never again allow myself to get into a relationship that had a locked door on the exit. A divorce. Maybe I would lease a wife with options and a choice of accessories and specific "functions on demand" some time in the future, but I wasn't about to "buy" into a relationship that suggested that there would be even a hint of it being driven by a woman. Divorce doesn't have a good residual value.

I've never been good at remembering dates and times, but I can say with certainty that this first encounter with Eva and the jazz band must have happened in July of 1988. I'll tell you why soon.

The "I wish you wouldn't smoke when you're with me" request was received with a very slight hesitant beat and a stare as I put the damn thing out. Help! I may be sinking.

We were halfway through the second set when I said I had to get going and settle in for the night. By this time Norma had told her I was living in my car. The other members didn't know and I made sure they weren't told. I just didn't want anyone to doubt this practice. I knew this homelessness was my pattern, my destiny, throughout my life, and I did not want anyone to doubt Buddhism because of me. Eva asked me to wait for a couple more minutes, and then she and I left for the parking lot to get in our cars and go on our way.

Outside, I walked her to her car and opened the door. As we were saying good-bye, she leaned over and started to give me a kiss. I quickly turned my head and her lips landed on my cheek.

Let me say something at this point. My recollection of what happened with the kiss and a little bit later is as I know it. But if you ask Eva, you'll get another story. In my defense I'll just say that she has a slight problem with short-term memory and leave it at that. And of course, Eva will probably respond with, "Don't forget. He was still drinking in those days."

W-h-a-t-e-v-e-r!

The kiss caught me off guard and I think it froze me in my tracks. After what seemed like a hell of a long pause I said, "Do you know what the hell you're doing."

She looked straight at me and said, "No. But it seems to be right."

"Eva, I'm a bum."

"No you're not. You're too happy to be a bum."

The rules went out the window when I put my arms around her and we kissed. There are all kinds of kisses, but this one had eternity attached to it. It had the excitement of a first kiss, the ancient history of something that happened a long time ago and the expectation of a future that would last forever. We must have stood there folded in each other's arms for quite a while before Eva said, "Let's sit in the car."

Here comes my instinct. I knew in a split second I wasn't going to get in that car with her. If I had gotten in that car, it would be over. I'd have lost all control. I can only imagine what would have happened, and I wasn't going to let that be. I stayed on the driver's side, kneeling outside until my knees hurt while she sat behind the wheel as we talked. Now we get into more detail about who said what. She says we talked about marriage. I say we didn't. She says she remembers it clearly. I say I remember no such thing. I say that I wanted to talk to a senior leader in faith and get guidance before this thing goes any further. She says OK, she will too. We both did just that, separately, and later compared notes to find that the guidance to each of us was the same.

"It seems like something is happening very naturally. Don't push. Chant and see what the future brings."

That was the guidance and that's what we did. Need I say more. Two years later we got married on July 28, 1990. But a lot happened before that.

I drove that Festiva to San Jose to see the children. I wanted to tell them that I had found someone I was interested in, and we were discussing the possibility of getting married. I drove to their house to find a very unhappy situation. Lynn was having a very difficult time with her marriage.

Very soon after our divorce she had married a man she met in Los Angeles but who lived in San Jose. She sold our house and moved with the kids up north. The unfortunate thing for her was that although he, in her words, "Adores me, and he's very ordinary," he didn't adore the idea of our children. The result was that although she put her heart and soul into the relationship, he wanted all her attention put on him, not on the children.

And it showed. Lynn was a mess. I was very concerned for her safety. The house looked like it hadn't been straightened out in quite some time. The kitchen was piled up with dirty dishes and the general feeling was downcast. She and I talked for a while and she let me know that she was very unhappy.

Here I was getting pretty serious about a woman in Los Angeles, and my ex-wife and mother of my children was in

San Jose miserable. For a moment or two I actually wondered if there was a message being delivered to me by the universe that I need to reconsider my situation and perhaps think that this could be a moment in my life when I needed to go back and reach out to Lynn and protect her by letting her know I would be there for her. At the same time I was very concerned for the protection of the children. They had already gone through a failed marriage with their mother and father, and looking around it was obvious this domestic environment must be very hard on them.

In the course of our conversation about her life, I told her about Eva. I wish I knew what was going on in her mind, but to me she said, "Why do you want to marry her?"

I thought it best not to discuss it in detail and just said something like, "It just seems right."

That wasn't the cleverest answer, but it was the best I could come up with at the time. When I got some time alone with the kids, I told them I wanted them to meet someone when they came to Los Angeles. Again I didn't get into too many details other than it was someone I thought very highly of.

Seeing Lynn so unhappy made me very sad. I looked back and saw that girl at Corriganville, very unhappy and very sad, very confused. I still wanted to do something or say something to make her feel better. I also wanted to apologize for any unhappiness I caused her, but it wasn't the time. Her husband walked in the house loaded and was trying to look sober as he climbed the stairs to go up and maybe sleep it off. That time to tell her how sorry I was for anything I said or did that caused her pain hasn't happened yet, but maybe it will if she ever reads this book or letter or story or whatever it should be called.

I drove back to L.A. with my mind traveling quite a bit faster than the speed limit. Eva, marriage, career, Lynn, the children, Buddhism—just about everything that had anything to do with my daily life raced through my mind like a hurricane, leaving me with a mess to clean up and put in order. I had a lot of loose ends and a lot of polishing of myself to get on with. Time didn't seem to be on my side, but it was. Time was telling me I needed to get my shit together and stop dreaming…now.

One of the first things I needed to do was to get a job. Just the thought of it made me shudder. I hadn't worked in film since the movie I did in Florida in 1985. After that I left the house and the kids and moved into the street again. My thoughts were that I had no business marrying Eva if I didn't have a job that came with health insurance. It amazed me to think this way.

What happened to Never Again.

I also found out that Lynn and the kids were going to be coming to Los Angeles, and I wanted the children to meet Eva. I had no doubt that they would like her and get along, but I wouldn't find that out until it happened.

It was also becoming apparent that my drinking was getting the best of me and that I had to quit. Each day I would make a determination that I wouldn't drink that day, but by the time evening came around I was back at it. As a matter of fact, it was getting worse. I was drinking more in a shorter period of time. I didn't drink before evening prayers or an SGI activity, but as soon as I could, I would get a bottle of vodka and put it away. It was also obvious to me that it was a big obstacle in the relationship with Eva and me. In her childhood, her father had been quite a drinker and apparently not a kind hearted one. The effect on her was apparent when she realized to what extent booze affected me. I had to quit and I knew it. I just wasn't doing it. I was no longer drinking the drink. The drink was drinking me.

How much time and energy and money did I spend carrying this drunk around inside of me. How much creative value did I piss out the window. I had to whip this devil residing inside me. And I was determined to do it myself without getting involved with any of the addiction clubs, clinics. I had the boneheadedness of a Bulldozer.

It was also around that time that I recognized that the drinking was at the very least one of the primary reasons I didn't challenge myself to change whatever it was about my life that had stopped me from creating a better marriage with Lynn. Buddhism teaches that no one is responsible for my problems but me. I believed that, but as far as the marriage was concerned, I certainly hadn't taken that responsibility seriously enough with my ex-wife to do something about it. I can't change my past, but I can do a hell of a lot better with the present and the future.

When Lynn and the kids came down, I went to their grandparent's home and picked them up. On the way to Eva's, we decided to stop at a Carl's Jr. and get a quick bite and something to drink. We parked the car and were making our way toward the entrance when Andy noted that there was a group of young Mexican boys standing around talking and laughing.

He began to slow down and in a low voice said to me, "Dad look, there's a bunch of 'beaners' over there."

All I said was, "It's all right, let's go inside."

No problem. We ordered and sat down to eat.

"I think I better tell you. This woman I'm going to introduce you to is what you call a 'beaner.' She's Mexican."

At that point poor Andy must have felt lower than a skunk. It was a great lesson for him. And just to tell you how really great it was, he later met and fell in love with a beautiful Spanish woman. We finished our snack and went to Eva's house where the children were greeted with incredible warmth and a hug. To this day I have never looked back.

I hope you remember that when I first met their mother at Corriganville, she was running back and forth trying to find a tampon machine that worked and I bought her a huge box of Kotex. You won't believe this. We hadn't been at the house very long when Eva took me over to the side and whispered, "I think you had better go to the store and get some sanitary napkins for Kelli. I'm out and she just started her period."

Tell me if that's not the craziest thing that could have ever happened. It was better than the day I got the TV on my first day of chanting. I love it. It was almost an omen to illustrate just how wonderful the relationship between my children and Eva would be. And it is wonderful. So I grabbed Andy and the two of us went to the store. I got the item needed, but I couldn't get the boy to go through the line with me. I guess he didn't want to be associated with his father while he carried the "private female stuff."

Eva was wonderful. From the moment they met, she and

my children bonded in a relationship that has continued to grow beyond anything I could have expected. She and Kelli became friends from the start. I think Kelli today would say that she could come to Eva and know she can be totally open and candid about anything. Real good friends are very hard to come by.

Andy, on the other hand, has always been the cautious one. He looks over a situation and finds the best way to approach it, keeping in mind that he wants to end up winning. When he was about 6 or 7, he started going to the neighborhood self-service gas station and figured out that women didn't like pumping their own gas. He started a business by offering to help them for a small fee of one dollar. He's one smart young man.

The same was true when he met Eva. He just kept to the side and watched her. Within no time, he knew her heart and invited himself in. And he's been there ever since. These kids didn't get their smarts from their dad. They passed him up in the brain department a long time ago. Andy is my good friend.

I, on the other hand, was not being a good friend to myself. I continued chanting and making a new determination daily to stop drinking, but day after day I backed down. It was hard to stop, but it was even harder to realize that I was so weak that I couldn't win over this addiction. I was sure of one thing: my prayer would be answered. I also knew that if I didn't stop of my own accord, I would be stopped with some pretty tough love. Prayers in Buddhism are answered, one way or another. And that's exactly the way it happened.

The first five years of our marriage were very tough. The drinking was a big part of the difficulty, and the other great problem was that both Eva and I are very stubborn and boneheaded.

At one point she said to me, "What you see is what you get."

And that's the truth. She kept telling me how inflexible I was, but at the same time she mirrored the exact same quality. I had spent way too many years alone in my heart and mind. Other than my children, the only person who really had full access to me was President Ikeda through his guidance and teachings about this Buddhism. And now I was spending time with a woman who wanted to know everything in the world I had done, thought or imagined.

This thing called hindsight is always there if I think about it. Lynn didn't challenge my character. It seems she was very withdrawn into her own world and didn't really appear to want to partner with me. At least that's my impression. She may have given up on the possibility that our relationship could get better. Very seldom did she ask where I was going, or what I had done or what I thought. From the time I met Eva, she wanted to know what was in my pocket. I knew from the get-go that there would no longer be time to spend with my solitary self. My private life would soon be extinct.

The longer Eva and I spent time together, the more it became clear to me that I had to make some very fundamental changes in both my mind and behavior. I realized that in my marriage to Lynn, I never got beyond wondering when she was going to change. When was she going to wake up. When was she going to grow up. When was she going to care. This is my experience. It's not anything I hold against her. I was looking at everything from the outside instead of seeing the outside from the inside.

There are so many benefits that have come about because of my pairing with this wonderful woman Eva. To put it as simply as possible, I don't expect her to change and that's all right with me. I just love her the way she is. What used to drive me nuts and make me crazy still drives me nuts, but I love her for it. Now we laugh and have fun with those same qualities. It's like turning poison into medicine.

Another example of the change that has happened in my life is family, or I'd rather say my *familia*. For whatever reason, I have never been able to get attached to the idea that having a family is such a good thing. So far it's always been a disappointment. That doesn't include my children. They fall into a different category. It's the extended part that wasn't very attractive to me—uncles and aunts, cousins or brothers and sisters. And then there's the mothers-in-law and the fathers-in-law. With my first marriage, I did what I had to do, but I never volunteered for more. With Eva's *familia*, that would never work. If there was ever a chance for this marriage to work, I had to change.

Very early in our relationship she told me she had six sisters. I also noticed that practically every Sunday she would go over to her parent's house in the morning, and I wouldn't see her until mid-afternoon. She didn't invite me. And then she would say I had to meet them, but it just wasn't the right time. When would the right time be. I was getting curious. Then she started to warn me that the *familia* would not only be very curious about me, but would also be very suspicious as to what the Gringo's intentions were. I think she was more nervous than me when that "right time" came. It was now time to meet the Muñoz *familia*.

I can't remember what the occasion was but it had to be on a Sunday. There must have been 35 members of the *familia* and Eva had to introduce me to everyone, one by one. And one by one I felt the desire on their part to tear into me with every question in the book. On the outside they were welcoming, but on the inside they must have been very suspicious.

It's hard to illustrate what unity is like, but once you see it you never forget it. I tell you in the simplest terms I can think of, if one member of the immediate family were to get a cold, each and every one of them would be there with a box of Kleenex. I had never witnessed anything like it.

Eva's mother's name is Josefina Muñoz, and she has my total respect. This woman has raised seven daughters who are remarkable people. And she did it all the while working as a housekeeper. The love and respect and appreciation and feelings these seven women have for her is beyond what words can describe. And can she cook.

After the introduction, everyone stood around holding hands in prayer and then their father, Josemaria spoke. I was going to be having a couple very interesting conversations with him later. Wait, conversation is the wrong word. I was going to have a couple opportunities to receive a lecture from him. But now it was time to eat. And eat I did.

The carne asada was being pulled off the grill, and then we all got in line to go to the food that was waiting for us in the garage. Just about every time I've been to a *familia* gathering, it takes place in and around the garage. The food is all hot and ready and there's a makeshift table stretched down the middle, close-up to the door. It can accommodate about 22 people. Once all the chairs have been claimed in the garage, the overflow heads for the benches or an outside table or the house.

I really don't know how much attention I was getting that day because I was having the greatest time watching everyone. I was in a "Scorpion mood" for detective work. There were more happenings going on in this great backyard *familia* room than Walt had put into Disneyland. I just kept looking around and eating. I couldn't help it. The carne asada was the most incredible piece of meat I had ever eaten. There were at least two kinds of beans, BBQ'd corn, and potatoes—mashed or sliced—guacamole and chips, homemade soup, lots of rice, salsa and everything else you could imagine. I kept going back for a little bit more of this or that. I don't think I've ever loved eating beans before that day. I couldn't get enough.

I was really trying to figure out how to fit in. I also knew that I just didn't know anything about the Mexican culture. So I was also learning and just observing. I don't know how much you can learn in a crowd of 35, but at one point I moved up the stairs leading to the kitchen, turned around and could see the *familia* from a bird's eye view. I had heard President Ikeda say something about "looking at the world from the point of view of the sun." This was a great scene.

Standing on the steps, looking over this map of people, I knew I was in for a hell of a ride with my life if I was going to marry Eva because Eva did not come alone. In my heart, I knew I would be marrying the whole *familia*. But at that time, I honestly hadn't made up my mind that I would be going back there for another taste of a new culture. I also noticed while standing on those steps, that I was seeing a real image of the world. Those seven sisters, tied together by the golden string of the heart to each other and to their parents, were something I had never witnessed first hand—ever. I looked over to another part of the fiesta and I saw Eva. She was looking at me. And she smiled and I knew it was all over.

Food and I have a difficult time together, but we make do. I don't always want to eat. It has to dawn on me that it's time to eat. That food, that night will never be forgotten. It was perhaps the greatest food I ever ate. And also the largest amount at one meal.

For the rest of the night I was slowly trying to find a way to fit into the shoes of a culture. Watching was the only thing I could do. One thing I noticed, as the evening thinned out and many went home, was that those who remained were mostly just the seven sisters, the mother and father and all those directly attached.

The sisters took their cues from the mother. She picked the time when the cleanup should begin by being the first to take something to the kitchen. She was the leader and the girls responded. From my point-of-view, the mother worked harder than anyone and it made me uncomfortable.

All the men were sitting off to the side waiting to be waited on. The girls brought the dirty dishes into the kitchen while the mother started washing. The men were in the waiting stage. I made a plan.

I went into the kitchen and started to help the mother wash dishes. I consider that time as magical when I got to stand with her. That night we all got to know each other a little and the sisters, I think, were shocked to see me standing at the sink. But I think they liked what they saw.

The men still hadn't moved; they were still waiting. I probably didn't endear myself to them when they realized I was washing dishes, but I made headway with the women. Perhaps an unwritten notice should have been placed somewhere in the garage. "Real men don't wash dishes."

Too late.

28

WAIT
Don't Light That Match

I must have done something right that first day with the family. During the dishwashing ceremony, I ended up becoming the chief washer and the mother started drying. I never saw so many dishes in my entire life. There seemed to be no end to them. The sisters kept them coming and I kept washing. I didn't know it at the time, but I had started something that I would become famous for, at least within the *familia*.

Each time one of the girls came by to drop off a dirty dish, they would say something to let me know that I was, "so far, so good." I think I was passing the first test. And Eva with that smile would come over and give me a little rub. This was turning out to be a good night.

By the time we finished and put the dishes back in their right place, it was time to bring out the dishes for dessert. Finally, we were done with the last dish for the night. I was exhausted. Now is the time for all the girls to sit around in the living room and relax. It's also the time for the men to come out of the garage and pass by me in the kitchen without a word being spoken. I think I went over and sat next to

Eva and listened to the chatter. One thing was very clear; the love and warmth this family felt for each other was a direct result of the mother's heart.

After 20 or 30 minutes Eva asked me if I was ready to go. I certainly was. That evening, that day was a lot to swallow at one time. As we got ready to leave, Eva packed the food she was going to take home with her. When these people gather for a birthday or a holiday, there is usually enough food left-over to feed everyone for another week.

We said our good-byes and each and every one of the girls came over to give me a hug or at least to say something like, "I hope you come again."

That's a good thing. At least they didn't wish me luck for whatever I decide to do with my future, or say something like, "Don't mess with my sister."

Eva and I got in the car and headed for her house in the Valley. She did ask me if I had a good time, but for most of the trip she talked about her sisters and her mother and father. I had told her I did have a great time and I wanted to ask her why she and each of the sisters say, "My mother." Never did any one of them say, "Our mother." And to this day it still goes on. I have yet to figure it out.

As I write this part of my experience with my new *familia*, I want to mention the sisters by name. The first born is Leticia and as of this writing she is recovering from surgery to remove a cancer from her body. She is doing well and getting better each day. She has challenged herself by using her illness and the separation from an unhappy marriage to open up her heart. Tisha is a school principal. That first day when I met all the sisters, probably around New Year's 1989, she appeared to me to be the most withdrawn. I had the impression she had a lot of personal issues on her mind, and I was later to see that was indeed the case.

It's very important to pronounce the next sister's name correctly. It's spelled Irma but pronounced Ear-ma. I hope you get it right. If you don't, it's my fault. Now we're talking about the politician in the *familia*. Getting into a discussion about world affairs with Irma requires that you had better have done a little reading and have gotten your facts straight. I remember when we were first introduced, I felt that she was the one who would be the chief interrogator if I were going to be questioned about my intentions. Fortunately, Eva had told me that Irma had at one time given serious thoughts about running for mayor of San Diego. I went into this encounter with the *familia* prepared to listen and learn and certainly not to pretend to know what I didn't know.

The next sister in line was called Petie. She pronounces it Petey. If someone really wanted her attention they called her Patricia. Petie was dressed as if she was trying to turn herself into a fiesta. She had very carefully made sure that when she walked in the door, you knew you were face-to-face with someone who was very comfortable with herself and the way she looked. And if you had any doubts about that, the moment she opened her mouth, all the uncertainty of that thought would disappear. "My way or the highway" could very well be her mantra.

Next in line by age would be Eva, I think. Evita would also be a wonderful name for her. She stood out like the sun in the sky. But it was the sun that shined from within her heart that drew you to her and warmed your life from within.

That warmth caused me and probably everyone else who ever got to spend quality time with her to hope that she wanted to be with you. Where this great fortune to share these years moment by moment with her ever came from, I don't know. I feel very inadequate when it comes to showing her my appreciation and gratitude for this time with her.

I think Dina, Armandina, is probably next in line although again, I'm not sure. The first word that pops into my mind is proper. She just seems so proper. She looks like she eats about the same amount as a canary and has a very striking aristocratic appearance. Dina is a teacher and speaks with that kind of authority although she doesn't speak down to you. If you ask her a question, she'll take the time to give it great attention before she responds. And her response is in as few words as necessary.

Now we come to the athletic one. Marquina. Quina. When I first met her she had one outstanding physical characteristic that got your attention immediately. She had a nose that made me think she could have been the chief of a tribe of Apaches in her last life. I liked it. She has since had it adjusted through plastic surgery. Now, with a body like that of a centerfold and the face of a cover girl, it's doubtful that the first thing that strikes you is her nose. Quina is a nurse specializing in the compassionate delivery of newborns.

And now we get to the baby, Jessica.[7] Also a teacher, she works with the very young at a daycare. I think if you had to leave a child with someone outside your family for the day, it would be your great fortune to have Jessica looking after and taking care of your young one. She has an ever-expanding

---

[7] Rick never mastered the Muñoz sisters' order of birth. The correct order is Leticia, Irma, Armandina, Eva, Patricia, Jessica and Marquina.

heart of concern and protection and of compassion. A child under her care would have an edge on many others as she offers a well-adjusted growth in this society as a beginning to their education.

The men faded into the background when in the company of the girls and their mother. For a while as I got to know the family, I had the impression that the men were second-hand citizens. The women were the foundation of the family, and the men had the opportunity to go along with their plans. Each of the women had a mind of her own, and it appeared that the men either went along with their direction or waited until they returned from completing their intentions. If these quick observations were correct, I knew immediately that it was going to be an interesting ride if marriage was going to be on the schedule.

Watching the family that first time, one thing stood out like a thumb in a pickle jar. The interaction between the girls and their father was nothing like that between them and their mother. With Josefina and the girls, there was no distance from heart to heart. But with the father, Josemaria, it was guarded and polite rather than warm and wanted. It was obvious that the distance had been there for as long as he was around.

I was the new face at the gathering. The father through his manner was doing his best to let me know he was the central figure and the voice of authority. It was clear to me that he wasn't, that it was the mother who guided and protected this wonderful family. I also knew I had better just keep my internal responses to him pretty much to myself. I knew that it wouldn't be too long from then that I was going to have a one-on-one with him. I could smell it coming. And I was so right. It was probably during my third or fourth attendance at one of these *familia* gatherings that he said to me that he wanted to have a serious talk with me.

The fact that Eva and I were falling deeper in love was becoming obvious to everyone. The idea that we might get married was out on the table, and the father was getting a little anxious about my coming into the family. The mother was worried as well. She didn't tell me directly, but she was very concerned about my being 15 years older than Eva. She was worried that I might get sick in my old age and that it would be very difficult for her daughter. When Eva told me of her concerns, I knew that along with the age and health issues, my being a Buddhist wasn't something she had envisioned as her daughter's mate. Raised Catholic, living as a Catholic, thinking as a Catholic, it just didn't sit well that the next newlywed in the *familia* would be a Buddhist. Eva had been a Buddhist for many years, but she didn't let it become a subject of conversation very often. Everyone knew but she kept it pretty much in the closet.

After that first meeting of the *familia*, it was time for Eva and me to go back to her place and turn in for the night. We had just reached the top of the hill on the 405 freeway, headed for Reseda, when I noticed a slightly uncomfortable pain in the pit of my stomach. Eva continued talking about her family as we went along. I was listening intently because I figured the more I knew, the better equipped I would be if there was to be a future for us. The only thing that disturbed my concentration as she went on was that this little pain was beginning to get a little stronger.

By the time we were pulling into the driveway, the pain that had at first gotten very uncomfortable had now started to disappear. By the time we got in bed and were relaxing, it was out of my mind. After about five minutes though, it started coming back. This time it felt as if my stomach was beginning to swell. I lay there thinking that I may have to get up pretty soon and go to the bathroom. Three minutes later and I knew I had to get the hell out of there.

I already loved Eva, but if I was to let this monster laugh its way into the air around the bed, I will bet my last dollar that the chances were good that I wouldn't be sitting here in our home writing this story. But at that point I figured we just didn't know each other well enough to take the chance that I would be back to sleeping in the Festiva that night.

Eva can go to sleep in seven seconds if she wants to. I did nothing to draw attention to the fact that I was getting up. By this time the pit of my stomach felt like a weather balloon that was getting ready to blow up.

I made it down the hall to the bathroom, hoping I could get to the other side of the house or better still the garage. But No. I got to the bath wondering what was coming next. I sat down; the seat was cold. And in a split-second it started. At first it sounded like a whistle. Then a tuba. Then it erupted into the sound and echo of an entire herd of buffalo making their way out of a porcelain canyon. And from that moment on, I began to have one of the most wonderful primal experiences of my very, very narrow life. And it went on and on. After I finally got up on my feet, I took a long walk around the house.

I went outside in my shorts, stood by the pool and took

a minute to look back and wondered what was next. That woman I was with had my heart and she knew it. I knew it too. She had my heart and I was going to go through some serious human revolution in order for this to work. I had to let go of my security blankets, my bad habits, and put my faith to work. Drinking and smoking were real close to the top.

As I stood there in my shorts next to the pool, knowing that Eva was inside in bed, there was not a bone in my body that wished I was somewhere else. This was all new to me. I've always been able to lean on the knowledge that I know how to survive, and that gave me a clear picture of where the door was whenever I wanted to get out of a place or a situation. Standing there by the pool with Eva in the house, all I really wanted to do was go back in there. With a smile that only relief can form, I crawled back in bed.

We got through that night and many more. I moved out of the car and into a loft at a friend's house. Bob and Susie Little and I have known each other for a good many years. Unfortunately, we haven't spent much time together for a while. But I love them. I lived in that loft comfortably until one night shortly after Bob had me take a drink of something that was at least 155 proof. In the middle of the night I rolled out of that loft straight on top of a small table. There's that actual proof again.

I'ze gots-ta stop.

Eva and I talked about moving in together. It was too soon for me, but more importantly, I didn't think that was what I wanted to show the SGI members at that time. Let the members see us together, and later something could change that showed it would be the best thing to do. I'm glad we didn't actually move in together until we got married. I use the word actually because I had been invited to set up residence in her converted garage with kitchen and bath. All we had to do was walk 20 feet to be together.

Another good reason for not moving totally in was the fear of not following through and making a marriage work. As long as I stayed outside, it meant I hadn't made up my mind that I was going to be able to keep the promises of marriage. I needed to make that promise to her and to myself before I could go through with another failure. And I could keep my stash of trash, smoking and drinking, close at hand. I wasn't ready to hang up my habits and I knew they wouldn't be at home in Eva's house.

I had lost my SAG status, couldn't afford to reinstate and hadn't been close to an acting job in a long time. I had promised myself that I would get a job with benefits before I would marry Eva. I kept that promise. I got a job at a now defunct home improvement center called Home Base. I worked as hard as I could to earn the benefits. I stayed on that job for five years and did pretty well as far as doing my best and treating the job with respect. Home Depot was wiping out the company, and I got a chance to be a part of the cutbacks.

I was soooo happy to get out of there. I was going nuts realizing this job was going nowhere and they would soon be out of business. And I thought it was time to take another stab at the film business. That artsy-fartsy part of me was beginning to come up to the front of my mind again. It's very difficult to maintain a happy mind when all you want to accomplish in society is always out of reach. One of the characters, as a part of the series I sculpted, "Just Some of My Friends," was named William Joseph. William Joseph was one of the few white men in town who braided his hair. His dream was to become a blind, black jazz singer. I think I understand this guy. This desire to satisfy the craving for creative fulfillment got my head spinning and out of that I think I just made a web that I caught myself in.

I think it was around that time that I read something President Ikeda said that truly pointed my nose and prayer in the right direction. He said something like, "Master the art of living." Such simple words, but they hit me like a ton of bricks. And at just about that same time someone, I think it was my son, said to me, "Why don't you take that first step again and think about becoming an extra, a background player?"

The wisdom and love of my son has always been there.

I followed this young man's advice and did just that. I registered as a non-union background artist. The first job as an extra became another one of those starting over experiences.

The last acting job I'd had was the film I worked on when I went to Florida. A lot of years passed, and the first background job I got at $40 a day was on a Miller Lite commercial with around 200 other extras. I may be exaggerating a bit, but I think there were two Andy Gumps and one bagel for each of us. By the end of the day I decided I didn't need this crap. But just as I was about to take a hike, a little bird with the sound of my son's voice spoke up.

"I thought you wanted to get back to the film business."

The next day I started work on a Michael Douglas film, "American President." We got the same food and treatment as the stars.

During the lunch break I sat with some of the SAG extras and listened to them bitch and moan about the work, the hours and the food. They were making three times the money I was, and I just listened until I was done eating and couldn't resist saying as I got up with my tray, "Try listening to yourselves. You might just consider the good fortune you have being able to work in film at all. You may be just an extra in this life, but the chances are pretty good that in your last life you were probably nothing but a prop."

The work as an extra provided a wonderful opportunity to watch the making of a movie that I had not examined before. That new POV, or point of view, was wonderful on one hand, but at $40 a day it wasn't enough.

It was time for that encounter with Eva's father, Josemaria. He pulled me off to the side and said he wanted to talk to me. I said OK. I said OK very loudly. Jose is about 99 percent deaf, and he uses it to his advantage. The mother and the girls have probably bought him a dozen hearing aids, but he refuses to use them. I don't know if he disables them intentionally or if they just break in his hard hands, but they stop working pretty soon after he gets one. And then of course he can't find the batteries. There was little or no determination at all for him to get one in working order.

So when he said he wanted to talk to me now; I said, "No, not today. If you want to talk, you'll have to get some batteries first and then we'll talk."

I think I caught him off guard but he said OK. We made a deal to talk the following Sunday.

I was looking forward to this opportunity for the two of us to get to know each other. That Sunday arrived and after everyone who was at the house got comfortable around the table in the garage, Jose and I slipped into the den for the talk.

I think it should be noted that Jose Muñoz is a big man. Not too tall but built like a bull. He was about 66 or 67 years old in 1988 when this talk was to take place, and I was about 47. It was easy to see that this man was tough, and if he decided to take a swing at me and even came close, the wind might make me take a step backwards. He had a hat, a fedora, that made me think of Don Corleone, the Godfather, and he knew it and used it to set himself up in that position.

We sat down on the couch, and he immediately started in by telling me that there was no way for me to ever become a part of his family. He spent the next thirty minutes saying the same thing in as many different ways as he could think of. His daughter had been married before and, according to Jose's Catholicism, she can never marry me because even though she had been divorced for many years in the courts, in his mind there is no such thing as divorce. He went on about that for another ten minutes and then it started to become clear to me that the biggest sin was that I didn't come to him first and let him know what my intentions were.

That was it. I had insulted him to the core of his being because he was the Godfather of the family and, as such, nothing is sanctioned unless he approves of it first. I probably could have kissed his hand or his foot at this point and all would have been forgiven. But his interpretation would be that I had kissed his ass. No way, Jose.

At least 30 minutes had passed, probably 45, before he wound down. He had repeated himself in as many ways as he could, and I think he just couldn't think of any other words to say that would make him any clearer. I waited until the silence became heavy enough to make him uncomfortable and said in as clear a voice as possible, "I want to apologize to you, Mr. Muñoz."

I could see him kind of sit up with that attitude you can get when you reach the conclusion that you have won and are getting the response you want.

"I want to apologize to you for asking you to get those batteries for your hearing aid because you certainly aren't interested in hearing a fucking thing I have to say."

I got up and left the den but turned just as I started out to the garage. He was following me with his eyes and I knew I had his attention. I also found out I had his respect. And from that day on, a love began to blossom between us that just gets better each time we meet. As a matter of fact, the bully of the family has changed his approach to his daughters and wife quite a bit. He's just a little more considerate and a little more giving and a little more gentle with the girls. He still wants to be the Don, but in a much improved way. He's now trying to earn it with a little respect. We also must thank his father for that. His name was Cruz Muñoz.

I got to meet this gentleman when he was hospitalized. He was the real Don of the *familia*. Looking into his eyes, scanning his face as Eva was introducing us, was like seeing an encyclopedia of his life. The details weren't necessary to know that this man had experienced just about every hardship a person could expect. His smile was very warm and welcoming, and I felt the same toward him. Without demands he immediately had my respect.

Some of the other sisters were there to visit him as well,

and listening to them, it didn't take a genius to see how much they loved him. He was The Don in their eyes as well. Soon Eva and I were left alone with him for a few minutes, and I knew I had to let him know how much I loved and respected Eva and that we were planning on getting married in the near future. I don't remember what I said to him, but I do know what I wanted to say. I do remember that I had told Eva that I was going to have to introduce him to chanting. I couldn't pass up the chance. I may never have this opportunity again. He was already in his late 80's.

"Sir, I love Eva with all my heart and I want to spend the rest of my life with her. I need to tell you that I'm not a Catholic nor am I a Christian. I'm a Buddhist and I study and practice the Buddhism of Nichiren Daishonin."

When he heard me say that I chant *Nam-Myoho-Renge-Kyo*, I knew that from that moment on, all formality between us was gone, and we knew we would know each other forever. I didn't want to cause him to tire, so after a few minutes we decided to leave so he could rest. I don't remember what else we might have said, but I was aware that Eva was just a little nervous, waiting for his reaction, as was I.

His response was without hesitation. He said, "That's wonderful. I hope you'll be very happy together."

I did get to see him a couple more times when he attended gatherings at the Muñoz garage. I also saw the interplay between him and his son. Again, I saw he was The Don. And this man played a very important part in Eva's happiness.

The son, Jose, and I were getting along better and better as time passed, and he even began to relax a little about the idea of Eva and I getting married. But there was one important part that he wouldn't budge on: he was not going to attend the wedding. This was tearing Eva apart. She wanted her dad there no matter what. And she chanted her heart out to make it happen, but Jose wouldn't even consider it. The grandfather, Cruz, got wind of his son's' boneheaded mind-set and came to the rescue. He knew his boy's heart and history and knew he just wasn't conducting himself with the greatest wisdom.

Jose had overcome a number of bad habits like his love for booze. He apparently wasn't a pleasant man to be around when he was loaded, and much of his mean-spiritedness would come out toward the girls. They all had issues that kept a distance between them and their father. He also had a bad habit of disappearing for as much as a couple weeks at a time whenever he got a couple bucks in his pocket. He had a love for gambling and whatever. He did return, but no one ever really knew where he was and apparently he didn't offer any information. How Josefina was able to put up with this behavior is still a mystery. But she kept the door open for his return.

When the real Don of the *familia* found out about his son's refusal to attend Eva's wedding, he got him off to the side and with no record of what was being really said, it became clear he gave Jose something to think about. We do know he at least posed a question to him, "What if no one ever gave you a second chance?"

Eva's prayer was answered when both her father and grandfather attended the wedding.

I was a little disappointed with the results from my side of the family. I didn't have any great desire to develop a better relationship, but I had been calling my mother more frequently. The result was that I just didn't want to continue trying. Sometimes it made no sense to me, but I must admit that I was aware of the fact that this was a challenge I had to face if for no other reason than to rid myself of the negative feeling in my heart toward my mother. My desire to experience all that Buddhism offered was stronger than any distaste I had toward her. I needed to truly polish this part of my life. Another interesting part of this exploration of my mind and heart was that I really did begin to care for her happiness. It wasn't the thickest kind of caring in the world, but it was going in that direction.

When I knew for sure that Eva and I were going to go for the gold, I called and let my mother know. Knowing she had many negative feelings toward many different races and cultures, I still wanted her to be there. That was probably the right time to get more serious about changing the space between my mother and me. Another fresh start. I had the drinking, the smoking and my mother. And let's think. Oh, and I was going to get married again.

When I had gone back to my mother's as a teen and went back to school in the 11th grade, I remember walking down the sidewalk with her when she noticed a man coming toward us whose hair was braided. He was wearing a hat and a long coat, and it was easy to identify him as a man of the Jewish faith. She waited until he had just gone past us before she spit out, "matzo ball." My mother had a disgusting way of spitting out slanderous words through her teeth. She always had something negative to say about anyone who didn't meet her standards. And here I was marrying a Mexican.

Of course, she didn't come to the wedding. Later she told

me that she had forgotten. Still later, she let it slip that she had gone to Vegas with a busload of seniors from her mobile home park association. I'm sure she wasn't the winner on that weekend.

My son and daughter were there and although I don't know exactly what was going on with all the ladies, I'm sure Kelli was right there in the mix. I do know Andy and I were having a great time trying to help each other get dressed and tie the ties. He is one great kid and now a great man.

The wedding was wonderful and Eva was so serious during the Buddhist ceremony that she scared me. I thought she might be thinking about finding a hole under the altar and sneaking out of there somehow. Maybe she was just becoming aware of what the hell she was doing. She made it, didn't run, and I'm a very fortunate man to have been brought together with her. I have no doubts that the coupling of the two of us was an extension of our sincere prayers and commitment to do all we could to help this faith gain a foothold in the world's population. We share a great mission together and are still, after 20 years, more committed to each other and to our faith than ever before. It's an amazing thing to be human and to find love with another. Some people love golf balls more than they care for people.

We had invited Mr. Kikumura to the wedding, and we asked him to say a few words.

He said something like, "If they had asked me to say something before the ceremony, I would have probably said something like, get outta here before it's too late. But since I'm saying a few words after the ceremony has been completed and it's all finished and legal now, I'll just say the same thing. It's too late."

The reception took place at Eva's house. I had already moved in and the party began. Eva was in her element, and when she wants to loosen up and party, she knows exactly how to go about it. I was recently looking at our picture album of that shindig, and it brought back a lot of wonderful memories. It also made me realize that I didn't share my appreciation very well for all the effort of so many friends from our relationships with members of SGI, *familia* and just good friends. I think a lot of people worked their butts off putting this together and keeping it going. There are too many to name here, but I'm going to make it a point to express that appreciation again whenever I have the chance.

Within three years of our marriage, each of the drinking, smoking and mother problems I mentioned came to a head. Within a couple months after getting married, Eva and I moved to a very unusual, charming, small house up in the hills behind a golf course. It was a wonderful experience to drive home to this place after facing the world of Los Angeles for the day. We could head to the hills with the feeling that we had just separated ourselves from the concrete life and were going to spend the night in the country just a stone's throw from the dirt road part of Mulholland Highway off Topanga Canyon.

It's time to move on again. This time I will leave nothing behind. This time I won't be running from a past I hated but toward a world I wanted to create. Now was the time for me to become the change. I wanted to upgrade my life from someone who could clown or detour or hide his life behind anger or even the fear of failing. It's not unlike coming out of a closet. Inside, I knew there was a different me than the one I didn't like. That other character and person who poked out of my heart on occasion was someone I wanted to bring to the surface and put to work for the sake of my family and for the sake of humanity. I think this is when my human revolution really began.

29

TWO CANCERS

After more than 40 years of practicing and studying this Buddhism and participating as a member and leader in the SGI-USA, I hear some people refer to me as a pioneer. Not me. A junior pioneer? Maybe. I have known too many real pioneers to ever call myself one. I don't think I'll ever be able to repay my gratitude for these amazing true pioneers of American Kosen-rufu—world peace through individual happiness. I do know that I never want to stop trying. Without the Gohonzon, the Gosho and President Daisaku Ikeda, I truly believe I wouldn't be alive today. The Gohonzon is the scroll inscribed with Chinese and Sanskrit characters— the link between the Buddha state within ourselves and in the environment. The Gosho is the individual and collected honorable writings of Nichiren. Daisaku Ikeda is president of SGI, a Buddhist leader, peace builder, prolific writer, poet, and educator. Those true pioneers steered me toward this Buddhism. To name one or two of them would be unfair to all. Let me just say, "Thank you," and promise to do my best to inherit the Spirit of Soka, or value creation, and share it with as many as possible throughout my life.

On August 2, 2006, I found out that I had non-Hodgkin's Lymphoma and it was very aggressive. By August of 2007, after 21 treatments of chemotherapy and a stem cell transplant, I was cancer free. I describe my encounter with non-Hodgkin's Lymphoma in more detail later in this story. My experience was published in the January 1, 2008 issue of the World Tribune, the SGI-USA weekly newspaper. From August, 2007, to August, 2008, I was challenged daily with the recovery from all the treatments as well as the side effects that go along with the journey to get back to being able to participate regularly in SGI activities. Thanks again to the training I received throughout my practice and the good habits of faith, practice and study, by August, 2008, I was ready to do a lot more physically.

Although the chemotherapy and stem cell transplant had made me free of the lymphoma, my one-year checkup revealed that a new cancer had formed in my left lung. Lung cancer. I wasn't surprised. I had started smoking and drinking by the time I was 8 years old. I stopped both of those habits in the early 1990's. During my first encounter with cancer I made a determination to clear out all my negative health karma if I was going to extend my life for Kosen-rufu (World Peace). The lung cancer was my prayer being answered.

During all this time President Ikeda's guidance and lectures on letters written by Nichiren Daishonin, kept the fires of my faith growing—"On Attaining Buddhahood In This Lifetime," "The Opening of the Eyes," "The Heritage of the Ultimate Law of Life," "The Drum at the Gate of Thunder" and "On Prolonging One's Life Span." Each of these lectures just reached out to my heart and asked me to open the treasure in my life more and more each day. "Reply to Sairen-bo." I couldn't get enough. Again I prayed like I was trying to get that blood out of a rock. I wanted to have every cell of my life reveal the wonder of these teachings of Nichiren. To share these treasures in my heart is my greatest desire. Again, it is with my deepest gratitude to the Pioneers of SGI-USA who took the time to help me overcome the limitations I placed on myself. Although I have been striving to live the oneness of mentor and disciple, teacher and student, for some time now, it was when first I got cancer that all the efforts of practice and study came to the forefront as my greatest benefit yet.

A couple of months after my lung cancer was detected, we took more scans and found the spot was growing. A biopsy determined that surgery was necessary as soon as possible. On November 10, 2008, I had surgery to remove the new cancer along with over 22 percent of my lung. That was on a Monday. The following Thursday evening, I slept in my own bed. I had again been declared cancer free.

The real benefit of this entire adventure is what is in my heart. I can't wait for the next lecture. In the meantime I read the latest over and over—"Hell Is the Land of Tranquil Light" and "On the Buddha's Prophecy." The order and the clarity these lectures give to the teachings of Nichiren amaze me. My life is filled with good fortune. My greatest good fortune is to continue on this incredible journey of practice and study.

When I first started to practice and heard members talk

about President Ikeda, I became very concerned. I was very reluctant to let any individual have a way into my life. It was the warmth and sincerity of these wonderful pioneers that kept me on the right track. They would show me their trust in President Ikeda's guidance through their behavior and would share his words with me. They encouraged me to pray and read and see how the humanism of his direction and guidance was all for my benefit and growth. Mentor and disciple began to take on new meaning as I started to chant to apply the guidance to my own life.

Over the years, the accumulation of experience and reward of this Buddhism is beyond anything I could have ever expected. The fortune and the treasures I have in my heart are beyond words. The faith I have in the Gohonzon through all these years just keeps growing. President Ikeda is guiding me through my life.

And I have Eva, the most wonderful woman in the world, as my wife and partner. Living with her is like living with a poem. Our hearts are as one. United together forever. One of these great pioneers told us, "Don't spend too much time looking at each other. Hold hands and face in the same direction together." We are putting that wisdom into practice. Each day we face the Gohonzon together and study the guidance of President Ikeda. With her prayers, her heart and a smile that could make the sun squint, she insisted that I get well. Just how fortunate am I?

Once more, "Thank you." I will spend the rest of time repaying my gratitude to Nichiren Daishonin, President Ikeda, my *familia*, and the pioneers and members of SGI-USA.

30

WHAT'S NEXT?

For most all of my life, I've been looking outside myself
for whatever my needs or wishes were. If I wasn't looking
for what I needed to get through the day and night, I was
at least keeping one eye open for anyone who might try to
get in my way. When I began my exploration of Buddhism,
I approached it with the same mind. I approached it with
excitement and curiosity about the way the universe works
and how I fit into this unexplored wilderness of my spirit.
My approach was as selfish as it could be. I approached it
defensively as well as with curiosity and wonderment. Trust
is not something I had a lot of experience with. I didn't know
how to put expectation on someone other than myself. I
didn't know how to trust that what someone was saying was
the truth. I had to find out for myself. And at the same time,
I didn't see myself as someone anyone else should have much
faith or expectation in as well. I was very comfortable within
my solitary self.

By the time I met Eva, I had 20 years of chanting and
studying Nichiren Buddhism behind me, but I still had

that tendency to look for something conspicuous to happen or appear. The fact that I had been drawn into her world and she into mine was more proof that prayers were being answered. I just didn't realize how thoroughly, how deeply, those prayers were affecting my inner life. Now I had to make a greater effort to awaken the inconspicuous results that I needed to come into play in my life.

It is only due to the collective benefit of our faith and practice that we were able to make it through the first five years of our marriage. We both wanted it to work but the process of change wasn't easy. It's better when Eva speaks for herself, but from my vantage point it became clear that if I didn't change my habits, there was no way she was going to live out her life with someone like me. No matter how much we loved each other, it didn't make any sense to continue on that level without my doing my best to climb out from under the negative weights that were keeping me from challenging those habits. And it was extremely clear that Eva wasn't going to let me get away with my bullshit. The walls had to come down.

It's April, 2010. Today I'm writing about twenty years ago. When I started this writing in September of 2008, I was looking back at what was going on in my life more than 60 years ago. It seems that it was easier to think back to those days than to write about things that happened just twenty years ago. Recently, I got the news that my son's marriage had fallen apart and his wife of just one year had already filed for divorce. My daughter hasn't found her mate either. It doesn't make much sense to go out buying baseballs or dolls or a pony for the "little ones" yet.

When I started writing this adventure of my life, I had it in my mind that I would leave some kind of record for my grandchildren to read at some time in their lives. I knew that I might not live long enough to meet them in person, but this way they would know a little something about Grandpa from Grandpa. Now there has been an extension added to the drama. Perhaps the possibility of "never" has arrived. Something tells me not to give up. I never got to know my grandfather and he never left me a note, so I'll just go on, thank you.

Eva and I were struggling to make this marriage work. I was still at Home Base and had worked my way up to a management position. The drinking was getting more out of hand and I was becoming very angry with myself. The phone rang and I answered.

"Dad, can I come live with you. I need to start over."

It was my daughter.

"Of course".

No matter what I might have been going through with my personal problems, her problems were my problems. And there was nothing I wouldn't do for this child who was now graduated from high school and needed to start her life over. This little girl meant everything to me. With her birth, she caused the awareness of a before unknown part of me to appear from inside my heart. Of course she could come live with us.

Us.

I neglected to discuss this with my wife. I didn't hesitate to respond to Kelli's need, but I didn't even take the time to consider my wife's feelings or thoughts. Not the smartest move when you're trying to solidify a wobbly foundation in a marriage. When I broke the news to Eva, she didn't reveal a moment's hesitation. That response is a perfect example of the depth of her heart. I think it also shows how much she thought of me.

It wasn't long after that when Kelli arrived in her U-Haul, looking like she had been through the mill. When Kelli moved in with us she was almost untouchable, unreachable. This girl had been through enough to make your hair stand on end. I didn't have to know more than that she was extremely unhappy. I was afraid for her. I was afraid she would do something to herself that would take a long time to heal.

When I would put out my arms for a hug, I sensed a deep restriction concerning me coming into her territory. I felt that I was trespassing. I know this feeling very well. Almost any effort to talk with her, to get her to open up, went by the wayside. I was lost as to what to do until I woke up to the realization that I had to depend entirely on prayer. Again, prayer is the way. Prayer can't be refused.

I knew Lynn's marriage wasn't a good one, but there was little I could do to help. She had given up her practice and was starting her exploration of Christianity. I wasn't surprised, just disappointed. What I didn't know was that Kelli and Andy were not part of what Lynn's husband had in mind when he met her and their attraction began.

There may have been a lot of disappointment in Lynn's heart when it became evident to her that she could no longer continue with our marriage. And when she remarried I think she turned her disappointment in me into a determination that this new marriage was going to work "no matter what."

Unfortunately, after a lot of effort on her part, it had to end in divorce.

Neither Kelli nor her brother were protected from Lynn's husband. He was abusive towards them, and they had to experience that. They needed love and guidance from their parents and it didn't happen. They began to find kinship outside of their home. As their father, I am able to understand their suffering because I experienced many of the same feelings at that same age. It bothers me that I didn't know what was going on in San Jose. Perhaps I could have done something. But I didn't know and I didn't do anything. That might have been a little bit of a benefit because if I had of known, I might have hurt someone. I haven't felt rage since I began chanting, nor have I been in a fight. But I would hate to be the one to get me pissed off, let alone angry.

I didn't know much about anything. But as I deal with what I know and see now, it's all been for the good. Andy moved down here about a year later and immediately got himself situated. I only got to see him when we were surrounded by family or in some other type of social situation. One fine day, I showed up at his apartment unannounced. He took one look at me and started jumping around like a fish that just got hooked. He started running around his place trying his best to gather up and hide the empty beer cans and bottles and all the other paraphernalia he would never want his father to see.

This young man ended up coming pretty close to the point of no return with the drinking and drug use, but on his own, got himself some help. He also became very skilled as an actor and became a winner in society. I think I'll just shut up and let him tell you his story.

Kelli also got herself caught in a net of some pretty bad habits, but today she is a mindblower. She is one hell of a woman who has taken charge of her life and has built a solid foundation of both heart and mind. On top of that, she's worked as hard as anyone I know. When she accepted the challenge to educate herself in the healing art of Chinese Acupuncture, I held my breath and prayed with a hope that came from every cell of my body.

Every day I would watch her attack the study of her chosen art as she spelled everything out in Chinese with her dry chalkboard. The books, the classes, the driving, the expectation when tested—all this while holding down a full-time job. She had to not only be able to master the Chinese language of her medicine and the herbal pharmacy, she also had to be able to sync it up to English terminology and anatomy. To watch this beautiful young woman develop her life has been one of my greatest wishes fulfilled.

My drinking problem was foremost on my mind and had been for about two years. With the arrival of Kelli it became obvious that she was very angry with me for many things, and the fact that she saw me as a drunk didn't help make our relationship a very pleasant one. The prayer was there, but my lack of effort betrayed the determination. Each and every day for two years I made a fresh determination to not drink that day, and each and every day I went back on my word. And I knew the tough love was right around the corner. Surrounding me were two determined and powerful women who were not going to be satisfied until I got off the booze. What's a drunk to do?

By then I had gotten to where I was able to have at least a pint or more at night after activities. I couldn't afford to drink out at a bar very often, but I was able to get that bottle at night and get ready for sleep. I think I remember that I had two full pints the night the tough love arrived by messenger.

I don't know how many innings I had listened to, but the Dodgers were playing on the car radio and I was sitting on the top of a hill on Mulholland Drive. I had the vodka with me as Vin Scully and I watched the Dodgers on the radio together.

The next thing I remember, I was lying on the road looking straight up at the face of a man looking down from the passenger window of a Cal Trans truck asking me if I was okay. I think I must have said yes and pushed myself out from under the truck. Either it had run over me while I was lying in the middle of Mulholland, or they had knocked me down first, and then had run over me. I have no way of knowing. I made it back to my car, got it started and began the 100-yard roll down the hill to our house. As I pulled into the driveway an LAPD patrol car pulled up behind me, and I was busted. Since her stay with us, Kelli had become as fed up with my drinking as Eva. I don't know her exact words but Kelli said something like, "Take him."

I'm not sure if Eva chimed in, but she didn't offer any resistance to what the officers wanted to do. They took me. On the way out of our canyon-hunting lodge, (they dried out the deer downstairs), the officers got lost. I helped them find their way out and when we got to the station, they booked me and had already made up their mind that I was of no harm to anyone but myself. They told me that someone had called to alert them that a man was drunk on Mulholland. They were very thoughtful when they spoke to me. They had seen way too many people go down this path, and they were very strict. At the same time, they showed great concern when they spoke to me about the future of my family and me if I didn't do something about the problem soon. After a couple of hours, they let me go. I called Eva to ask her to come and get me.

"Why?"

"They released me."

"Why?"

She didn't believe they had let me go but finally came and got me. I was so glad to be home. I had to sleep. Waking up became a whole different matter. The truck had run over my left foot and right thigh. It could have just as easily run over my head. It took some time before I was able to be comfortable on those legs. That was tough love at its best. It wasn't my last day of having a drink, but it was near. And it did happen. I did quit drinking. And it wasn't long before I saw the benefit. Things started to be clearer, especially in the study of Nichiren's writings and President Ikeda's words.

During that two-year period when I knew the drinking was drinking me, I think that one of the reasons I didn't quit sooner was the fear that I was going to lose a part of my character and personality, that I wouldn't be able to know and like the new me. It was that one great thick blanket of familiarity and comfort that I had draped around my life for so long. If I lost it, I felt I would be exposed to the bones and there would be nothing left for me to offer to anyone. I was afraid I would lose my creativity and at the same time reveal an empty shell of a self that no one would want to spend any time with. Perhaps I only liked myself when my real self was buried under the influence of booze. And that was my great lack of faith in myself.

Now I feel very clearly the effect of exorcising that poison from my life. Although I would have benefited from not drinking far earlier in my life, today I find that my experience gives me a great advantage when listening to others tell me about their various addictions. I really know what they're talking about. I can get into their shoes with them and confidently tell them that I know the way out of that hell.

Next on the agenda was my mother.

The problems with my mother were no longer center stage in my life. I knew where she was. She knew where I was...that was enough. I just didn't have the feeling of wanting anything more. I had decided long ago not to expect anything from my mother. It's very difficult to feel appreciation when that appreciation isn't there. I knew this wasn't a healthy way to be, but I was spending a lot of time each day of my life trying to help others get out of their personal hell, and I didn't take a lot of time working on the hell that she and I shared.

At the same time, I couldn't get her out of my prayers. In one way or another she was always on my mind. I knew that it was time to get this monkey off my back and turn it around. This was going to require an in-depth internal journey to find the compassion this Buddhism suggested I aspire to. I could cry at the drop of a hat toward a horse or maybe even a stranger, but I never shed a tear for my mother. I had been going on quite a few of those internal journeys lately, and this one was going to be one of the most important trips I would ever make.

The most interesting part of the path I went along was the undeniable existence of the apple that fell from the tree. Many of the same things about my mother that I couldn't stand were stuck like glue to the sides of my own nature. As the sincerity and depth of my prayer multiplied, so those character traits in me began to emerge. My good fortune of being a leader in the SGI and doing my best gave me many experiences that let me know that I would experience good and beauty and happiness from this encounter, and so would my mother.

I had been reaching out to her for some time, not a lot but every so often. It wasn't the most important thing on my mind, but I did reach out. She never reached out. I was beginning to experience a little something from inside as I prayed to change this ongoing tug of war with her when I came up with what I thought was a great idea.

The December before the January 17, 1994, Northridge Earthquake hit in the San Fernando Valley, I called my mother after talking it over with Eva, to ask her if she wanted to come for Christmas. This would also mean that she might be able to meet my new *familia*. There was a little pause on her part, but everything was fine. She'd think about it.

When it was time for us to say good-bye and just before I hung up, I think I said, "I'll call soon. So long. I love you."

A deadly pause. Then in a voice that sounded like a toilet gargling, "Don't ever call me again."

BANG!

She slammed the phone down and that was that. That

was the end as far as I was concerned. It was over, that was it, no more. Didn't need that. It was over!

I wish.

OK, skip to January 17, and the quake hit hard. I called my mother as soon as possible to tell her that her two grand-children were okay. The moment she recognized my voice she slammed the phone again. BANG! That was enough. I didn't need that. I didn't want that. I just had to keep going. For the next couple of years we didn't speak. Those are the times when only daimoku—chanting—and prayer can be used to change the course of a stampeding herd of buffalo before it hurts someone.

When I called again, she answered and didn't bang the phone down. We ended up having a pretty decent conversation. My mother was beginning to suffer from macular degeneration, a condition that impairs vision and can lead to blindness. We started to talk more often as I would call her after she had an appointment with the doctor. So we got along a little better and a little more civilized. I began to visit her every couple of months. I could feel it in my prayer that everything was turning around. One year, she sent me a birthday card and signed it "LOVE, Mother." We won. I don't want you to think everything was perfect from then on. She never lost her mean streak, but she was much easier to be around.

My children had stayed with my mother for a week during the summer when they were around 13 or 14. No sooner were they in the car after I picked them up when Andy said, "I don't believe she's your mother."

The anger in Kelli was close to going off. She could have

exploded in holding back her feelings. I think Kelli and Andy found something they agreed on. They would never be dumped off on my mother again.

Much later, as a family, Eva, Kelli, Andrew and I visited my mother in the hospital once when she was admitted for a procedure. During that visit, it was as if we were talking with the sweetest elderly lady in the place. She was warm, kind, gentle, and totally open. It didn't dawn on me that nothing had really changed until the next time I visited her at her home. She was back. Just as ornery as she could get. And then I got it. It was the morphine. I bet she loved that morphine.

When I got sick with cancer, it was at the same time that my mother's life force really began to wane. She had spent most of her life after retiring from the Aerospace race living in a mobile home. And as it became apparent to the other members of her park that she needed some care, they stepped up and took care of her. The prime move was when she was placed in a nursing home as she got weaker.

My illness made it impossible for me to visit her, but it would have been nice to say good-bye. One neighbor, who was there for my mother as she was admitted to the hospital, told me later that one of the last things my mother said to her was, "I know my son loves me and he chants *Nam-Myo-ho-Renge-Kyo* for me every day."

I do. My mother truly was and is one of the greatest treasures of my life. Thank you, Mom. Hope that doesn't get her mad.

I'm looking forward to the next life and time when my mother and I meet. I wonder what our physical appearances will be. It really doesn't matter; we will find each other one way or another. It's our karma. I do know she had a side to her that was loving and caring and wanting to be a good influence on some people's lives, but she had a mean way of going about it. I want to somehow lead her to this Buddhism and let her experience the other side of the fence. She has been unhappy with herself for too long. I want to introduce this Buddhism to all my ancestors. It's my mother who helped me want to even wonder about the rest of the people I have as ancestors, and it's Nichiren Buddhism that has taught me to not just think of my family, but to think of all the families of the world. Each and every one of us has this incredible life condition of a Buddha within us. Why not share it with all the people?

I have got to thank my mother and share this Buddhism with her. If my life with her had happened any other way, I would have never found or even considered a spiritual life. How do you repay your debt of gratitude for that? I think I must just keep trying.

· · · · · · · · · · · ·

The Los Angeles Equestrian Center has been my home away from home many times. Sometimes I just had to go down there to smell the world. I like to go from stall to stall and say hello. A lot of wonderful memories come to me when I think about that place. Every once in a while, a trip down there still becomes almost a necessity. I can feel one coming now.

I have an ego and pride like everyone else. One thing I prided myself on was the ability to do just about anything athletically and that I very seldom got sick. I've done some pretty crazy things in my life, and I've never treated my body with respect. The drinking, the smoking and just the general wear and tear on my body started to show its ugly head one day in 1998 while I was at the Equestrian Center.

I wanted to write two letters that day, and I wanted to be near some horses at the same time. The first letter was to Robert Redford. I had just read The Horse Whisperer and I decided I would be perfect to play the lead character's brother in the film version that he was going to direct. The other letter was to Roy Rogers. It was time to say thank you. I remember writing that I thought it was time for his life story to be put on film and even suggested the country-western singer Clint Black to play him. Black's wife Lisa Hartman would be perfect as Dale Evans. I told him that I would like the part of Trigger, but I wasn't sure my legs would hold up. As I was writing the second letter, I suddenly felt as if the flu had flown into my body. I started to feel really sick and quickly decided to get in the car and head home. Whatever this was, it was coming on fast.

I was driving Eva's Toyota Supra. By the time I got in the car, my left foot started to go numb. The next bit of news was that I needed to get gas. I got to the nearest station and after having decided that I was going to put $20 worth in the tank, I changed my mind when I noticed my left hand was beginning to go as well. I decided that it didn't make sense to fill up. I might not make it home, so I got $2 worth instead. Why waste all that gas? I got out of the car to pay and I fell down. That left leg was dead to the world. The right one was still good so I got up and hopped my way in to the cashier.

Hopped back out, pumped the gas, and headed for home.

I think that Eva, deep in her heart, had a hidden desire to be a racecar driver. She loved to shift the gears of that Supra. And she loved to put the pedal to the metal on occasion. But with a numb leg, a hand and arm that isn't working very well, shifting this thing became an arcade type of game. Once I got the car on the freeway, I began to chant only to find that half my face was no longer cooperating. I kept chanting but I sounded like a man who had just put away a fifth of Johnny Walker Black in the last couple of minutes.

I made it to the house, pulled into the driveway, got out and hopped to the front door. Once inside, the first thing I did was to make my way to my altar and chant. That is where I wanted to be. The fact that I got there was everything.

I have no idea how long I chanted or how long I was in the house, but when Kelli got home from work and saw what kind of shape I was in, she let out with a few words I hadn't heard before and let me know in no uncertain terms that she was calling 911. I got her to wait by telling her I wanted to do my evening prayers before I figured out what to do next. I needed that time.

By the time I was finished, there was a slight change in the numbness. First, it seemed that there was a little more feeling in my facial muscles. The hand and arm were also becoming a little mobile. The leg was taking a longer time to shake it off. By the time Eva came home that night I had a good limp but other than that, I didn't show many telltale signs. So I told my wife I had a groin pull. I don't know how I did it, but I had convinced Kelli not to say anything to Eva and that it would give me an opportunity to see what I should or needed to do. Of course I didn't do much except begin to chant a little more seriously about health.

Another big concern was that I had been set to do a commercial for Globe Insurance in five days after that minor stroke. I waited until the next day before being assured, in my mind, that I would be able to pull it off without jeopardizing the production. Added to the situation was that I had to speak for a full 60 seconds on camera as the insurance company's spokesman. I needed the money and it was a buy-out agreement...cash—$3,000. I chanted as if it was my last day on earth for my mouth and lips to work. I made it. But I don't think I learned my lesson. The shoot went well and no one on the production was any the wiser. Including me.

About a year and a half later, I was in our house when I noticed that one of my eyes was closing to the half way mark while I was chanting and would remain like that for a couple of minutes before going back to normal. It was as if someone had lowered a curtain causing me to not be able to see out of that eye. That happened a couple of more times and then one day my eyes decided to cross. OK, that was enough. I found a good doctor and he surgically cleaned out my right carotid artery. That was 1998. When he described the procedure and what it entailed, I told him that I was concerned about the scar that was going to be at least six inches long on my neck. I told him that it could hurt my chances of getting an acting job.

He said, "Don't worry. You're an old actor. I'll put the scar in one of your big old wrinkles and no one will notice."

Everything was fine after that. Somehow Eva didn't find out about the first little stroke until about the time of the surgery for the second experience when the eye closures forced me to go to the doctor again. I didn't want to worry her. It's not easy for me to share when things aren't going as expected.

Skip to May, 2006. I was driving on the freeway going to Palmdale when the other eye started to shut again. I chanted and it went back to being able to see out of it in a couple of minutes. I was going to an SGI meeting and I decided to continue. The meeting went well, I thought. On the way home, the eye closed again and that's when I called the same doctor again. Another surgery to clear out the second carotid artery, hoping that it would be the last of the repair work needed on this used body of mine. Maybe not.

For a couple of months before that, I noticed that I didn't have the energy I used to have. I was slowing down. I was close to 65 and maybe that was to be expected. That second surgery didn't do what I had hoped. I had expected to feel better and have more energy, but my vitality level continued to wane. At first I thought it was my body telling me to take time to smell the roses. I was always running out to one meeting after another and didn't take time to relax. My wife was also very busy with her work and activities. We tried our best to keep Wednesday evenings for our date night. Wild Wicked Western Wednesdays. That was our day.

The slowing down of my system got to the point where I began to think there was a little more going on than just aging quickly. I had filmed the commercial where I rode a BMW 1150 through that imaginary Ethiopian desert just outside of Palmdale a couple months before and noticed that I had a difficult time recovering my energy from what had been a very draining experience. Didn't think too much about it, but now with the sluggishness and even with the walking slower, I figured it was time to have a physical. I made an appointment at the Motion Picture Hospital for an exam.

Strangely, it was right after making that appointment that the waning of my life force picked up its downhill speed. I was really beginning to feel the body begin to give up on me. Physically, I didn't recognize myself. Never before had I not been able to leap on a horse, ride a bike or fall from a tall building. I had never experienced the thought that I couldn't do anything athletically if I put my mind to it. But now I was worried about blowing my nose. I figured I'd probably drop the Kleenex.

My agent, Heel—great name for an agent—called me to go on a callback for a FedEx commercial that would film in New York in a couple of days. I got dressed in my best suit and headed out the door. By the time I parked my car in Santa Monica, I was exhausted. Then I found I couldn't make my way half a block down the street without sitting down. There was a set of stairs I had to climb to get up to the casting office, and it could have been a mountain as far as I was concerned. I got up there, and why I even went in for the session I don't know. But I did and I was a mess.

By the time I got back in my car and headed home, I could think of nothing other than wondering if I was going to make it through the day. Chanting while driving had been a habit I started when I was a new member. I don't recall it being any more sincere than it was that day. I think I chanted my way home just as I had when that first mini stroke hit me at the Equestrian Center.

When my wife came home from work and took a look at me, we both sat and cried. We knew this was it, and I had to go to the hospital.

Eva called my son and my daughter, and they got me there. I honestly have very little memory of the events over the next three days and have to rely on my family for details. I was told that the Motion Picture Hospital didn't think they could give me the care I needed because they didn't have an intensive care unit. They sent me to a nearby hospital in West Hills. It apparently took three days to determine that I had a very rare, possibly deadly, blood disease called listeriosis. During the time spent testing to find out what was wrong with me, I understand they almost lost me a couple of times. In the meantime, it also became clear that with all the tests they had conducted, I had non-Hodgkin's Lymphoma. They started me on a diet of chemotherapy. Unfortunately, a bone marrow biopsy had not been performed and they gave me the wrong chemo. It was like being hit by an 18-wheeler head on.

31

THERE IS NO END

... So Far

Buddhism is about winning. It's about taking each and every incident in life, whether positive or negative, and turning it in the direction of good, value and beauty. From the beginning of my practice I have heard this and have experienced it on many levels, but never did I have to go so far into the depths of my life to prove it to be true.

As I discussed in an earlier chapter, I entered the hospital on July 26, 2006. Talk about getting in rhythm with the universe. On July 1, 2006, my insurance through the Screen Actors Guild was elevated to Plan 1, and now I had this protection for the rest of my life without a chance of it being dropped for any reason, even if I don't work another day. On August 1, 2006, my Medicare coverage began. One day later, on August 2nd, we were told that I had cancer, and the very next day my wife handed me a copy of our monthly SGI-USA magazine, "Living Buddhism," that contained the first installment of President Ikeda's lecture, "On Attaining Buddhahood In This Lifetime."

There is nothing in this world that will ever convince me

that my receiving that lecture from President Ikeda, on that day, was anything other than a result of my consistent chanting, prayers, study and efforts to help others practice and study. That lecture was a letter from President Ikeda to me. In the clearest way possible, he was saying to me that I didn't have to die from this cancer. He made it clear that Nichiren Daishonin's Buddhism had all the power I needed to release all the power from within me that I would need to win. And I believed him. I knew it was true. And I decided I would prove that these words of the law of the universe were true. Now all I had to do was do it. I was in the rhythm to be a winner.

As all this unfolded, I woke up to realize I already had the greatest fortune in the world. I had my wife with me, I had my children with me and I had President Ikeda with me in my heart. I had the prayers of many members of the SGI. And I had a multitude of experiences to show me the greatness of this Buddhism. How I'll ever be able to repay my debt of gratitude, I don't know, but what I do know is how and where to begin. And it's right here, wherever I am and whatever I'm doing.

I vow to carry out this practice—"At all times I think to myself: How can I cause living beings to gain entry into the unsurpassed way and quickly acquire the body of a Buddha?"

This is all I want to do. Living and practicing this Buddhism opens up the possibility of unlimited potential. And it is not only my aim to experience this limitlessness for myself, but I want to influence as many people as possible to strive to do the same. In particular, I want to be an indestructible pillar of support to the young people of SGI.

The SGI is a remarkable organization. Everything about

it is of one mind. Its total purpose is to provide an environment where people can be introduced to Nichiren Buddhism, to be available to help with questions, make available the entirety of Nichiren's writings and provide a forum to facilitate discussions. And it's the people who do all this. You can't get the people to continue a practice like this if the religion isn't producing results. The theory is enlightening on its own. The history and documentation is recorded and available, but it's the actual proof, the actual facts, that are the clincher. Without results, it's just words.

I also had a lot of the results of the negative baggage I had accumulated over my travels in this lifetime as well as those that I brought with me when I entered this world. As I began this encounter with all these health issues, I had the distinct feeling that I just might be getting to the bottom of this negative baggage I carried into this life plus the karma I had created in the last 60-some years. Long ago I had to learn about the law of cause and effect. It was my past causes that were coming to the surface. Believe me when I tell you that there is a great freedom in not blaming others for what occurs in my life. It actually gave me more strength to fight to win by not splitting my mind into putting responsibility for my survival on someone else. As I later told one doctor, "I'm not putting my life in your hands. I think we need to partner and multiply our opportunities."

I had a big chunk of karma to work out, but this piece of it was a complete surprise. I think it must have been one hell of a life I had led at some time, somewhere, that would present itself this way and at this time. For quite a while before all this illness hit the fan, I had been thinking a lot about what I must have done to end up coming into this world with my mother, my father and the life I had lived. It's hard to pin down all the many details, but it seemed clear that I had obviously been very abusive to someone, somewhere, sometime.

Nichiren Daishonin had written a letter to three of his disciples titled, "Lessening One's Karmic Retribution." I experienced the truth of that letter over the next couple months at a level that I hadn't planned on, but because of my experiences of practice and study as a member of SGI over the years, I was a lot more prepared for this emergency than I knew. There is a lot that happened that I missed because of the medications I was given, but there's a lot that I remember very clearly.

As I'm getting closer and closer to coming up to the present as I write, I find that I'm changing my approach to this story, and I'm enjoying it. It's a good thing that I'm not writing this letter for anyone other my grandchildren. That's not true, is it? I hope this time spent that has been so good and so valuable for me will somehow be instrumental in helping others help themselves.

I lived to leave this hospital in the West Valley. I do have to say that there was a lot that happened that didn't have to happen, and it's clear that human error was the constant. I don't think the errors were intentional but were made by not thinking, not paying attention—by the hospital making its first priority the business of being a hospital, not the welfare of the patients. That's how I saw it. First and foremost, the heart of compassion should motivate a healer of any type. The one thing that stood out like a rusty nail was the disrespect for the profession of healing. But they didn't miss a beat when it came to the billing. I got invoices from doctors I never met.

One of the things that got to me while I was at this hospital was that the doctors don't listen. They depended on their intellectual knowledge to treat me but didn't take the time to listen. I felt that no one knows better than I how I feel. I wasn't pretending to be a doctor, but I felt it was very important to express what was going on with me. They didn't have the time. The patients on my floor were as if on a Lazy Susan, and the parade of doctors had only so much time to spend before they had to move on. It's contrary to the communication needed to foster the relationship between the healer and the subject to be healed. It must be as much of a partnership as possible.

I ended up spending more than three months not being able to sit up in bed. I couldn't lie on either my back or stomach. I could only lie on one side or another. No one checked to see if I had been turned. I developed a bedsore that turned into an ulcer about the size of a half dollar on my butt. I would think someone would have caught that before it happened, but no.

Without a bone marrow check and other tests, they made a big mistake when they gave me the wrong chemo. It caused my kidneys to shut down and within eight days I went from 169 to 199 pounds—a 30-pound gain! By the time I left that hospital I was down to 128. My heart function went down to a 20 percent level and my left lung began to develop scar tissue from the combination of steroids and the chemo they gave me. I could go on with a lot more details but I'll just tell you, I can't recommend that place. Maybe just one more little

450

incident. One early morning, about 3 a.m., my wife got a call from my night shift nurse.

"You better get over here and take care of your husband. I don't have time for this."

It seems that she intended to see that I slept the whole night so she wouldn't be overwhelmed with too much to do. She gave me a double dose of Ambien sleeping medication. Apparently, I had a negative reaction, got out of the bed, fell down because I was so weak and caused the IV medication and equipment administering it to crash to the floor and break. Eva freaked, drove like a mad woman to get there and took charge. I'd like to bill them. How much should the bill be for the stress she caused my wife? If you want to see what it's like to not care, I believe that nurse should teach that class.

That's a pretty dark picture of my time in that hospital if I let it be. But I can't. The entire experience and even what I am experiencing now in my journey to revive this bag of bones and create the proof of this Buddhism with my life is the most valuable experience so far. I can't tell you all the benefits I have had since going through that hell. It was while there that I found my life. The inner journey into my mind and heart and body was extraordinary. And then there was the experience of uniting with my wife.

Without her prayers and her heart I don't think I would be able to tell this story. She just decided I wasn't going to die, and that was that. When she walked into the room to see me, my heart would leap with excitement. When she was there, everything was okay. The power of her love helped pull me back from a very narrow ledge that my life was clinging to. The doctors didn't know what to do when I began fading down to 128 pounds. But she did.

With the knowledge that I had no idea what was coming next, I lived completely in the moment, and that allowed me to release myself from a part of my heart that had been frozen for as long as I can remember. I let Eva in and my heart defrosted and we meshed into one. And we have continued to cause this love to grow and blossom. I've never looked up the meaning of the word "fusion," but I have to believe that in our case it has to include a oneness of our hearts and prayers. We became our prayers and determination. That fusion has never retreated.

This Buddhism of Nichiren Daishonin as explained by President Ikeda is all they say it can be. It's up to the person to reveal its truth. As I expanded, as I built a life with Eva, my relationship with my children also expanded. I know that there were more than a few reasons for the kids to feel a separation from me because of the divorce, but from my point of view, those reasons didn't exist. The gratitude and appreciation that had escaped me for so many years now came out in full force. There were more than a few times when I would just break out in tears of delight at the sight of them. I later saw a couple pictures of myself in that hospital, and I was in bad shape. How they could stand to look at me I don't know.

The children's mother came and visited a number of times. I was told that Eva asked her to come and keep her eye on me during a hairy time when she couldn't be there. I understand that I gave Lynn a pretty rough time. I'm sorry. I wasn't myself during much of that stay when she visited, and I think I let my resentment for her having moved away from L.A. with the children come out. I must have revealed that to her and topped it off by being really delusional. The meds didn't help. I know Lynn prayed for me during that time, and for that I will be forever grateful. That's another wonderful experience of my life. The children's mother and father continually pray for them and for each other's happiness. How can life be all that good when around us we keep seeing and hearing about what is bad? I think I may be beginning to get the point that "the shadow never moves until I do."

I also remember, to some degree, that I had a conversation on the phone with my mother and tried to make her feel like trash. I think it was one of my kids who overheard the conversation and I apparently said something like, "Who is this?"

"It's your mother."

"Which mother? There are all kinds of mothers. Which one do you want to be today?"

I cut off at that point and hung up. Fortunately I was later able to apologize to her for that. But I've never had a sit down talk with Lynn to get all the stuff we need to discuss out of our system. I feel that I need to apologize to Lynn for my part in the divorce while at the same time I want to say to her how appreciative I am for the time we spent together as husband and wife and mother and father.

I do need to apologize to her for how I treated her while I was in the hospital. She deserves all the happiness she can handle, and her new marriage was just such a chance to catch the brass ring. I hope Lynn and I can forever move forward and not hold ourselves back because of any negativity resulting from our relationship.

Kelli has always been a protective force in my life. It was just inborn into our relationship. There were several times when she would, at 6 or 7 years old, show me with her words or actions that I was going in the wrong direction. She just seemed to have a certain wisdom that would appear when I most needed it. And there I was in the hospital without much optimism coming from the staff and doctors. It was very difficult for me to understand the medical language of the professionals, but there was Kelli to explain it to Eva and me in plain English. All her study of medicine, both Chinese and English, became my good fortune as well as hers. Hearing her explain what was going on enabled me to shuffle it in my mind and see it from the hope-filled teaching of Buddhism.

With all this happening at a pace I couldn't keep up with, Andrew was my line of communication with the business of hospitalization. It just so happened that he was by now one of the leading marketing people at an HMO. Don't try to tell me I wasn't protected from all sides. He would come see me during his lunch breaks almost every day, at least whenever he could. One day, he came in while I was in one of my most delirious states. Apparently, I had turned my head and noticed that there was an electric shaver sitting on the table next to the bed. How I was able to get out of the bed, I don't know, but when Andrew came into the room, he found me sitting on the floor, leaning against a wall, shaving. He freaked and ran for a nurse. They came into the room to find in my hand a plastic applicator for an underarm deodorant. In thinking I was shaving, I had covered my face with the stuff. I must have looked like a foaming skeleton. It wasn't so funny at the time, but now it's good for a laugh.

When I got down to 128 pounds, I decided I'd had enough of that place. The doctor was coming around and giving me injections saying, "Let's see what this stuff does?"

That was enough.

"If you don't let me out of this place now, I'm going to die here, and that's not acceptable. Either you sign me out or I'm going to crawl out, but I will be out of here."

Eva got there and in as little time as possible we were on our way home. I didn't know heaven had a driveway, but there was one when I looked up and saw our home. I couldn't get myself out of the car and up the one step to our house, but with the help of Eva and my children I was home. Another step on the way to winning.

It's been said that Buddhism is a practice of turning poison into medicine. I did that on the deepest level when I discovered that the cancer was the medicine I needed to find all the powers of Buddha in my heart and mind. And then there is the medicine of being home with the love of family. And there's the medicine of being able to pray to my Gohonzon at home, and there's the medicine of good food.

While in the hospital, I would feel nauseated by just the smell of the food. I couldn't eat it and that's a fact. But the moment I got home, the first thing that happened was I got hit with a craving for Jerry's Deli's chicken noodle soup. Eva got me some and I think I was having liquid gold for my first meal. I couldn't get enough, and if left alone, I would have eaten until I exploded. For the next few months, I ate and ate and loved and loved and chanted and chanted. And by January, 2007, I had gained about 45 pounds, was able to get a little muscular strength and balance and was strong enough to handle the next obstacle. The cancer, which they thought they had gotten, was now coming back and growing aggressively.

It was now that the results of "Lessening Karmic Retribution" truly revealed its truth. A chance conversation my wife had with a co-worker brought a recommendation to make an appointment with The Angeles Clinic and Research Institute in Santa Monica, California.

With a complete copy of the records of my stay in the West Valley hospital, my wife, my daughter and I met with Dr. Lawrence Piro and his staff. First impressions have rarely proven to be false in my life, and within the first few moments of introduction to Dr. Piro, I felt as if I had just met one of the stars of "Beach Party Bingo." This was the original surfer dude. No surfboard in sight but the rest was all there, other than the fact that he was in a suit and looked like he should be on the cover of GQ. The hair was bleached by the California Sun…I think.

He studied the records for what seemed like a long time, looked up and spoke with the voice of wisdom.

"You've been through it, huh?"

Eva, Kelli and I didn't have to look at each other to know that this man was the one. I immediately had full confidence that I could partner with him and the clinic on the deepest level. And if there was a chance of beating this devilish function known as cancer, his heart, mind, medical wisdom and compassion were the answer to all our prayers. This new fortune presented itself as a protective force from here on referred to as Dr. Lawrence Piro. You just can't have too many good friends.

In that first hospitalization in the West Valley, I found one of the most disturbing things about some of the doctors was that they didn't have time to listen. If I was trying to report something about what I was experiencing at the time, they would invariably interrupt and begin to give me some intellectual gibberish about what they learned in medical school 20 years ago. At one point I had to tell two of them not to come back in my room until they were ready to listen to me. I wanted dialogue, not a lecture that they have repeated a hundred times.

With Dr. Piro it was a completely different story; he listened. With him I felt that we hooked up and both of us were headed in the same direction at the same time. We partnered with the same goal and intent. I felt the power of healing was multiplied ten-fold. Although my spiritual base is Eastern and his Western, it became a "medical marriage" without differences. It was refreshing not to be examining our differences but uniting with sameness. It became very apparent why so many celebrities like Dick Van Patten, Farrah Fawcett and Ryan O'Neal had looked to him for his wisdom and knowledge. He has been asked to speak for them to the media as well. But you never feel that they take priority over any of his other patients. I believe Dr. Piro is the good fortune I've been able to accumulate through the years to turn my medical problems from a poison in my body to a medicine for my life.

Briefly, I'll tell you that under the direction of Dr. Piro, I had four sessions of chemo treatments. The tumors were now very aggressive, and Dr. Piro consulted with Dr. Auayporn P. Nademanee at City of Hope in Duarte, California, about 20 miles east of Los Angeles. Dr. Piro thought that I might be a candidate for a stem cell transplant. When I met her, I knew I had run into another of the top generals of medicine.

The treatment Dr. Nademanee guided me through was a system to separate my own stem cells from my blood over a two-week period, and when they felt they had enough, freeze them. Then I was hospitalized and given a regimen of three chemos a day until my physical system was in the right condition to accept my stem cells back into my system. This procedure allowed doctors to begin harvesting new stem cells from my own bone marrow. I was released from City of Hope on August 4, 2007, free of the cancer.

Throughout this entire time the foundation of study in the teaching of Nichiren Buddhism and the wisdom of President Ikeda's guidance kept fortifying my faith and belief. It kept my mind clear from doubt and gave me the strength to continue on the path of determination and declare the truth of this Buddhism. All this time, I could feel the power of the prayers of my wife, my children, their mother, Lynn, and the wonderful members of SGI-USA. The direction of my life had completely changed from an untimely death to a life filled with dreams and wishes. My greatest wishes then and now are to become an indestructible pillar that will never allow this organization to hesitate in its quest for world peace. I will do this by sharing my experience and faith with as many people as I can.

It will soon be Eva's birthday. She loves her birthdays. She celebrates them for one week each year. I have a hard time understanding the degree of celebration she has for this day. I know there's a lot of appreciation involved, but it's very difficult for me to relate to. I've never been very happy when my birthday came around. I still try to ignore it, but with Eva's heart leading the way, I can't get away with that any more. I think most of the time I tried to make sure I was not going to have a good time on that day just to spite my mother.

Knowing that Tuesday, May 18, 2010, will soon be here makes me look at myself and realize I can't give her all that I want to give her. I never have. And that doesn't feel good. What does feel good is that I want to give her all I have.

My health still isn't what I would hope for by this time. It's been a hell of a ride for these last four years and it's far from over.

Recently Eva said, "We've got to saturate your bone marrow with *Nam-Myoho-Renge-Kyo*."

It's true. My bone marrow has been compromised by the chemo. Twenty-one treatments is a lot of chemo, a lot of chemicals, and my body is worn out. Right now we are trying to kick-start the marrow to produce new cells and get them into the blood. Without this natural production, the body begins to wear out and subsequently the possibility of getting healthier and having more energy when needed slows down. My wife's imagery paints a clear picture. I'm going to include that picture in my prayer.

From what I've been told, when I first got sick and they put me into intensive care, Eva became very upset and immediately began to communicate with people of faith and understanding of this Buddhism. They had many experiences with tackling problems in their daily lives. And as leaders who had taken on the responsibilities of communicating Nichiren Buddhism to many people, they have heard and seen the results of chanting many, many times. One the SGI's national leaders, Linda Johnson, cleared her way into Eva's heart and gave her words of encouragement that brought her out of the shock and got her on the playing field of winning. Eva also was able to listen to the words of Mr. Kikumura and another great woman, Mrs. Takakuwa. This is the heart of Buddhism. The people of the SGI are just about as compassionate and as wise as you can get. If I ever forget my debt of appreciation for this organization and the people, I should have to forever walk with horse shoes nailed to my moccasins.

Eva told me later that one of her first visualizations was of her chanting and sending *Nam-Myoho-Renge-Kyo* into my body by pouring it into me through a hole in my head. I have often been aware that I had at least one hole in my head, and I guess she found it. Here I am, hole and all.

I hope to stop writing this letter—or by now a book—very soon. I've pretty much brought it up to the present, and just to keep writing for the sake of writing doesn't seem to be the thing to do.

I don't think I've given enough attention to the grandchildren. I think I would like to learn to write better. All the way through this journey I was thinking about them, but I didn't write directly to them. I'd like to do that now.

"Kids, my ulterior motive in this package of words is to introduce you to Nichiren Buddhism and the SGI. By the time you find any interest in exploring the world with the dreams of joy and happiness in your hearts, I hope you'll take time to look into this teaching that holds the key to celebrating your highest potential of your life. It will, at the very least, be a wonderful experience of looking into the mystery of life."

It's now the end of June, 2010. I'm getting healthier every day. Dr. Piro and I have addressed the bone marrow issue, and we have reversed its tendency to weaken and are getting the production of the cells almost back to normal. Another victory based on faith and practice and the partnership of patient and doctor.

Soon after making the determination that I was going to bring this writing to a close, something happened that I feel I must share with you. Earlier I went through a very quick description of the sisters based on my impressions at that first meeting with the *familia* in the garage. At that time, I didn't refer to the men by name. I made a general statement that the men seemed to be the "second-hand citizens" of the family. Remember, that was my first impression and that was 20 years ago in 1988.

The first sister I mentioned was Leticia. She was also the first-born and I sensed a deep unhappiness in her heart. Tisha was married to a man who struck me as someone so involved with himself that he had little or no time to give to the effort needed to continue building on a relationship. I'm sure it was Leticia who instigated and led the action to adopt a wonderful boy they named, Alex. Since then, Alex has grown to be a fine creative young man. The husband has gone and revealed his true nature by trying to take everything important to Tisha out from under her. As I mentioned before, she is free of her cancer and happier and more creative than ever.

Irma (Ear-ma) wasn't married at the time but later fell in love with a long time family friend, Lanz. I met Lanz when Eva worked for him as a business management accountant. It was pretty soon after Eva and I started taking our relationship seriously that I went to her office to take her out to lunch.

As soon as she introduced us, Lanz and I got into a little

conversation, and I thought to myself: This is the quietest, whitest, black businessman I think I'll ever meet. There is nothing jive about this guy.

I would have predicted that he had no rhythm and that he couldn't snap his fingers and tap his foot at the same time. I can't tell you when it happened, but it seemed that almost overnight he became hip-hop. But it's a beautiful picture to see Irma happy and holding hands with him.

Next is Petie, Patricia, again. When she gets dressed she can wear all the colors of the rainbow and make Baskin-Robbins 31 Flavors look like they missed something. And her partner is silent, unassuming Jerry. I don't think this man has ever started a conversation unless he's asking you if you're hungry. This man can cook better than an ugly woman, but like all the other men, after he's made sure the food is ready, he just fades into the background at these *familia* gatherings around the table in the garage.

There is one man who doesn't fade. It's Scott the gambler. He's married to the athletic sister, Marquina. Scott is also athletic. He is and has been the National Paddle Tennis Champion. He has held all the major titles for many years. He is also like one of the sisters. He's always in the mix asking questions about this and that. His mind works so fast that he has a difficult time waiting for answers. And before you can respond he's off on another planet. This man has a heart of gold. He's also always hoping someone will drop a nugget in his lap. That's just Scott.

Jim is the husband of Dina and the father of their three wonderful children. Again, quiet would have to be another word for Jim.

And then there's Jessica and Phil. In many ways a person who didn't have a relationship with them probably would never guess they were a couple. They have been together since high school, and she could easily be the cheerleader of the family. With a heart as warm as the sun and a smile to melt ice, Jessica brightens up any room she walks into. Whatever it is, she's got it. Phil on the other hand, from my experience, was the most difficult to get to know. At all the gatherings I had been to over the last 20 years, I could always find him standing pretty much off to the side keeping his eyes wide open for anything. Mostly, I think he just couldn't keep his eyes off his lovely wife. When he wasn't at one of the gatherings, I missed him. If I didn't see him I figured he was on duty.

Phil became a California Highway Patrol officer about 27 or 28 years ago. I think it was in the early part of May, 2010, that Jessica had found a lump in her breast, and upon medical examination it was found to be malignant. Of course everyone was concerned, and she had all the support from the family she would ever need. I remember asking her if she would have any reservations to chanting, and her reply was that she was very satisfied with her doctors and her religion.

A short time later I decided to call Phil to offer my support to him. I would also have asked him if he would consider chanting for his wife, but I was only able to leave a message. Either he never got it or for whatever reason, I didn't hear from him. That was shortly before June 9, 2010, when California Highway Patrol Officer Philip Ortiz was run down by a motorist shortly after getting off his motorcycle to address a traffic concern on the 405 Freeway in Los Angeles.

The family swarmed to the UCLA hospital where he was

taken by his fellow officers, many of whom he had personally trained. That was one of his gifts. He had become a mentor to many of these men in gold and blue.

The tears flowed without end from the *familia* as well as from his family of CHP officers. For the next two weeks, there was 24-hour vigilance by the family and a 24-hour posting of officers to serve and protect the family and to be on constant alert to provide whatever the needs of Philip or Jessica were.

The story of the affairs of the heart that took place during the time of Philip's hospitalization needs to be told. From all I saw and heard, the spirit, the heart and the actions of the members of the CHP, from the newest recruit to the top of the leadership, displayed the kind of extraordinary caring and protection you would only expect from a parent to its child. They took care of their families.

One of the most outstanding things to take place during all this turmoil was the change that took place within the core of the family. From Scott there was a depth of maturity that had not been revealed before. His consistent vigilance and concern for all was remarkable. Dina's Jim and our Chef Jerry found their voices. Their words and presence provided a sense of security that may have been unexpected. Lanz also played an important role in keeping the family united. No longer did my early impression of "second-hand citizens" seem to apply.

Gina Ozanne, another great friend of the family has to be recognized. Gina has to be as close as the girls will ever get toward having an eighth sister. They have all been tied together since childhood. She was there through this whole ordeal, and not for a second did she relinquish her full support. She is married to a CHP Officer and shares a very common thread of experience with Jessica. If there could have been an eighth sister, she would have been the one. I also want to mention my daughter, Kelli. From the moment she heard of the accident, she was there day and night. One person after another would tell me how much she was appreciated for all her efforts. She meshed into the *familia* and made her father very proud. And when he could, Andrew also did all he could as well as offer prayers from his heart.

I mention all this because of a deep sense of gratitude and appreciation to Philip. Without his even being aware of it, this man who would always stand off to the side, keeping a watchful protective eye on his wife and the *familia*, had instigated a closeness and a unity that wasn't there before. Several of the girls and the men have told me that there has been a distinct change in the depth of consideration for their partners in marriage and toward the entire family. I also feel a oneness with my *familia* that wasn't there before. Thank you, Phil.

On the 22nd of June, two weeks from the time of the accident, Philip passed to a new beginning for his next appearance. On the 23rd, Jessica had a successful surgery to remove a tumor from her breast.

As Nichiren Daishonin has written, "We living beings, right down to crickets, ants, mosquitoes, and flies, all possess life that is without beginning or end. "

Another of the revolutionary teachings that hit me very early in my relationship with Buddhism was that life is eternal. Birth and death are two phases of the continuing drama of our eternal existence. Philip's life had a manifest form we all experienced with him, and now he has a latent life we cannot see. The life of Philip also exists in the hearts of those who loved him and most assuredly in the heart and mind of his Jessica. His life is eternally without end as are the lives of all living beings.

To imagine and then to know that death is not the end, but the beginning, is perhaps one of the greatest rewards of my faith. Whatever my concept of death may be, it will permeate every activity and thought of my life if only on the subconscious level. Perhaps the most significant gift of my illness was that I was able to see that the entirety of my existence depended on me. With the clarity of prayer and the determination to eradicate these devilish functions of illness, I was able to pray on the most fundamental level and awaken to the eternity of my life.

Now when I pray for Philip's enlightenment and happiness and his return to continue to fulfill his mission in life, I am able to fuse with his eternal life force. I also feel very strongly that with his death, Phil is still fulfilling a very important part of his mission on this earth.

In a general sense, little time is spent studying death. It appears that it is one of those subjects we just don't want to deal with. Death represents darkness, fear and suffering to most. Very few are looking forward to dying and because there is so little time given to discussion and reading about the possibilities, those fears grow deeper and occupy more of our thoughts as we get older and have to face this very unavoidable fact of life. Parting with family and loved ones is one the most difficult of life's necessities. And in my *familia* this is the first time the experience has hit so close to home.

If I were ever asked what the greatest gift in my life would be, I would have to say it is the quest to unite with the life of the universe. My mentor in life, Daisaku Ikeda, reveals through his words and behavior that his relationship with his mentor, Josei Toda, was his key. And the Buddhism of Nichiren Daishonin has revealed the truth through practice and study. None of the teachers of the law of the universe are ever satisfied with theory. They needed to experience this true law with their entire life. I feel the same. Without actual proof, actual fact, it would just be words. My greatest determination is to have a oneness of heart and mind with my mentor, Daisaku Ikeda. It would probably be better to say that it is the quest and intent of my life to experience—in its totality—that oneness.

I want to share with you one more great wish that I have. I want the first grandchild to be the arrival of my mother coming back so we can finish the unfinished business of loving each other. That is my prayer and dream.

And when that baby comes around, the first thing I will do is love her, hug her and whisper in her ear, "*Nam-Myoho-Renge-Kyo.*"

There is only one-way to stop writing, and that's to just stop…for now.

Rick

EPILOGUE

My husband Rick Richards passed away at 1:52 a.m. on December 30, 2010 of respiratory failure—a consequence of the extended and extensive treatments he went through in his challenge with cancer. On January 15, 2011, nearly 1,000 friends and fellow Soka Gakkai International members paid tribute to Rick at a memorial service at the SGI auditorium in Santa Monica, California. In a statement read at the service, SGI President Daisaku Ikeda praised Rick, writing that his "exemplary way of life based on fervent faith will surely shine eternally within the hearts of numerous fellow members."

Even as his illness took an ever-greater toll on his body, Rick continued to write. He wrote well into the summer of 2010 before deciding that it was time to stop, that he had written enough. His manuscript began as a letter to his yet unborn grandchildren. As Rick wrote, his son Andrew had been married and divorced. At the memorial service, Andrew reconnected with Melinda Hernandez, a former girlfriend he hadn't seen in 10 years. Their love for each other rekindled the moment they saw each other. Two years later we welcomed Andrew's and Melinda's baby girls—fraternal twins Avery and Madison—into the world. I really believe that Rick's fierce determination towards the happiness of his children made this reunion possible.

As I was going through the journals Rick began writing in 1968, I found his entry on how the idea for this book and its title began to take form. In writing about the origins of his title "The Butterfly and the Bulldozer," he said he felt his first wife was like a delicate butterfly, and saw himself as a bulldozer, full of anger and prone to violence. He approached problems with brute force, trying to run over or smash whatever he saw as an obstacle. As his life began to transform through each experience, slowly, perhaps even subconsciously at first, he began to recognize that he could not run over his problems or away from himself. He told me he eventually realized that he was both the delicate butterfly and the strong bulldozer.

His years spent feeling abandoned, discarded as worthless and pathetic, were necessary steps in his struggle to emerge from his own chrysalis like a butterfly. And I believe that is a struggle one must overcome alone. No matter how good anyone's intentions are, enlarging the opening of a chrysalis—sometimes mistakenly called a cocoon—to help a butterfly emerge, destroys the butterfly's ability to fly. The butterfly has to struggle and force its way out through a tiny opening in the chrysalis to force fluid from its body into its wings. Only then will the wings be ready for flight.

This is such an amazing metaphor for Rick's transformation and for the teachings of Nichiren Buddhism. Within each of us is the power and grace to live victoriously and become absolutely happy.

Rick had earned his physical wings as a paratrooper in the 101st Airborne in 1965, but his spiritual wings came later. His transformation, as profound as a butterfly's metamorphosis, came with his discovery and revelation of his enlightened true identity and his embrace of Nichiren Buddhism. Rick practiced this Buddhism for more than 40 years and as he describes in his life story, he continued to open and reveal his life to himself and to the world, even to his very last breath.

"There is absolutely no doubt that your husband, who has devoted his life for the sake of kosen-rufu [world peace through individual happiness], will be embraced by immeasurable good fortune and virtue, having attained enlightenment," President Ikeda said in his statement. I see how our fortune has continued to unfold even now.

At Rick's memorial, my sister Marquina poignantly described his attitude toward his illness. Most of us, she said, "would be paralyzed with fear, but Rick and Eva always focused on the victory. He mentioned many times that he would not change his diagnosis for the world because it gave him so much more purpose in life." His free spirit, she said, allowed him to gallop "like a thoroughbred through the greenest pastures during his treatments."

When I met Rick, my heart knew him already, although my brain told me stay away. We couldn't help but fall in love and fight for our relationship to work. We were married for twenty years, five months and two days.

The first five years were tumultuous, with us trying to figure how this marriage would ever work. The next five years were spent knowing it would work, but thinking the other had to change to make that happen. The following ten years were about becoming one, supporting each other, teaching each other and learning to love unconditionally. Together, we fought his illness with every ounce of strength, courage, prayer and hope we could muster. His daughter Kelli and his son Andrew were right by our side.

Rick's cancer was the beginning of my own profound inner transformation. I have been practicing Nichiren's Buddhism since I was 20 years old, but I had only scratched the surface of revealing my true potential as a human being. All the things in life, which kept me in fear and locked into my own world, vanished. Life and death situations can do that to us. The heartbreaks and challenges that cause so much pain, anxiety and anger are ultimately irrelevant. What really matters, and what I have learned to focus on, is the heart, the love. Give your true self wholeheartedly and fearlessly to your partner in life, your family and your friends. The reward for this effort is a deeply rich and fulfilling life.

To our granddaughters Madison and Avery, I loved you before you were here. I am so fortunate to have you girls in my life. And to our future grandchildren, you are equally loved.

My e-mail screen name is forevarick. Rick's is forrickeva. Rick made these up, and I first thought it was a sweet thing to do. But I have come to realize that he felt I was forever and forEva and Eva. He would sign all his cards to me that way.

Thank you . . . gracias . . . my Rick Richards! I can still hear you calling me with that delicious voice of yours.

Your wife in lifetime after lifetime!

Rick's love of the Los Angeles Equestrian Center gave us the idea to dedicate a bench and plant an oak tree in his honor.

The engraved plaque on the bench welcomes passerbyes to sit and enjoy the the beauty of the equestrian center as Rick did for so many years. The bench faces an arena where he took his children and taught them about the horses he loved so much.

The engraved quote on the rock by the tree, is one that he referred to often.

Avery and Madison, our grandchildren at a few weeks old.

Andrew, Melinda, and our grandchildren, Avery & Madison.

Madison and Avery Christmas 2013.

**Andrew, his stepson Hayden, Melinda, Hayden's mom,
Avery and Madison, Thanksgiving 2013.**

Acknowledgements

To Rick's and my own Sensei:

Daisaku Ikeda, our teacher, our mentor. He continually teaches us to believe in our life, to never give up, to see and act on our innate wisdom and enlightened selves. Thank you, Sensei!

To My friends who out of the kindness of their hearts and much patience with me read and re-read and edited and re-edited my husband Rick's "Butterfly".

Ed Boyer, our primary editor. Thank you for being patient with me. I know I have not been easy. You did not give up on me.

Norma Sanders, my friend who loves me unconditionally and is always there for me no matter what. Thanks for reading, reading, reading.

Jennifer Kang, for all your encouragement to keep moving forward and for helping me open up when I saw no opening.

Ellen Brown, I only have tears of appreciation for all you have done and keep doing for me. Thank you for designing Rick's book from cover to cover.

Carol Chastang, my Carolina, thank you for your thoughts and encouragement and of course editing, too, most of all for introducing me to this amazing philosophy of Buddhism. You have been so much a part of my life since we were kids.

To Rick's children, who have allowed me to be in their

lives as a step mom and *lita*, Kelli and Andrew and his wife Melinda. And you too, Hayden.

To my Avery and Madison, I am so in love with you both. You have transformed my life in so many ways. Your grandpa loved you before you were even here!

To my parents, Josemaria and Josefina Muñoz and my sisters Leticia, Irma, Armandina, Patricia, Jessica and Marquina. Thank you for being there through each one of our challenges and for me when Rick passed away. I can only say a million thank yous and *mil gracias*!!! *Los quiero muchísimo*. I love you very much!

To our SGI family, thank you, thank you, thank you to each and every one of you!

And to everyone else I missed here, I am most fortunate to have so many people who cared for my husband Rick and me. Thank you!

Eva Richards
June 2014